The Voice

The Voice

40 Years of Black British Lives

EBURY
PRESS

1

Published in 2022 by Ebury Press, an imprint of Ebury Publishing
20 Vauxhall Bridge Road,
London SW1V 2SA

Ebury Press is part of the Penguin Random House group of companies
whose addresses can be found at global.penguinrandomhouse.com

Text © The Voice Media Group 2022
The Voice Media Group has asserted its right to be identified as the author of
the work in accordance with the Copyright, Designs and Patents Act 1988

The publisher has made serious efforts to trace all copyright owners
and is willing to acknowledge any rightful copyright owner on
substantive proof of ownership.

This edition first published by Ebury Press in 2022

www.penguin.co.uk

A CIP catalogue record for this book is available from the British Library

Hardback ISBN: 9781529902426

Typeset in 11.5/17 pt Sabon Next LT Pro by Jouve (UK), Milton Keynes
Printed and bound in Great Britain by Clays Ltd, Elcograf S.p.A.

The authorised representative in the EEA is Penguin Random House Ireland,
Morrison Chambers, 32 Nassau Street, Dublin D02 YH68

Contents

Acknowledgements

Over the last four decades, *The Voice* has given a voice to the Black community in the United Kingdom by fighting racial injustice, campaigning for equality, informing our community, supporting Black businesses and recognising new and varied talent.

Importantly, *The Voice* has been pivotal in empowering the Black community to tell their own stories and celebrate their successes.

It is intended that this book, which gives an account of the lived experiences of our community through the pages of *The Voice* newspaper, will remind many and educate others of seminal moments in our history.

The Voice acknowledges that without our avid readers, devoted supporters, talented contributors, welcomed critics, committed advertisers and sponsors, dedicated followers, loyal subscribers and generous donors, we could not have operated for four decades and thus unable to produce this book.

We thank you all!

We pay homage to Val McCalla, the visionary who launched *The Voice* in 1982 in the aftermath of the 1981 uprisings and brought many on board to fulfil his dream.

It is also important to pay homage to previous management and staff who have contributed to *The Voice*, both in print and online, over the years as they laid the foundation on which we are now building. Our legal representatives, designers and printers are not to be forgotten, as without them there would be only words but no pages.

We extend sincere gratitude to the contributors, project team and publisher:

To Sir Lenny Henry for writing the foreword; Michael Eboda for contributing the introduction; and Richard Adeshiyan, Dotun Adebayo, Winsome Cornish, Vic Motune and Rodney Hinds for reviewing the archives and compiling the decades.

To Petrina Dale of Mahogany Services Ltd for meticulously cataloguing the archives and reviewing content and images. To Elizabeth Bond, Fionn Hargreaves and Mia Oakley from Penguin Random House for their invaluable support and guidance.

We also extend heartfelt gratitude to the current Voice Media Group Team who have kept the flames going: Executive Director Paulette Simpson; Senior Manager, Corporate Affairs & Communications, Paula Dyke; Editor Lester Holloway; Sports Editor Rodney Hinds; Entertainment Editor Joel Campbell; Senior News Reporter Vic Motune; News Reporters Sinai Fleary, Vernon Graham, Leah Mahon and Richard Sudan; Advertising's Sylvester Amara; Sales and Advertising's Garfield Robinson, Getnet Kassa and Trevor Raymond; Graphic Designer Thierry Lagrin; and Accountant Winnie Phua.

We also thank our numerous dedicated columnists and freelance reporters who are valued members of our team.

The JN Group, that owns *The Voice*, has supported the newspaper's rebirth and growth during the last decade. *The Voice* team extend their heartfelt gratitude to the Board of Directors for believing in the vision as we look forward to the next 40 years and beyond.

Foreword

By Sir Lenny Henry

When *The Voice* approached me to write the foreword for a book commemorating its fortieth anniversary, I literally jumped at the chance.

After more than ten years campaigning for media diversity and having co-edited the 2021 book *Black British Lives Matter*, I am in no doubt of the importance of *The Voice* in British society and Black history globally.

The truth is that in the UK, less than 1 per cent of journalists are Black – a meagre 0.2 per cent to be precise. There is not a single Black editor of a national daily British newspaper and according to a study that looked at headlines of national newspapers in one week of July 2020 – at the height of the global Black Lives Matter protests – just six of the 174 front page bylines were attributed to a journalist of colour.

It is against this reality that *The Voice* is so important. Let me explain with a small personal story.

I first broke into TV by winning the talent show *New Faces* in 1975. Back then I was almost always the only Black person on set. Just under 40 years later in 2013, I infamously found myself sitting at a BAFTA ceremony feeling like nothing had really changed – the only other Black people there either seemed to be offering me food or checking my coat.

And so, after drinking a little more than I should, I went to leave the ceremony, thoroughly pissed off. At that point, I was approached by a journalist who asked me the most innocent of questions: 'What did you think of the BAFTAs?'

And I answered: 'I guess it was . . . All White on the Night!'

Hardly my greatest comic moment – but I was pissed.

The next day the story appeared in all the papers. The *Telegraph* went with the headline, 'BAFTAs were a disgrace for not celebrating Black talent, says Lenny Henry', while the *Daily Mail* said: ' "What were the judges doing?" Lenny Henry blasts BAFTA for not recognising Black talent at this year's television awards.'

From that night onwards 'Lenny Henry had become political', at least that is how many of the mainstream newspapers seemed to present it.

The truth is I had always been political and wanted to talk about the racism I have faced, but that was rarely reflected in mainstream press. But it was reflected in *The Voice*.

The Voice has consistently been the place that has covered all of me, not conveniently editing out the inconvenient parts that might make certain parts of British society uncomfortable. *The Voice* has allowed me to talk about the racism I've faced and the lack of diversity in the industry even before 'diversity' was a common word.

The Voice feels like family, where a Black person can just be themselves.

Born a year after the Brixton uprisings of 1981, *The Voice* has been 'home' to the Black British community for the last 40 years. It has reported on issues and events that other newspapers simply ignored and invariably given a unique Black British perspective on major events, providing invaluable insights into our understanding of British society.

It is no coincidence that during the early days of the COVID-19 pandemic, it was Vic Motune, a reporter from *The Voice* newspaper, who first raised the issue of how the government's hostile immigration policy might be exacerbating the spread of the virus. He, like so many other *Voice* journalists, saw links and offered a new perspective that escaped other journalists.

On a personal level, this has translated into me having a unique relationship with *The Voice*.

The Voice not only consistently showcases great journalism, but it has also acted as a crucial platform for nurturing and incubating some of the best journalists in the country, from Gary Younge to Afua Hirsch, and Henry Bonsu to Nadine White.

The Voice is an ongoing testimony to the strength of the Black British community, surviving against the odds and being an invaluable part of British society.

If Black British Lives Matter – which we believe they do – then Black British newspapers and journalism have to matter.

Enjoy some of the best journalism, produced by some of the best journalists.

Long live *The Voice*.

Introduction
The Importance of the Black Press

By Michael Eboda

While Winston Churchill famously said, 'I shall leave it to history, but remember that I shall be one of the historians', the former publisher of the *Washington Post*, Phil Graham, noted that journalism is the 'first rough draft of history.' Considering these two quotes gives you a sense of just how important it has been for the Black community to have our stories chronicled through newspapers written by Black people, for Black people. They also illustrate why the opposite doesn't bear thinking about. The Black British press has, in various guises over the past 60 years, reported our story in our words.

The first recognised weekly newspaper to be made for Black people living in Britain was the *West Indian Gazette and Afro-Asian Caribbean News*, which was launched by the inimitable campaigner Claudia Jones in 1958.

Sadly the *Gazette* failed to survive Claudia after she passed away in 1964 and it would be seven years until the next Black publication, the *West Indian Digest* launched. In 1973, founder Arif Ali acquired the *West Indian World* from its owner St Vincentian Aubrey Baynes. Ali went on to launch three more journals in the early eighties, the *Caribbean Times* in 1981, the *Asian Times* in 1983 and *African Times* in 1984.

Up to that point, the one thing all the Black newspapers had in common was that they were primarily focused on an audience we have come to know and love as the Windrush Generation – people who had emigrated from the Caribbean from the 1940s to the 1970s. They still largely considered themselves immigrants in Britain, a country that was only too keen to keep them feeling that way.

In 1982, in the wake of the Brixton uprising that had rocked the country a year earlier, a young Jamaican accountant turned news reporter called Val McCalla launched *The Voice*. In the words of the paper's longest-running editor, Steve Pope, McCalla 'identified the emerging culture of the Black British identity and honed it into tabloid form.' By the early 1980s a generation of young Black people were born and grew up in Britain. As a result, they had a very different outlook on life to their parents. We were Black and British, but didn't really understand what that meant.

Gary Younge in his foreword to Peter Fryer's *Staying Power, The History of Black People in Britain*, articulates it brilliantly:

> For the longest time the central distraction for Black Britons was insisting on our existence. That we were Black was unarguable. That we were in Britain was acknowledged if only to be contested. But the notion that we could be Black and British . . . confounded many, if not most.

By launching *The Voice*, McCalla helped us to achieve a degree of clarity, a proof of concept so to speak. It showed us the many things we had in common. It empowered us with information about people like us, and we trusted it because it was owned and written by us.

As veteran journalist, broadcaster and writer Henry Bonsu explains: '*The Voice* launched at a time when the community was coming of age. It was a turning point in the maturity of the community. The paper reflected that.'

If the 2020s is the era of fake news, for a Black British newspaper the 1980s and 1990s was the era of real news, real people, real issues and real stories. Back then Britain was a very different place than it is now. From 1980–99, more than 100 Black people died in police, prison and psychiatric custody. Some of you will remember the names: Colin Roach, Cynthia Jarrett, Orville Blackwood, Joy Gardner and Oluwasiji Lapite to name a few.

The police, who are far from perfect now, were a law unto themselves and regularly meted out terrible beatings to Black people – men and women – who had the misfortune to fall into their clutches. Racism, in all aspects of life, was the norm: in education, the judiciary system, housing, workplaces; and *The Voice* reported on everything. It exposed injustices, it ran campaigns and gradually more and more of these stories made it into the mainstream consciousness, making many of the national media outlets rethink how they reported on events involving Britain's Black communities.

In doing all of this, the newspaper also became a fantastic training ground for Black journalists, so many of whom have gone on to have successful media careers. Sharon Ali, Brenda Emmanus, Asif Zubairy, Joel Kibazo and Rageh Omaar spring to mind immediately, but there are many more. Latterly Nadine White has been appointed the first 'race correspondent' of the *Independent.*

Over the years, *The Voice* gradually increased circulation, to the point where in the mid-1990s it had audited sales of more than 55,000 per week. It sold so well that left-leaning local authorities, keen to attract Black jobseekers as the idea of equal opportunities in employment began to take hold, advertised their vacancies in *The Voice*. Indeed, many readers bought *The Voice* because it was the only place at the time where decent jobs were advertised for Black people.

The Voice had little competition until 1996 when *New Nation* was launched by Rupert Murdoch's Ghanaian son-in-law, Elkin Pianim, who promised a paper that would focus less on racism and more on some of the positive things that were happening in the community. I was editor of *New Nation* for eight years and the two publications did battle journalistically, but the real fight was between the advertising departments. Eventually *The Voice* won and *New Nation* folded in 2007 due to dwindling commercial revenue.

Fifteen years later *The Voice*, now a monthly publication with a regularly updated website, is the only title regularly reporting on Black-interest news. Some may argue that there are also blogs and 'Black Twitter', but do they really count?

'It's not journalism, you need an authorised version. Checks and balances,' says Bonsu. It's difficult not to agree with him. The need for strong independent Black newspapers has never been more evident. A single newspaper clearly isn't enough. But as *The Voice* soldiers on, perhaps we should be grateful for small mercies.

Nicola Rollock, Professor of Social Policy and Race, King's College London, sums it up beautifully:

> In a society in which we are otherwise rendered invisible – or only made visible when deemed a problem – the Black British press has been essential to

determining and reflecting who we are on *our* terms. Our cultures, identities, norms and desires – infused with tales of 'back home' – are captured not just in articles, interviews and advertisements but in the names of the journalists and editors who have graced their pages. This is the news – our news – documented for the present and, crucially, as an enduring legacy for generations to come.

Therein lies the importance of a strong Black press.

1982–1992

A Defiant *Voice* in the Wilderness

By Richard Adeshiyan

In 1963, US civil rights leader Martin Luther King Jr. said: 'Injustice anywhere is a threat to justice everywhere.' Yet his words could easily have been used to echo the experience of Black people in 1980s Britain, who faced injustice at every turn. To fully understand the importance of *The Voice*'s entrance into the media landscape, you have to also recognise that it emerged in the midst of a fractured society still trying to adjust to multiculturalism. Two critical events in 1981, the New Cross Fire tragedy followed by the Brixton riot, had magnified an already-strained relationship between the Black community and the Metropolitan Police. The country was three years into a Conservative government under the leadership of Margaret Thatcher and, not unlike the previous decade, the climate was particularly unforgiving towards Black people and other minority communities.

Following incidents such as these, the Black community could not rely solely on reports from most newspapers, as they rarely had the depth of understanding, the inside track or, more importantly, the trust of Black communities. The harsh reality was that, for the next decade, the Black community would be at the mercy of a sneering popular right-wing tabloid press whose reports were often malicious and blatantly racist. This mindset sadly permeated the social fabric of British society. In 1982, unemployment topped three million with Black people disproportionately represented. The dreaded 'sus' law, the source of indiscriminate policing, had created a hostile environment. It was during this decade that the right-wing tabloid press would turn their jingoistic fire on Britain's Black and Asian communities, publishing stories that showed a callous disregard for balance or fairness. When it launched, *The Voice* was 'David' pitted against Fleet Street's 'Goliath'. Throw in the fascist and far-right groups and the picture could not be clearer.

When *The Voice* made its belated entry into this particularly corrosive environment in the summer of 1982, the newspaper would be charged with updating the evolving Black British story. The person who took on this huge responsibility was a child of the Windrush Generation. Val McCalla arrived in the UK from Jamaica in May 1959, aged 15. In a rare interview for Derek Burnett's *Millennium People*, McCalla recalled: 'It was springtime in London and yet the minute I stepped off the plane dressed in my new rayon suit I started to freeze.' Within a year of his arrival he had joined the Royal Air Force (RAF). Although his parents wanted him to become a doctor or a similar profession, he had always longed to become a pilot. Sadly, a perforated eardrum took him into the less glamorous world of accountancy and bookkeeping. He worked in supplies for the five years he served and appreciated the opportunity the RAF gave him to acquire a professional skill. These skills proved invaluable when establishing *The Voice* many years later.

Leaving the RAF in the mid-1960s, he held a variety of admin, accountancy and bookkeeping positions, and was generally drifting along until he reached a pivotal point in his life – the break-up of his marriage at 34. He began to reappraise his life, thinking about what he had achieved and what he still wanted to do. That all changed when a circular dropped through his letterbox canvassing for volunteers to help start a new community newspaper. He offered his services to the paper, *East End News*, in his spare time and would end up on the paper's management committee. His regular feature 'Black Voices' aimed at the local Bengali community and other ethnic minorities formed the majority of the paper's readership. He declared in that interview, 'This was effectively the birth of *The Voice*.'

McCalla was particularly inspired by feedback from the paper's Black and ethnic minority readers about issues raised in 'Black Voices'. *East End News*, which survived largely on local authority grants, would eventually run into serious financial trouble. Unable to breathe new life into the paper, he resolved to start his own. His aim was to establish an independent newspaper targeted specifically at the Black community. Mainstream newspapers, he felt, gave scant coverage to Black issues or perspectives and existing Black newspapers in circulation were aimed more at the older generation of migrants. They focused more on issues 'back home' rather than the interests and aspirations of Black people either born or living in Britain today. He initially thought it might only be an East London newspaper existing more as community service than a commercial venture, and that he could get it off the ground in his spare time while continuing his freelance accountancy work in the City. Instead, it would become a successful commercial operation. Operating from a 'little hut in Hackney', McCalla worked with a staff of fresh young graduates who offered their services for the reward of a Chinese restaurant meal at the end of the week. McCalla told Derek Burnett in 1999: 'It was an exciting period, although it was a struggle. I look back on those days with affection. People were so energised.'

After securing a £60,000 loan from Barclays Bank, *The Voice* officially made its long-awaited public appearance on the August Bank Holiday at London's Notting Hill Carnival in 1982. Initially 150,000 copies of the twenty-eight-page debut issue were distributed for free at the two-day event, which is considered one of the capital's true celebrations of African Caribbean culture. However, the following week only 4,000 copies of a 50,000 print-run were sold. It would take the majority of its first decade for the newspaper to carve out a niche for itself. McCalla added somewhat poignantly at the end of that interview: 'I am not interested in personal glory, I am more interested in seeing *The Voice* read by the next generation and for it to become a British institution.'

From the outset the newspaper was tasked with many roles and its responsibilities went well beyond just publishing a weekly newspaper. It would take on a Hansard-like function on behalf of the Black community as a publication of record. It was part radical clenched fist, part community confessional, concerned counsellor, educator and campaigner. The Greater London Council (GLC) had been established in 1981 and in the wake of the derisory Scarman Report commissioned after the Brixton riots, the landscape started to shift. *The Voice*'s arrival could not have been more perfectly timed, especially as the 'equal opportunities' mantra was being espoused by local and central government. The newspaper would showcase the rising stars of entertainment, music, arts and sport, and followed many taking their first steps on their entrepreneurial journey. The newspaper also attempted to push back on tired stereotypes and held up a mirror to Black Excellence, but its news pages refused to sugar-coat Britain's Black reality. The first issue provided a real reminder of the task in hand. Surprisingly, the very first front-page story was not a Black African or Caribbean one, but was a story that would resonate throughout the decade. Under the headline, 'Living in terror', the front-page story revealed that police were investigating racist gangs' repeated attempts to burn down the home of a Pakistani family living in Waltham Forest. In those early years, *The Voice* often took up the cause on behalf of Bengali and Pakistani communities regularly targeted by fascist far-right groups. The choice of story was hardly surprising, as at the time McCalla was living alongside Asian families in London's Bethnal Green and was well aware of the community's challenges when working at the *East End News*.

The second lead story, 'Dying on the dole', made for equally grim reading as it was revealed unemployment in Britain had reached an all-time high of 3.2 million. The report highlighted a survey that made the shocking claim that unemployed men were more than twice as likely to commit suicide and 40 per cent were more vulnerable to cancer. Within that article Lord Scarman esti-mated the rate of unemployment among Black people under 19 in Brixton to be as high as 55 per cent. The resolve of the Black community would be severely tested that summer at Notting Hill Carnival, but thankfully the event passed without any trouble. This was acknowledged in the second issue with four simple words: 'Carnival speaks for itself!' The newspaper's editorial com-ment dubbed it 'the miracle of Notting Hill', declaring:

The 1982 Notting Hill Carnival was a triumph for the organisers. It was a source of pleasure to thousands that attended, and one, ultimately of relief to the vast num-bers of police who had been drafted in anticipating the worst. It was also seen as a miracle in the context of the next 363 days of unemployment, social inequality and oppression of Britain's Black population.

More significantly it was the reporting of the tragic death of 21-year old Paul Worrell, which gave the reader a grisly glimpse of things to come. The headline read, 'Sobbing mother says her son was killed', and the full story included chilling words from the family's solicitor, who said: 'God help anyone in the medical wing of Brixton Prison'. Paul Worrell was found dead in his prison cell earlier that year and the newspaper would follow this story with beady-eyed intent. Brixton, long considered the spiritual home of Britain's Black community, had garnered a reputation for resisting heavy-handed policing. Regular drug raids on Railton Road, the area of resistance known simply as the 'Frontline', would often make headlines in the newspaper, with many convinced that the police used these raids as a show of strength. However, if the 1981 disturbances had proved anything, Brixton was an abject lesson in how not to police.

But, there was no pretending that street crime and robbery were not a huge problem in Lambeth, and the combination of rampant Black youth unemployment and oppressive policing produced an unpalatable cocktail. An early *The Voice* news article revealed 80 per cent of street crimes involving violence were committed against women between 30–70 years old. By September 1982 unemployment had hit 3.4 million and a Lambeth Council report showed unemployment among young Black people in the borough had risen by 79 per cent over the year. In Brixton alone, an increase of 71 per cent had been recorded for those aged between 19–24. Official estimates for Brixton were that 50 per cent of all Black people under 24 were out of work, but it claimed the real figure could have been as high as 75 per cent. John Tilley, the MP for Lambeth Central described the figures as 'frightening':

> Black people were in a worse position for employment before the recession and their relative position is getting worse. I think these figures give the lie to the Government's claim that they have done a great deal for Brixton. Peter Davis, Lambeth's Tory Deputy Leader, agreed that the figures were 'deeply disturbing' and that 'Blacks were suffering disproportionately.'

While the Greater London Council (GLC) and the government refuted any reports suggesting that they were not helping the country's Black population, the figures spoke for themselves. When GLC leader Ken Livingstone was interviewed by *The Voice* in 1982, he agreed Black employment was a major issue and was being addressed, but when asked how many Black people there were in senior positions at the GLC, he said:

> There isn't a single Black person in a senior administrative position in the GLC. The highest Black paid officer must be Herman Ouseley, the head of the Ethnic Minorities Unit. After the election, we asked how many out of a total of 7,000 firemen were Black and we found out there were only 10. We changed the recruitment methods, we advertised posts for firemen in the ethnic press and we now have 30 Black firemen.

Previously, these posts were very rarely advertised and invariably passed down to family and friends. It would take another three years to get 100 Black firemen and -women.

The newspaper also committed to covering international news as 'it recognised that large numbers of London's Black people look towards horizons far beyond the boundaries of their adopted city, maintaining an interest not only in the land of their birth but also in places where racial struggles which parallel their own experiences are in progress.' The 1982 story, headlined 'Non-stop Vigil', showed the newspaper's early support for South Africa's Black struggle against apartheid. Protesters were pictured outside South Africa House in London's Trafalgar Square demonstrating for the release of three Black South African freedom fighters locked up in Pretoria Prison's death row under South Africa's notorious security laws.

However, the paper had not forgotten that it was also in the business of attracting paying customers. Marketing and promotions would become important arsenals in reaching a new younger audience. Running down the right side of the front page was the obligatory flash: 'Coming soon in your *Voice*: Win! A Ford Capri, a holiday for two, video and TV and designer clothes.' Inside readers got a glimpse of the future under the headline 'Boateng shines at memorial reception', with a report on the Marcus Garvey Memorial Trust event held at Brixton's Abeng Youth Centre to mark the ninety-fifth anniversary of the birth of Jamaica's visionary hero. The prominent Black lawyer Rudy Narayan, the charismatic founder of the Afro-Asian and Caribbean Lawyers Association, which became the Society of Black Lawyers, was present. But it was fellow lawyer Councillor Paul Boateng, Vice chairman of the GLC Ethnic Minorities Committee, who stole the show. Following his speech, the paper reported that the audience applauded heartily. 'He's an alright guy', a young Rastafarian remarked. 'Anything happens to him now, Brixton burns again.'

The debut issue also introduced its 'Voices Profile' section, which celebrated the significant contributions of Black women from different walks of life. The profile of mother and house-wife Josie Harriott begins: 'Whatever title we use some of us remain *just* housewives, but some can turn our humble role into the art of living. I met one such woman the other day, Josie Harriott. She is one of those remarkable people who know how to turn disadvantage into advantages.' Harriott spent her child-hood in a children's home unaware of the existence of her parents. However, she maintained that she 'was not deprived of anything' and went on to work in hospitals most of her adult life. She married at 27 and brought up five children more or less single-handed.

Early in its run the newspaper had no hesitation in becom-ing the proverbial Rottweiler fighting injustice on behalf of the Black community. During this decade, The Commission for Racial Equality (CRE) was producing countless damning reports, which were all subsequently covered in the pages of the newspaper. Along with a long list of societal injustices faced by the Black community, one of the newspaper's most revisited subjects was deaths in police and prison custody. The news-paper started making the police accountable for their role in the deaths of Colin Roach and Paul Worrell. Despite the news-paper's tireless campaigning, the deaths kept coming and many of the stories had a familiar ring to them. The verdict 'death by misadventure' was often heard at inquests and became part of the vernacular. The place of death was predominantly a police cell and over 70 Black men lost their lives in custody in the 1980s.

There were also constant reminders of the key events that immediately preceded the newspaper. *The Voice* ran a front-page

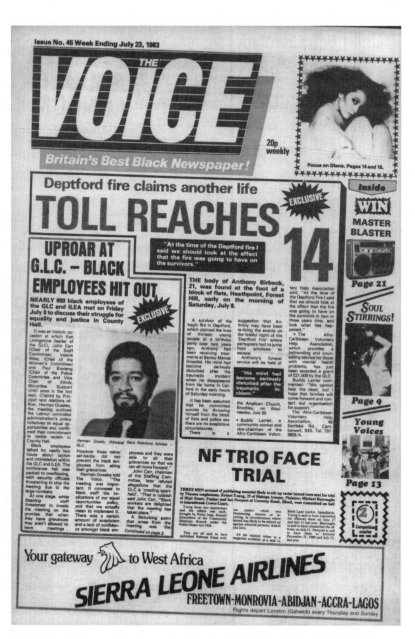

The Voice *was launched a year after two tragedies shook the Black community –
the Brixton riot and the New Cross fire. In 1983, the paper reported that a
fourteenth person had died as a result of the fire*

story commemorating the deaths of 13 children who died in the 1981 New Cross fire, marking the start of the newspaper's focus on this tragedy. The report announced that the New Cross Parents Committee would be holding an ecumenical service at St Mary's Parish Church, Lewisham with the participation of Wilfred Wood, Archdeacon of Southwark. Sadly, the community received another unwanted reminder in July 1983, when the newspaper ran the front page announcing: 'Deptford fire claims another life – toll reaches 14.' The body of 21-year-old Anthony Berbeck, who had become seriously disturbed after the traumatic event, was found at the bottom of a South London tower block. The newspaper would follow the story with 'A decade in mourning', marking the tenth anniversary of the New Cross fire featuring pictures of the 13 young lives lost. The newspaper clearly understood that the New Cross fire was a uniquely Black British story and reflected the resistance and resilience of a new generation.

The newspaper very quickly shone a light on injustices in the Black community, often moving swiftly to douse inflammatory and misleading reporting at a time when the term 'institutional racism' was not yet common parlance in the UK. In its second issue, the story 'Not all scroungers' corrected biased national news coverage, which reported a Department of Social Security (DSS) swoop in Oxford. It claimed police had netted 400 unemployed 'fiddlers' and gave the impression that ethnic claimants were scroungers. At the time Oxford had a population of 100,000, of which 5,000 were Asians and 3,000 African Caribbeans, but just two people of colour were detained and charged. Despite this, the news story that appeared in the *Sun* also included a cartoon of a magistrate's court depicting the majority of the accused as non-white. Elsewhere in that issue the story

The paper was keen to highlight instances where other national newspapers had unfairly painted people of colour in an unfavourable light

'Stop and search – protest over new Home Office proposals' revealed that police would be able to take fingerprints of anyone over the age of ten, by force if necessary, should Home Office proposals be implemented. These two stories merely scratched the surface and as the months unravelled it was clear that the newspaper had disturbed a previously untouched hornet's nest.

But amidst the early gloom *The Voice* also reported stories that delivered unexpected levity. Not unsurprisingly, it was an annual cricket fixture between a West Indian side and the Brixton Police in 1982, which presented a metaphorical 'ceasefire' in a historically strained relationship. It was the first and only time a match report appeared on the newspaper's front page, and was appropriately titled, 'No sweat!' The sizeable picture of Police Commander Fairbairn of 'L' Division and Lloyd Coxsone at the match would have made a worthy entrant for any caption competition. The match report was equally convivial and the Brixton West Indian side, which included esteemed soundman and record producer Coxsone, ran out comfortable winners of the Leslie Walker Shield at the Kennington Oval. The newspaper made reference to the match in its editorial comment. It read:

> The real result of the friendly cricket match between Brixton Police and Brixton West Indians last week should not be the figures on the scoreboard. All sports are capable of engendering amongst participants a mutual respect for the opponent's ability, and none more so than the noble game of cricket. If even a little goodwill and mutual regard is carried back to the Frontline where the real hostilities take place this pleasant annual event will have served its true purpose.

Meanwhile, the newspaper was not so charitable in exposing endemic police corruption, racism and brutality so evident in the Mangrove Nine case more than a decade earlier. In truth, some of the policing of Britain's Black communities would not have looked out of place in apartheid South Africa or America's Deep South in the 1960s. Terrifyingly, the reports were so voluminous, it was impossible to gauge the true figure. Disturbingly, this was a police force that was no respecter of age, sex, profession, cultural origin or disability. On closer scrutiny there was a common denominator in the majority of police assault cases – the victims were charged with assaulting the very policeman that had assaulted them. Invariably, these assault charges were thrown out by the courts because the police were found to have blatantly lied. What was particularly noticeable was the large number of police brutality stories covered in the newspaper that featured attacks on elderly and middle-aged Black women. Young Black men were always the prime police target, but these reports revealed that the real miracle was that there had not been more outcomes similar to that of Cherry Groce, who was shot by police in 1985, and Cynthia Jarrett, who died of heart failure in 1985 as police raided her home.

Two stories, 'Gran in cop terror' and 'Granny-bashers' also illustrated the worrying trend. In 1989, 65-year-old Carmen Robinson stepped in when she saw one of her grandson's being arrested by police in Notting Hill. She told *The Voice*: 'I wasn't near anything, I hadn't said anything, and they just pushed me to the ground. I was hurt. But I didn't know how badly at the time.' Later, bumps and bruising were found on her head and back. In 1992, 73-year-old great-grandmother Marie Burke was assaulted by police and later awarded £50,000, one of the highest damages payments at the time. The court found that Mrs

Burke had been viciously assaulted, falsely imprisoned and maliciously prosecuted. Barrister Courtney Griffiths said that the compensation sum highlighted the extent of police dishonesty and incompetence. In reality, when police failed to get their assault case over the line, they turned to the tax payer's war chest to bail them out. The 1986 story 'Coppers pay up – mum wins substantial damages' presents police officers not just content with physically abusing a defenceless woman, but taking delight in her humiliation. Lora Lucas, a Sunday school teacher who was awarded £26,000 after being violently assaulted by police officers, urged Britain's Black community to follow her example and 'get off their backsides and fight for their rights and principles'.

The 46-year-old mother of three, said: 'Many people said to me you can't fight against the police, but I believe you can. It was a horrible case and I was badly abused. But I believe in fighting to the death for what is right. I would do it again.'

Lucas was badly beaten by three police officers in August 1981 who arrested her for staging a sit-in protest in a builder's office where she had gone to complain about 'shoddy' repair work to her home. She was kicked, hit in the eye, punched in the mouth and dumped in a cell. In the High Court her counsel Adrian Fulford said: 'When she arrived at the station her mouth was bleeding, her wrists were swollen and she was bruised.' The article went on to add that as she was carried protesting from one police station to another, officers forcibly pulled her legs apart, looked up her skirt and said: 'What a sight this is before breakfast.' Mrs Lucas was then charged for assaulting the police. Cleared on the charge of assault, she sued Sir Kenneth Newman, the Metropolitan Police Commissioner for damages for assault, false imprisonment and malicious prosecution. Mrs Lucas was awarded £10,000 for assault by three police officers, £1,000 for false imprisonment and £15,000 for exemplary damages after finding that the police had lied to Camberwell Magistrates when unsuccessfully prosecuting Mrs Lucas for assaulting them. Mrs Lucas said: 'It has been a long five-year fight, but I was determined to go with it for the principle of the thing. I was outraged when they looked up my skirt. I am now very bitter. These sorts of people should be wiped out of the police force.'

Sadly, these were not isolated incidents. In 1984 *The Voice* told the story of 46-year-old Clementine George, who received £8,000 damages in the High Court after being beaten up in her home by police four years earlier. She told *The Voice*:

> One of them held me against a radiator while the other hit me in the stomach. I fell to the ground and passed out. I came round soon afterwards and heard them going through the kitchen and lounge. I went up to them to ask them to stop, but they just hit me and knocked me to the ground again. I was in so much pain I couldn't call out.

She was left with a Black eye and severe bruising, and the attack had aggravated her existing angina condition. The judge was shocked at the behaviour of the police and that they had 'concocted a false story' when they realised Mrs George might bring them to court. 'I live in fear. Whenever I hear a knock at the door I start to tremble. I can't sleep and I'm nervous all the time – it's a nightmare,' she added. In 1984, 32-year-old nurse Claudette Whittingham also suffered a beating in her home, when five policemen and three customs officials raided her flat in search of a non-existent drugs haul. She told *The Voice*: 'One of them started hitting me on the hand with a truncheon, while another grabbed me around the neck. When I felt the breath leave me, I bit him. He shouted, "she's stabbed me," and the rest started to hit me.' Her 25-year-old neighbour, who witnessed the incident, said: 'I thought there was someone inside trying to kill her. It was like a siege, there were four patrol cars and five vans. It was like a pack of wolves on a dead carcass. The police left her no dignity at all. I don't know what effect this will have on the children.' After being treated at the hospital she returned to the police station where she was released without charge: 'They wouldn't treat a dog like that. It makes you angry. No human being should be treated like that. I never had much confidence in the police. I have no trust in them now. I would never go to one again.' Because many of these assaults took place in front of young children, the legacy of distrust would be passed on to the next generation.

In 1987 an article in *The Voice*, headlined 'Getting away with blue murder', revealed that one of the five 'bully' police officers jailed at the Old Bailey for the attack on a group of schoolboys in 1983, had already escaped punishment for a similar attack on a Rastafarian man. In 1982 five police officers were involved in an unprovoked attack on Winfield Leon in Finsbury Park, North London. An internal police investigation had cleared the officers, but Mr Leon was awarded £1,200 in damages against the Metropolitan Police in a civil action case in 1985. On that occasion, Judge Marder QC said that the police had flagrantly abused their powers and then told lies. Judge Kenneth Jones was equally damning, describing the policemen as 'vicious hooligans' who had 'lied like common criminals' over the 1983 attack in Holloway, on a group of schoolboys aged 13–16. All five policemen were found guilty of trying to pervert the course of justice and received sentences between two and four years. Baltimore Ranger, who was 16 at the time of the attack, criticised the 18-month sentence given to Farr as a 'joke'. Outside the Old Bailey, he said: 'It does not renew confidence of the youths in the street'. But, he added: 'We were lucky. There are others that this happened to who give up. Our case was just one of many'.

Many of these cases were dogged by police inertia, so the road to justice was often long and tortuous. The 1984 story: 'Sorry – say police – Scotland Yard apologise for 'inhuman' attack', confirmed the belated recognition given to these cases. Stoke Newington couple David White and his wife Lucille, a middle-aged West Indian couple, had two years earlier received £51,000 in damages after successfully suing the Metropolitan Police for assault. At the time the judge said that they had been 'subjected to a catalogue of violence and inhuman treatment'. Scotland Yard's 'sincere apologies and regrets' seven years after the brutal attack, was a belated slap in the face. The couple suffered extensive injuries after 17 police officers from Stoke Newington police station entered the White's home without a warrant and assaulted the occupants in September 1976. One officer who admitted using unnecessary force during the incident was forced to pay a fine, while three other police officers were cleared of disciplinary charges because 'the case could not be proved beyond all reasonable doubt'.

Stoke Newington police officers were among the worst for brutality and corruption. The 1985 story, headlined, 'Assault probe demands MP', recognises a familiar pattern of behaviour by officers and as you read the story one thing becomes patently clear; the odds were not only stacked against Black people, but in this case – and many others – they were totally rigged. In the

Issue No. 123 Week ending February 3, 1985

THE VOICE

Britain's Best Black Newspaper!

30p weekly

'Assault' Probe demands MP

by Steve Pop

' I feel he would be better off taking civil action against the police, as I have no confidence in the police'

Trevor Smith with wife Jacqueline and son Simeon. "The whole thing has been a nightmare for me and my family."

AN MP is demanding an inquiry into the activities of some Metropolitan officers following allegations that they assaulted a suspect and caused over a thousand pounds worth of damage to his car.

Ernie Roberts, MP for Hackney, wants an investigation into the running of Stoke Newington police station after claims by local man Trevor Smith, aged 42, that he was beaten up by officers from the station when he was arrested trying to open his own car.

Mr Smith of Warwick Grove, Upper Clapton, was charged last April with assault, following an incident outside his flat when police believed he was trying to steal a black Daimler car. Mr Smith says he tried to explain that the car was his, but was still arrested by officers. While on his way to the police station Mr Smith claims officers

pushed him onto the floor of the van he was travelling in, stamped on him and pushed his arms hard behind his back.

Several days after the incident for reasons unknown to him, police towed away Mr Smith's Daimler. He claims that on collecting the car, there were dents and scratches all over it. Cost of repair work was estimated at £1,500.

At Old Street Court last October magistrates dismissed assault charges brought against Mr Smith.

Following the alleged assault by police, Mr Smith has lodged an official complaint with Scotland Yard's Com-

plaints Investigation Bureau and has instructed his solicitor to start legal proceedings to sue the police for assault, false arrest, and damage to his car.

Ernie Roberts said "I have had a number of complaints from constituents about the Stoke Newington police station and think there needs to be an investigation into its running."

"The problem is that there is no council or community cooperation with police in the area. I am very unhappy with the situation," said Mr Roberts.

Ian Haig of Hackney CRE who have supported Mr Smith in his case, said "I think he has a justifiable complaint, I feel he would be better off taking civil action against the police as I have no confidence in the police complaints procedure."

Looking back over the events of the last year Mr Smith said, "The whole thing has been a nightmare for me and my family. My children are

frightened when they see policemen, and I still suffer muscle pains from when they grabbed my arms.

"All I want now is justice. I no longer feel angry towards the

police," said Mr Smith.

Detective Chief Inspector D. G. Harrison, who has been appointed by Scotland Yard to investigate police actions in the case, said he could not

comment specifically about the matter, as his investigations were still continuing.

However he added, "Mr Smith can be assured that there will be a thorough and fair investigation into the

matter."

But MP Ernie Roberts hit back saying. "I don't see how you can have a fair verdict when you have a situation where by police officers investigate the actions of other officers."

Fast Eddie flies out...

HOLLYWOOD'S super cop Eddie Murphy left London last Thursday after a five day visit, with his attractive fiancee Lisa Figuerod.

The 23-year-old star was in town to promote his smash hit film Beverley Hills Cop which has already earned him £60 million.

Eddie is on the other side of the law for a change, after playing the clever chief in Trading Places to being a bright Detroit cop on vacation in Beverley Hills.

See Buzz Inside for more about Eddie's smashing film.

In 1985 Hackney MP Ernie Roberts called for an inquiry into the running of Stoke Newington police station

report, Ernie Roberts, MP for Hackney, called for an investigation into the running of Stoke Newington police station after claims by local Trevor Smith, 42, that he was beaten up by officers from the station when he was arrested trying to open his own car. Mr Smith was charged with assault, following an incident outside his flat when police believed he was trying to steal a black Daimler car. Mr Smith said he tried to explain that the car was his, but was still arrested by officers. While on his way to the police station Mr Smith claimed officers pushed him onto the floor of the van he was travelling in, stamped on him and pushed his arms hard behind his back.

Several days later the incident, police towed away Mr Smith's Daimler. He claims that on collecting the car, there were dents and scratches all over it. The cost of repair work was estimated at £1,500. At Old Street Magistrates Court the assault charges brought against Mr Smith were dismissed. Looking back over the events of the year Mr Smith said: 'The whole thing has been a nightmare for me and my family. My children are frightened when they see policemen.'

This reality was echoed in the 1988 story, 'We prayed while cops beat us up,' when three churchgoers, Samuel Massiah, 21, Trevor Palmer, 24, and Winston Brian, 23, were returning from a Seventh-Day Adventist holiday camp in Great Yarmouth and were stopped by police in Tottenham for allegedly dropping litter. They claimed they had been punched and kicked by police and called 'baboons, coons and Black bastards' and told that England was not their country. Massiah's injuries were so severe he had to take time off work. He told *The Voice*: 'The venom with which the police officers insulted us was terrifying and the racial abuse that they came out with was filled with real hate.' As the men were being taken to Tottenham police station they knelt and prayed in the police van. 'Our faith saw us through the ordeal. We prayed that God would look after us and make sure we were safe. When the police saw what we were doing, they laughed', added Samuel.

The 1988 story 'Thug cops in deaf kids "attack"' revealed that age was no barrier. Tottenham MP Bernie Grant called for the sacking of five Tottenham police officers who allegedly beat up two deaf schoolboys, Michael Slack and Roger Husbands, in a brutal attack after they were arrested while innocently looking over a garden wall for a ball they had lost two days earlier. The two youngsters, both 13, attended a special unit for hearing-impaired children at Gladstone Community School in Tottenham. Roger was able to relay the horrific details to his mother – they were beaten and kicked and punched in the stomach and chunks of hair pulled out and were held in custody for over three hours without anyone being informed. This style of policing was also evident when Tottenham police stopped Stedroy Williams in his car on his way home from work in 1991, telling him he was wanted for an offence. The story, 'Cops beat me up and then said sorry', goes on to say that the officers punched him in the neck, broke his car phone and held him in a cell for nine hours. After realising he wasn't their man, they apologised and sent him home. They had mistaken the 14-stone Williams for a nine-stone man.

The police's targeting of young Black men took many forms and being totally innocent was never a good enough excuse. Many ran the gauntlet just leaving their homes. One friend recalled an incident from the 1980s when he was running for a bus with a friend in Hackney. In those days you could literally chase down the old Routemaster and grab hold of the handrail at the back of the bus. No sooner had they gone upstairs and sat

Police brutality to disabled man

A JUBILANT Patrick Wilson was cleared last week at Tower Bridge Magistrates Court on charges of obstruction and assaulting a police officer.

The charges arose from an incident in the Old Kent Road. Mr Wilson, 29, severely handicapped (suffering from sickle-cell anaemia and arthritis), had driven his girlfriend Susan Farbridge to work. After saying goodbye to her, he noticed a police car approaching from the opposite direction.

The police car soon did a u-turn and proceeded to follow Wilson, eventually turning on their siren and lights. On pulling over to the side of the road, he was approached and ordered to "turn off the engine and get out". He tried to explain the fact that he was disabled but the officer replied: "shut your mouth, you black bastard".

Patrick then decided that if he was to entertain the officers any further it would be with witnesses so he drove off, making his way back to the minicab office where his girlfriend was working.

The police had by now requested assistance, and on arriving at the 'cab office his car was surrounded by a large group of police officers.

The officers then held an impromptu conference before deciding their next move.

Susan Farbridge, who had been told earlier by a colleague who had seen Patrick stopped, and having searched fruitlessly for him, arrived back at the office to find a group milling around his car. She too tried explaining that her boyfriend's disabilities, asking them to show some consideration. She was told to clear off.

The police, in the shape of PC Patterson, had now got into the car through its hatchback and after "subduing" Patrick, opened the doors for his colleagues, another four police officers clambered into the car. In the ensuing melee, it was alleged Patrick bit PC Rossiter's hand in the hope of breaking free.

Susan, who had protested throughout at the treatment being meted out to her boyfriend, was eventually arrested and placed in a waiting van, followed later by Patrick, who was "thrown into the van like a slab of meat". During the trip back to the police station, PC Rossiter in particular continued with the torrent of abuse "why don't you f— off back to the sunshine, you f—ing Rasta".

On their arrival at court, the couple were further charged with obstructing another police officer — this too was thrown out.

In discharging, the magistrate went on record stating "no credence can be given to the evidence of the police officers involved — in particular that of PC Patterson".

John Paisley

Patrick Wilson being helped into court by Susan Farbridge.
Pic by John Paisley

Cont. from page one
"BECAUSE I'M BLACK"

Sandra Luke.   Pic by David McCalla

. . . And another case, 27-year-old Doreen Bogle

TWENTY-SEVEN-YEAR-OLD Doreen Bogle has worked in the BBC's engineering department for four years.

Although she has known of it, it is not until now that she is experiencing what she describes as the "subtle racism" practised by the Corporation.

Some weeks ago, Doreen was provoked by a white workmate and a fight ensued.

Many insulting words were exchanged, not least of which was the word "wog" that the white girl used referring to Doreen.

There were three witnesses to the event.

The white girl reported the incident to the personnel manager, who summoned Doreen and promptly suspended her from work, in order to "sort things out".

The white girl, however, was not sent home.

After two-and-a-half days suspension, Doreen appeared at a disciplinary board meeting, where she was informed that fighting was not allowed on the premises but as this was the first time it occurred she would not be dismissed.

But then, last week, Doreen was asked to sign a report, taking full responsibility for the incident.

Doreen refused, on the advice of her union (Association of Broadcasting Staff) representative, and asked why the three witnesses to the event were not called forward.

She was told they did not wish to be involved.

In the meantime, Doreen is waiting for an amended report to be submitted to her to sign. She told The Voice: "They are not interested at the disciplinary board — they asked me when did I last have a fight — as if all black people fight.

"I told them that the last fight I had was when I was 11 — during my first year at school."

FERNANDES BARRED OVER 'RACIST ROOKIES'

DESCRIBING LEAKS to The Voice and other media regarding racist essays by police cadets as a breach of conduct, police chiefs at Hendon Police College have barred Asian lecturer John Fernandes from the building.

Mr Fernandes, who has been teaching at Hendon for eight years, was given two hours to clear his possessions and leave for what Scotland Yard described as "a substantial breach of trust".

A working party from Brent Council, made up of five Labour, one Liberal and one Conservative councillors, are looking into the affair and Bryan Stark, Chair of the Education Committee, has mentioned the possibility of withdrawing all of the 28 lecturers working at Hendon Police College.

Mr Fernandes made it clear that he intends to continue to attend the college.

Leader of Brent Council, Martin Coleman, said: "The real problem is not John Fernandes but the failure of the police to take seriously the racist attitude in the cadets essays.

"Rather than attempt to discuss a way of dealing with the problems, the police have acted in an arbitrary manner.

"Brent would still be willing to discuss all aspects of the situation providing there is a return to the status quo — that is, lay instructors reinstated on the course of multi-cultural education and John Fernandes goes back to teaching the course he was responsible for devising.

"Even at this late stage, I would urge the police to take a reasoned view so that the whole affair can be settled amicably and we can develop a police force which has the confidence of all sections of the population."

SDP's racial justice

THE SOCIAL Democratic Party has recently held elections for its Social Democratic Campaign for Racial Justice for the coming year.

Re-elected as Chairman of the Campaign is Michael Golder, who said: "We will continue to ensure that the ethnic dimension is considered at all levels and play our full part in convincing the electorate that a SDP/ Liberal Alliance Government is the only hope of eliminating poverty and promoting greater equality in our society."

One of the Joint Secretaries to the Campaign, Paul Mathurin, told The Voice: "Basically, the group is something like a pressure group — to ensure that the ethnic dimension is considered when policies are being made by the SDP.

"Our aim is to make sure the ethnic minorities are represented within the party — in fact, it was due to the group that Roy Evans is on the National Steering Committee."

Paul Mathurin — Secretary.

Michael Golder — Chairman.

Disabled driver Patrick Wilson was cleared of obstruction and assaulting a police officer in 1982

down in their seats they were joined by two men, one sitting next to him and another beside his friend. They were plain-clothes police and flashed their cards, proceeding to ask why they were running for the bus. They both played it cool, and with no case to answer the police went about their business. Caught 'running while Black' joined 'walking while Black' as another lame excuse for the police harassing and stopping young Black men. Getting stopped by the police for, effectively, 'driving while Black', was also a very common occurrence and these stories would appear regularly in the newspaper.

The 1982 story 'Police brutality to disabled man' once again exposed the police's use of underhand tactics to secure a charge. The jubilation of the defendant Patrick Wilson, who was cleared of obstruction and assaulting a police officer, told only half the story. The charges arose from an incident on Old Kent Road, South London, when 29-year-old Wilson, who suffered from sickle cell anaemia and arthritis, had driven his girlfriend to work. Driving home, he noticed a police car approaching from the opposite direction. The police car performed a U-turn and proceeded to follow Wilson, eventually turning on their siren and lights. He was pulled over and ordered to 'turn off the engine and get out'. He tried to explain the fact he was disabled, but the officer replied, 'shut your mouth, you Black bastard'. He decided to drive back to the cab office where his girlfriend worked to ensure that there were witnesses, but by this time the police had requested assistance and on arrival he was sur-rounded by a large group of police officers. His girlfriend tried explaining her boyfriend's disability asking them to show some consideration, but was told to clear off. PC Patterson managed to force his way into the car, and after 'subduing' Patrick, opened the doors for another four officers to enter. His girlfriend who had protested throughout was eventually arrested and placed in a waiting van, followed later by Patrick who was 'thrown into the van like a slab of meat.' During the trip back to the police station, PC Rossiter continued with a torrent of abuse, 'why don't you f*** off back to the sunshine, you f***ing Rasta.' On their arrival at court the couple were further charged with obstructing another police–officer - this too was thrown out. In discharging them, the magistrate went on the record stating, 'no credence can be given to the evidence of the police involved – in particular that of PC Patterson.'

This case echoed another where police blatantly lied and were able to operate with impunity. 'I was framed' man's claim of police set-up' reported the acquittal of Derek Mullings, 25, a leading Black copywriter for top advertising firm Collett, Dickenson and Pearce. He was arrested along with a friend at the 1985 Notting Hill Carnival on charges of theft from a person unknown and possession of an offensive weapon. By September the mugging charge was dropped and the offensive weapons charge was dropped by the prosecution earlier the following year. Mr Mullings is convinced that their only crime was that they were Black. He said: 'The police produced a flick knife, a cosh and a cheap gold chain in the back of the van, and they began to discuss how they would frame us.'

The real irony of this case is that Mullings had previously worked on an ad campaign for the Metropolitan Police and his work had been rewarded with many awards and prizes. It was Mullings who wrote the catchy line: 'With today's criminals, it is more grey cells we need.'

In the summer of 1985 the Metropolitan Police also asked Collett, Dickenson and Pearce to prepare a series of radio commercials warning the public about the dangers of mugging at the annual Notting Hill Carnival. The script for the ad was written by Mullings.

Although this was the prevailing culture, another mid 1980s story, 'Rookie forced out, I was made an outcast – that's the penalty for telling the truth', spelled out the risks of going public, even if you were white. The report revealed how a young white police recruit's evidence was instrumental in the jailing of three corrupt colleagues. He claimed that, as a result, he had been pushed out of the force. PC Adrian Dart, 31, was key witness in a week-long trial in 1984 that involved the brutal injuries to 44-year-old British Leyland worker Junior Williams. He had been arrested on suspicion of stealing four light fixtures and taken to Longbridge police station, West Midlands, where the young constable fingerprinted him. At Birmingham Crown Court PC Dart described how in the process of fingerprinting the suspect, he was interrupted by three detectives who took Williams into the CID room where he heard sounds of a scuffle, shouting and sobbing. Williams then emerged with blood streaming down his face. The young PC's evidence was vital in convicting the detectives, who claimed that the British Leyland employee's injuries came from 'overexcited gestures of despair, caused by throwing his hands up to his face.' Since the three long-standing detectives were jailed for periods of up to a year, PC Dart claimed that a campaign of hate had forced him to resign 'in disgust' after 18 months' service with West Midlands Police. His car was vandalised, colleagues refused to speak to him, his wife had received malicious phone calls and even a drawing of PC Dart with a noose around his neck had appeared on a police notice board. The young ex-constable said: 'I was made an outcast. This is the penalty I have paid for telling the truth and playing things straight.' Williams had his theft charges dropped by the police.

If the behaviour of some of police rank and file was an issue, then Inspector Peter Johnson, senior race adviser to the Police Federation, scored a spectacular own goal. Speaking in front of 2,000 officers – some of them Black – at its national conference in Scarborough in 1984, on police training, he said: 'I was on a working party that was dealing with our coloured brethren, er, or nig nogs.' The chair of the meeting immediately jumped up, saying the remark in no way represented the views of the Police Federation. Inspector Johnson had spent 18 months on a Home Office working party, looking into race relations, and was the Police Federation's race relations officer. He also trained on the National Police Training Council. He later said: 'I am very embarrassed, and the remarks do not represent my view of coloured people at all. I talk at training schools to young police officers about coloured people and their problems, and tell them not to use words like "nig nog" or "coon."' He resigned soon after.

Sadly, policing of Black communities did not change dramatically with the introduction of the Police Evidence and Crime Bill in 1984. *The Voice* reported simmering tensions in several London neighbourhoods in early 1985, and there were similar concerns in Toxteth, Liverpool; St Paul's, Bristol; Handsworth, Birmingham; Moss Side, Manchester; and Chapeltown, Leeds. Although divided by geography, the shared Black experience often followed a similar journey and converged at the same destination. Surprisingly Handsworth was the first to erupt in violence after police allegedly punched a Black woman in the face. Two people died and 35 were injured in the riot. *The Voice*'s front page simply asked, 'What now?' featuring a full-sized apocalyptic image of the devastation. The newspaper had seen trouble looming in Brixton several months earlier and a 1985

Issue No. 161. W/E October 26, 1985

THE VOICE

Britain's Best Black Newspaper!

30p weekly

RIOT TORN BRITAIN

A special report starts on page 13

CALL FOR DAY OF ACTION

Community's response to Jarrett Death and Groce shooting

AT a recent meeting of the black community a decision has been made to respond to the police raids that resulted in the death of Mrs Cynthia Jarrett and the shooting of Mrs Dorothy 'Cherry' Groce.

Leading representatives of the black community, including many business people, met black youths at a hastily convened summit meeting in London last week to thrash out this joint response to the recent inner city troubles.

Three main initiatives emerged from the meeting, held in Westminster Bridge road. These include the setting up of a steering committee with a special emphasis on youth representation; preconditions for setting up a foundation for black action and a Black Media Association.

The latter, the BMA has since been formed after publishers and/or their representatives from African Times, Asian Times, Caribbean Times, The Jamaican Gleaner, Black Teens, New Life, The Voice, West Indian World, Root Magazine, Chic, Focus and West Indian Digest met at a later date.

The steering committee formed at the meeting was charged with formulating plans for:

1. A day of action to mark the death of Cynthia Jarrett.
2. A fund to help the families of Mrs Jarrett and Cherry Groce who was paralysed by a police bullet in Brixton.
3. The setting up of educational programmes for black youths.
4. The establishment of a Black Action Foundation with trustees drawn from the community.
5. A study of the conditions of gross deprivation black youths are forced to live under.

The steering committee are due to meet this Wednesday to announce further details of the day of action.

Thousands mourn Cynthia Jarrett

Mourners look on.

CYNTHIA LEONARA JARRETT, 48, who died as a result of a heart attack when police raided her north London home three weeks ago, was mourned by thousands of people at her funeral services.

Mourners who attended the service at St. Paul's Church, in Tottenham, were told by black Reverend Lamont Phillips of nearby St. Matthews Church, that reconciliation should be sought through her death.

"My brothers and sisters let us now with this farewell to Cynthia, build a monument to her and all those who died as a result of violence. Let this be our prayer," he said.

After the funeral, the public responded to the pleas of the Jarrett family for calm. People lined the streets in quiet dignity as the funeral cortège of ten limousines and cars made its way to Southgate Cemetery where Cynthia was buried.

Defence campaign started

NORTH London community leaders set up a defence campaign for justice last weekend and hit out at the policing of the black community following the death of Cynthia Jarrett and the subsequent unrest.

Bernie Grant, leader of Haringey Council, Dolly Kiffin and residents of Tottenham's Broadwater Farm Estate and local community leaders, supported youth action against the police and claimed that since the unrest black residents of the estate have been harassed.

The defence campaign emerged as a result of this local dissatisfaction with the police and was spearheaded by young people who aim to organise themselves and channel all their energies into one group to fight racism.

Spokesman for the Broadwater Farm Youth Association said, "Organisation is the key to fight our oppressors, rioting is not the way. It will get us noticed but it will not help us."

The BFYA have demanded that police funding in their district be withdrawn, a public independent inquiry into the death of Mrs Jarrett and an end to racial harassment and police brutality.

In 1985 the community was shaken by the deaths of Cyntha Jarrett and Dorothy 'Cherry' Groce, who had both died during police raids.

news report revealed that a recent raid on the Brixton 'frontline' had caused another conflict among the local community. Critics feared that it might be the spark for another uprising in the area. In October 1985, the police shooting of 38-year-old Dorothy 'Cherry' Groce in Brixton and the death of Cynthia Jarrett in Tottenham were incendiary and sparked disturbances and destruction in both neighbourhoods. *The Voice*'s front-page headline declared, 'Brixton burns again', alongside a large picture of the police arresting people. The images on the centre pages resembled scenes from a foreign war zone and the newspaper reported that 'an uneasy calm' had descended on Brixton following the shooting.

Angry residents told *The Voice* they would arm and protect themselves against the police because they were 'sick and tired' of officers bursting into their homes and treating them like 'animals'. A middle-aged woman who claimed the police forced themselves into her house looking for a former tenant, told *The Voice*: 'The police have no respect for our homes; they think they can just drop in at any time. I get confused now when I see the police, because I don't know whether they have come to protect me or to kill me.'

Cherry Groce underwent emergency operations at St Thomas' Hospital to remove a splintered bullet from her spine and her eight-year-old daughter Lisa told *The Voice*: 'When I woke up my mum was lying on the floor and a policeman had his gun to her throat, she said, "I can't breathe, I can't feel my legs".'

Lee, Mrs Groce's 11-year-old son choked back the tears, as he said: 'I said to the policeman 'you've shot my mum, haven't you?' And he said to me "don't be silly, it just a graze, she will be alright." A week later the front page splashed 'Attempted murder charge – demands Brixton's Black community, announcing that Brixton's Black community is overwhelmingly in favour of charging Inspector Douglas Lovelock, 42, with the attempted murder of Cherry Groce. The death of 48-year-old Cynthia Jarrett, apparently as a result of heart attack after police entered her Tottenham home, appeared on the same front page with the headline 'Search death'. The report said the fatal incident sparked unrest at the Broadwater Farm Estate, resulting in one death and over 80 injured. Mrs Jarrett's 23-year-old daughter Cynthia claimed that a policeman involved in the search pushed her mother aside, causing her to fall. Fifteen minutes later she was dead. On the Sunday, relatives of Mrs Jarrett led a peaceful demonstration of 400 people to Tottenham Police station. The demonstration produced a heavy police presence and by seven o'clock violence had started. The violence in Tottenham was the worst seen in the recent spate of inner-city disturbances. PC Blakelock, 40, was stabbed to death and a gun was fired at lines of riot police. Winston Silcott, wrongly convicted of PC Blakelock's murder as one of the Tottenham Three in March 1987, had his conviction quashed in 1991, after tests suggested the confessions had been fabricated.

The search of the Jarrett household came after her son Floyd was arrested on suspicion of driving a stolen vehicle. He is then alleged to have assaulted an officer. It was later discovered that the vehicle was not stolen and there was no stolen property found at his mother's house.

These cases united Britain's Black press into the Black Media Association. Publications represented at the association included the *African Times, Asian Times, Jamaican Gleaner, Black Teens, The Voice, West Indian World, Root Magazine, Chic, Focus* and *West Indian Digest*. The 1985 disturbances provided yet

The Voice *documented the devastation in the aftermath of the unrest in Handsworth in 1985*

another reminder of the insidious reporting of right-wing tabloids, which took every opportunity to rubbish the Black community, although they did not need the inner-city unrests as an excuse. An article headlined 'The Black and white media show' read: 'The white community's view of the recent spate of inner-city disturbances is determined either consciously, or sub-consciously, by the media – television, radio and press. This was a fact recognised by the Commission for Racial Equality (CRE) who published a report on this issue entitled 'Public Awareness and the Media' in 1981.' Elsewhere in the article, it reports on Home Secretary Douglas Hurd's ill-fated trip to Handsworth to talk to local people.

The booing which drowned out his efforts to speak was described in the Daily Express as a 'Zulu style war cry'. Continuing the South African and 'Zulu' type imagery, the *Daily Mail*, *Daily Express* and *Sun* continually referred to young Black British people as 'chanting West Indians'. In 1987 *The Voice*'s article 'Another Sun exclusive' attacked the racism spread by the *Sun*, and its targeting of popular Rastafarian poet Benjamin Zephaniah. A picture of Zephaniah appeared alongside a leader article in the *Sun* on 27 April 1987, with the headline, 'Would you let this man near your daughter?' recalling the ultimate question common in British racist folklore, 'would you let a Black man marry your daughter?'

The editorial focused on the fact that Zephaniah had been invited by Trinity College, Cambridge, to take up a fellowship. The paper indignantly quoted some lines of his poetry unflattering to the Royal family. 'Is this really the kind of man parents would wish to have teaching their sons and daughters?' The *Sun* asked before insulting his dreadlocks. The article read: 'From the picture Mr Zephaniah could do with a shampoo and set.'

However, to truly understand the paper's mentality and antipathy towards Black and Asian communities, you had to get inside the belly of the beast, which the left-leaning *New Statesman* achieved in November 1985. The piece, 'Daylight on The Sun', was based on a diary kept by Peter Court while he worked on the paper's arts desk as graphic designer for a few months. One of then-editor Kelvin MacKenzie's choice remarks noted by Court was: 'Well Botha has said the days of white power are over in South Africa. What he doesn't say is what's going to happen when the darkies come down from the trees.'

'No I'm not having pictures of darkies on the front page,' said deputy editor David Shapland, who was deputising for MacKenzie on the night an Asian man won *Sun* Bingo. 'That's the last thing our readers want – pictures of Blacks raking it in.' At the time, MacKenzie dismissed Court's diary as more 'crap' from the lefties, maintaining he was not racist.

Court wrote: 'This brought a wry smile from execs who had heard him ask at conference what happened at the end of the film *Ghandi* when it was shown on TV. He had switched channels before the end, he told them, because he was not interested in "a lot of fucking bollocks about an emaciated coon". To this day, it seems that these insidious views and reporting are still greeted with a severe case of selective amnesia. This was also a period when government-aided compulsory repatriation was being touted. With the Home Office minister David Waddington announcing in the story, 'Easier repatriation,' that the government would make it easier for immigrants to return from where they come from.

In response to this political climate, *The Voice* spent much of the 1980s shaping its own narrative. The newspaper covered a vast array of topics, from female circumcision and Black homosexuality, to domestic violence and abortion. There was an in-depth three-part series on Rastafarianism, plus the fascinating Magdala Files story, which highlighted Ethiopia's stolen Black history. Reader's letters, a 'Talkback' slot, along with the editorial comment and regular columnists, all reflected a different perspective on Black life. The 'Black Eye' column, which encouraged readers to send in any derogatory or racist stories, also made interesting reading.

Unfortunately, continual brutal policing resulted in the deaths of too many young Black men. They were disproportionately represented in the figures for deaths in police or prison custody and there remained far too many unanswered questions. In January 1983, the death of Colin Roach, who was found shot dead in the foyer of Stoke Newington Police station, would become *The Voice*'s 'cause celebre'. The potent front-page headline read, 'Colin Roach death sparks revolt', and *The Voice* was the first newspaper to talk to Colin Roach's family and friends. Initially, the case was said to be a suicide but after scrutiny by the family and the Black community, a demand for a full-scale public inquiry was requested by the Hackney Legal Defence Committee. After conducting its own investigation, the newspaper discovered inconsistencies and conflicting police reports. The story was reported on almost weekly following his death and a half-page article 'The Roach Affair: the fight goes on' appeared in the newspaper's 1983 review issue. Five years later the newspaper carried an article titled, 'How did Colin Roach die?' in response to an independent inquiry that cast grave doubts on the official version of his death.

Sadly, this pattern of police behaviour would become the norm. A 1987 story, 'Sisters sue for lack of care', reported that the family of a young man who collapsed and died in court

NEWS

Angry crowds gather outside Stoke Newington Police station to ask:

Who killed Colin?

ON FRIDAY, January 21, at 7.30pm, a meeting was held by the Hackney Black People's Association at the Hackney Town Hall, calling for an independent inquiry into the alleged suicide of Colin Roach.

The meeting was chaired by Pansy Adale and those in attendance included the Mayor of Hackney, Sam Springer, and Cllr Kodikara amongst others. There were over 100 people in attendance.

The main points of the meeting included the discussion of the need for black people to organise properly and thus execute a peaceful march. The background of racist attacks which is inherent in Stoke Newington police station was revealed by Pansy Adele.

On Saturday, January 22 at about 2pm, a mass demonstration was held, amidst enormous tension because of the huge numbers of police and the outrage felt by the black youth.

The demonstration was led by the Roach family and placards of Colin Roach's picture were seen. There was about 1,000 people participating, including a number of various community organisations and, at several points, it almost got out of hand.

A black policeman was called a traitor and had a few placards thrown at him.

The police orchestrated the march and people joined in as the march proceeded from Hackney Town Hall to Stoke Newington Common.

The plea for peace and strategic organisation were the sentiments expressed by various community leaders, including Cllr Dennis Twomey. Mr Roach said: "I want to thank you all for the support which you have shown . . . Colin did not kill himself, he had too much to live for", before breaking into tears.

COLIN ROACH AFFAIR

●A demonstrator from last Monday. About 40 arrests have been made in the week after the Roach tragedy.

Pics by Philip Wolmuth

ON MONDAY, January 17, at 2.15pm, about 60 black youths assembled outside Stoke Newington police station demanding a public inquiry into the alleged suicide of Colin Roach.

Despite Scotland Yard's report of drinking, abusive comments and consistent warnings, the demonstration was a peaceful one.

The Voice was on hand and witnessed the demonstrators walking peacefully down to Dalston Junction and back up Stoke Newington High Street to the police station. The police did "escort" the protestors and when they returned to stand in front of the police station, about three busloads of policemen were brought in and had already begun positioning themselves within the crowd.

The Voice witnessed the Commander giving the signal, and it was at that point that the "disturbances" started. Several of the demonstrators were openly fighting with the police and the black youths kept saying "Take your hands off me". The police ignored these demands and five of them bodily carried and dragged a number of demonstrators into the police station. One young black woman, who the police attempted to arrest, punched a policeman in the face in the middle of the road, and then four of his back-up team, including a policewoman, carried her into the station. "One on one!" cried a black youth to a policeman. He retorted: "I said to move along — move on!" He threatened

One youth being arrested at Stoke Newington.

"Take your hands off me"

The 17 demonstrators who were arrested were taken to different police stations immediately. The Voice spoke to both solicitors, Ms Gareth Pearce and Mr Erwin Adams. The first is handling the case of one demonstrator, whilst the latter is handling the case of 18 demonstrators. They informed us that all of the arrested demonstrators were released on unconditional bail and that their charges included causing actual bodily harm to a police officer, threatening behaviour and obstructing the pavement. Their case has been adjourned until March 1.

to arrest this youth and so, to avoid being senselessly arrested, the youth moved on.

Police reply

Dear Sir,
I have been made aware that a meeting to discuss the tragic death of Colin Roach is to be held at 1pm on Saturday, January 22, 1983, outside Hackney Town Hall. Leaflets have been distributed in public places.

You were one of a number of people who attended the meeting at Stoke Newington Police Station on Saturday, January 15, 1983, when police

gave full details of the investigation into Colin Roach's death and answered questions put by those present.

Despite extensive efforts by police to dispel mis-information and reduce tension, disorder has occurred. Criminal offences, such as theft and robbery have also taken place in the wake of the disorder.

I would urge you to exercise your influence to avoid further disorder and if present at the proposed meeting (January 22, 1983) do everything possible to ensure it is peaceful and lawful. The meeting should know that a public inquiry (an inquest) will be held.

Your assistance is greatly welcomed.

W. Moore

Hackney Mayor spearheads appeal

COLIN ROACH AFFAIR

AS THE Colin Roach death continues, with many questions unanswered, the call for a public inquiry is growing.

Heading the call for a public inquiry is Hackney Mayor Sam Springer.

"There are lots of questions that have not been answered", he told The Voice. "And the only satisfaction that I think that those who are showing concern can get is a public inquiry.

"The amount of complaints that have come out against Stoke Newington police — those that have been recorded by the police complaints board and those which have been recorded by voluntary organisations people go to for help and assistance — certainly point a finger at Stoke Newington police.

"There was a report which indicated that people of extreme views within the extreme right political parties are members of the law enforcement agencies and I have got no doubt that there is a possibility that we have got

Sam Springer.

some in Stoke Newington."

Mr Springer went on to say that the Colin Roach affair and the way Stoke Newington police work were two separate issues and that two public inquiries were necessary.

"The two issues are separate and I think the first issue is

basically to clear the air in respect of the Colin Roach affair because I think this is owed to the family. I think the family needs to be satisfied at the end of the day what actually did happen. But the wide issues in terms of policing Hackney needs another inquiry and I think it's about time it happened.

"The whole of the police force in Hackney aren't bad — they've got some genuine policemen who want to see things turn for the best. I've a lot of respect for the home beat policemen.

"But the police have got to create a public image that the public will respect — they've got to make the first move in declaring their activities open to public scrutiny.

"I would implore the police authorities concerned in this case to do that."

Speaking from the GLC's conference on the Police and Criminal Evidence Bill at County Hall over the weekend, Paul Boateng, Chair of the GLC Police Committee, told The Voice: "The death of Colin Roach is a tragedy and the treatment of his family is an indictment of Hackney Police.

"I fully support the demand for a public inquiry."

In its first decade, The Voice *established itself as a campaigning newspaper and regularly reported on the death of Colin Roach*

were suing the prison authorities and the police for withholding medical treatment. The court's unanimous verdict that the 27-year-old man would not have died had he received proper care was a familiar postscript. It was revealed that prison staff, including a physician, ignored the symptoms of a sickle cell crisis despite knowing the prisoner suffered from the complaint. He had been picked up by police several days earlier, but they were unable to find the arrest warrant and he was held without seeing a solicitor on an unknown offence. A week later, he was pronounced dead in the cells of Thames Magistrates, Court. Disturbingly, the widow of Winston Rose was still awaiting an apology eight years after he died at the hands of the police, although she received £130,000 in damages.

Regrettably, even when cases seemed clear cut, the final outcome could be totally unexpected. The report 'Anger over biker death – "The verdict was bloody rotten"' told the story of Black Hell's Angel biker John Mickelsen, who died in hospital after a struggle with police in 1985. He had been hit over the head with a truncheon, put into a police van and left in the charge room of Feltham police station. He died without regaining consciousness. The original verdict of 'unlawful killing' was quashed by the second inquest, which returned a verdict of 'death by misadventure.' Although these cases were predominantly in London, there were also young Black men dying at the hands of police in the UK's other cities. The death of 24-year-old Clinton McCurbin in Wolverhampton in February 1987, nearly 35 years ago, was Britain's very own George Floyd. McCurbin was suspected of using a stolen credit card in Next in the Dudley Street shopping precinct, and police were called to the scene. What started as a non-violent encounter resulted in McCurbin being pinned to the ground the same way Derek

Chauvin pinned George Floyd to the ground. Although his death bore all the hallmarks of the shocking US murder, this happened well before the advent of citizen journalism. Rather conveniently for the police, McCurbin's killing would not be captured on camera phone and go viral after being posted on social media.

Although the headline, 'Another death – Wolverhampton stunned by new police death,' was shockingly familiar, its level of newsworthiness at the time did not bring the world to a standstill. The report described Wolverhampton as 'a volcano ready to erupt', and that feelings in the Midlands town were running high following the death of McCurbin. West Midlands Police were reluctant to reveal exactly how McCurbin was restrained, but countless witnesses claim the two officers held him face down on the ground, with an officer kneeling on his back forcing his head backwards. Members of the public who witnessed the event stepped forward shouting that they were killing him. He was dead within minutes from asphyxia consistent with restraint. Initial police reports that the death had been the result of a heart attack induced by drug taking proved to be incorrect and led to angry demands that the statement be withdrawn. A leaflet distributed in the aftermath of the killing read: 'When he protested he was punched, kicked and dragged.' Witness Paul Brown said he saw two police officers holding McCurbin down, one on his back, the other holding his feet, and then 'all of a sudden he went funny.'

The killing triggered disturbances in the city for several weeks and the coverage in local newspaper *Wolverhampton Express & Star*, which supporting the police line and stoked up fear, angered the Black community. In the wake of McCurbin's death, *The Voice* followed up with the front-page headline,

'Demo call for police death', and interviewed the bereaved family and local community figures. A seven-day inquest into Clinton's death returned a verdict of 'misadventure' and, unlike Derek Chauvin, none of the officers involved were ever prosecuted. In the aftermath of the killing, the flagrant use of the neck-lock would come under the microscope.

The newspaper's 1988 story, 'New drive for Black cops', revealed a fundamental problem. Police recruitment of minority officers had hit the buffers, with no Black or Asian officers in 100 new recruits to the Brixton force. Out of 400 Black and Asian officers serving in London, just one was stationed in Brixton. There were similar recruitment drives in Peckham, Streatham and Croydon. The Metropolitan Police had committed itself to an Equal Opportunities policy in 1986, but the figures still told the real story. There were just 412 Black and Asian police officers out of a total of 27,366 in the force. If policing was an erupting volcano spewing hate and bile, then many Black employees found the workplace experience bittersweet. Advertising from the capital's borough councils along with the Greater London Council (GLC), NHS and the London Fire Brigade had helped stimulate the Black recruitment drive. Effectively, this recruitment push produced new buzz words, such as 'We are an equal opportunities employer' and 'We are serious about equal opportunities'. The newspaper's headline story 'Jobs galore!' greeted the news that the GLC had designated 1985 as the 'Jobs Year'. But often, the 'equal opportunities' message rang hollow for many who worked in both the public and private sector.

In 1984, the newspaper revealed council employee Lucille Guichard had accused Camden Council of racism in their employment policies. Guichard, who had worked for the council for 15 years had applied for the position of supervisor but was

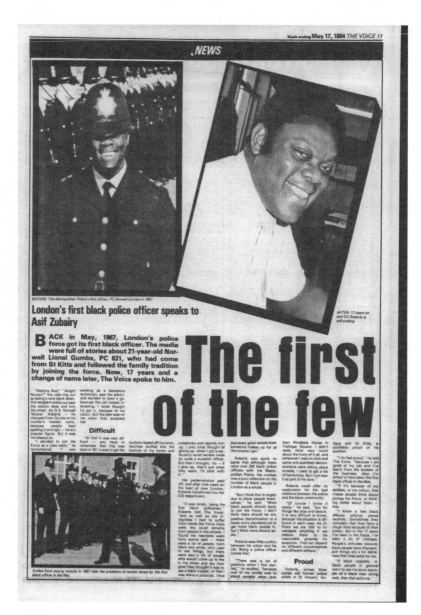

In 1984 The Voice *interviewed Asif Zubairy, the first Black police officer to serve in London*

given 'excuses' by the manager and the job was given to someone who, she claimed, had no experience. Guichard explained she was under constant pressure from the supervisor. She told *The Voice* that she had to have a time sheet while the other workers did not. When she handed her time sheet in, pages went missing and money was deducted from her pay. In addition to this treatment, she said she walked in one day to find a toy monkey sitting on her chair. She told *The Voice*: 'The other workers were sitting around laughing and making jokes such as "Hey monkey! Where do you come from? Why don't you go back to where you came from. Go on, go back and swing on your trees."'

Guichard accused her supervisors of personal prejudice and racial discrimination. She claimed her union could not do anything about it because even they were used against her. She told the newspaper: 'The years I have spent in this place have been some of the most soul destroying part of my life. More than once I was close to breakdown.'

Despite the extensive evidence in support of her case, the local law centre and the Camden branch of the National and Local Government Association all refused to take up her case. Guichard said: 'The worst thing was there was just no one you could turn to, no one would listen, and you were left to stew on your own.' The Camden Black Workers Group (CBWG) eventually took on her case and two-and-a-half years later it proved that everything she said was true. Confidential evidence showed there had been incorrect evidence used against her allegedly bad time-keeping when she had never been late for work in her life. In October 1986, as direct result of the CBWG, Guichard was awarded £24,000 in compensation.

The 1982 front-page story 'Fired 'because I'm Black' told the story of 22-year-old Sandra Luke, an illustrator who worked for a West End fashion salon for two months and then was told to leave. She had been told that her illustrations were satisfactory, yet she had noticed that a job advert had been placed in the *Evening Standard* for her role. When she quizzed them on the advert they told her not to worry, but then also hired a young white girl. Not long after, Luke was called into the office and told production was down and they would have to let her go. They told her that they were working on a 'last in, first out' basis', but she pointed out that she was not the last one employed. The management pointed out that the white girl had more experience, although Sandra claimed this was not the case.

In same issue, the newspaper also ran the story of 27-year-old Doreen Bogle who had worked in the engineering department of the BBC for four years when she got into an altercation with a white female colleague who allegedly racially abused her. Bogle was suspended and asked to sign a report taking full responsibility for the incident. She told *The Voice*: 'They are not interested at the disciplinary board – they asked me when I last had a fight - as if all Black people fight. I told them the last fight I had been in was when I was 11 – during my first year at secondary school.' Black men were equally challenged in the workplace and endured a culture that was almost Jurassic. Yet again *The Voice* published many examples of workplace discrimination, with the private sector in particular coming under scrutiny. There was the branch manager of a Dixon's store who felt it acceptable banter to call a Black worker 'chalky', 'nig nog' and ask him if he had had his 'coonflakes'. Another manager of a well-known construction firm believed that calling his Black employee a 'Black bastard' would make him work harder and would engender camaraderie among the workers.

In 1985 the story 'Law Society in row of Black lawyers' report', found an unpublished report by the Law Society that said there was no 'real' racial discrimination in the legal profession, in complete contrast to the scathing report findings of the race relations committee of the Senate Inns of Court and the Bar. Lawyer Paul Boateng said: 'If reports that the Law Society is about to deny racism and discrimination in the legal profession are true, it is alarming in the extreme because it reflects a disturbing degree of complacency and blindness to a continuing scandal in the profession.'

The situation for Black people working in the health service was equally concerning. *The Voice* found that the NHS continually overlooked the promotion of Black nurses and doctors.

One 1988 headline, which read, 'NHS spurns Black nurses – "I came across racism every day of the week from both staff and patients,"' revealed the extent of discrimination reported in a paper called *The Black Nurse: An Endangered Species*. Another story, 'Black doctors get a raw deal', revealed a CRE report found they were being discriminated against despite receiving good qualifications and were confined to low grade and unpopular jobs. *The Voice* also raised awareness for other issues that would often slip through the net of public consciousness. In 1988 a story headlined 'AIDS test shock' revealed anonymous AIDS testing on pregnant women could lead to the wholesale discrimination of Black mothers-to-be, according to leading expert and counsellor Vernal Scott. Scott, who ran the Black Communities AIDS Team, advised pregnant women to state that they did not want a HIV test and demand to know what tests will be carried on blood samples.

Far more concerning was a story that exposed a culture of shocking indifference within the health service. In 1984 it was

Issue No. 76 Week ending March 3, 1984

THE VOICE

Britain's Best Black Newspaper!

30p weekly

INSIDE THIS WEEK
A LOOK AT BLACK RADIO
See pages 14/23

Racist jokes 'sickening' says councillor

STUDENT'S CHARITY RAG BACKFIRES

Cllr Janet Boateng.

A FURIOUS row has broken out over amazing race hate gags printed in the charity magazine of one of the country's most respected hospitals.

The rag magazine of Guy's Hospital in London, printed a number of race-jokes.

One such item reads: "What do you throw a drowning nigger? His wife and kids". Another item included is "Why do wogs smell? So that blind people can hate them too."

The magazine was produced by a number of medical students at Guy's Medical School.

Local councillor Janet Boateng slammed the 'jokes' as 'sickening'.

"When one looks toward good race relations and unity between black and white, these senior people are expected to take a lead," she said.

Hospitals

"But instead, they are inciting racial hatred.

"I really do fear for the lives of black people in hospitals if this is the calibre of doctors this country is producing out of ratepayers money."

Councillor Boateng did not consider the 'jokes' to be at all funny.

The Peckham area has a substantial black population and is served by Guy's Hospital.

"There's nothing to laugh about," she commented.

The Member of Parliament for Peckham, Ms Harriet Harman has also reacted furiously to the magazine.

Ms Harman said of the offending magazine, "I think they are a disgrace and offensive to Asian and black people. But they are also offensive to all people interested in seeing a peaceful multi-racial society.

"There are a lot of black, Asian and Jewish people who use the hospital and work in the hospital."

Ms Harman intends to take the matter further.

Hatred

"I take this very seriously. It constitutes incitement to racial hatred. So I've referred the matter to the Director of Public Prosecutions."

If the DPP finds that the published items amount to the offence of inciting racial hatred this could result in the prosecution of a number of people at the hospital.

Apology

Mr A.W. Baker, assistant registrar of the teaching hospital told The Voice that he could not comment on the controversy.

The committee responsible for producing the 'Wag Mag' have said, "The Wag Mag was intended to be a lighthearted way of raising money. In retrospect we strongly regret any offence caused by racialist inclusions.

We've already written letters of apology to all those writing letters of complaint."

PLUS THE WILSONS

Your week's Buzzz pull-out

PLUS

PLUS Is he the richest black man in the world? Chief Nzeribe speaks out

A hospital's charity magazine was criticised by politicians when it was revealed to have printed a number of racist jokes

revealed race hate gags were being printed in the charity magazine of Guy's Hospital in London, one of the country's most respected hospitals. One read: 'What do you throw a drowning nigger? His wife and kids'. Another read: 'Why do wogs smell? So that blind people can hate them too'. The magazine was produced by a number of medical students at Guy's Medical School. Local councillor Janet Boateng slammed the jokes as 'sickening', adding: 'I really do fear for the lives of Black people in hospitals if this is the calibre of doctor this country is producing out of ratepayer's money'.

Harriet Harman, MP for Peckham, also reacted furiously to the magazine. She told *The Voice*: 'I think they are a disgrace and offensive to Asian and Black people. But they are also offensive to all people interested in seeing a peaceful multiracial society. Mr A.W. Baker, assistant registrar of the teaching hospital, told *The Voice* he could not comment on the controversy.

The committee responsible for producing the magazine said: 'The "Wag Mag" was intended to be a light-hearted way of raising money. In retrospect we strongly regret any offence caused by racialist inclusions'. Just weeks later medical students at Charing Cross Hospital in Fulham, West London, withdrew 20,000 copies of their rag mag after it was condemned as 'grotesque, racist and tasteless'.

Increasingly, mental illness and breakdown were often obstructive shadows stalking many young Black men, who were unable to deal with life's imposed 'strangleholds'. Since the newspaper's launch it had carried a series of articles on the escalating problem and had questioned why so many Black men were dying disproportionately in psychiatric wards in mental hospitals. *The Voice* revealed in a 1990 report that Black psychiatric patients had died in suspicious circumstances almost every year for the past five years, and an increasing amount of research showed Black people were far more likely than white people to be diagnosed as being mentally ill. Unfortunately, Black voluntary groups which provided an alternative to the frequent misery of mainstream health systems were battling survival. The paper highlighted the case of Broadmoor patient Randolph Ince who was prescribed powerful drugs at three times the recommended dosage while at a London mental health hospital. The hospital manager investigating said he was lucky to be alive. Sadly, this was not the case for Joseph Watts, a young Rastafarian described in a psychiatric report as a 'gentle giant', who died in the facility four years after arriving. In *a* 1987 feature from *The Voice*, 'When anger turns to madness', psychiatrists Maurice Lipsedge and Roland Littlewood said they believed Black people were more likely to be offered drug treatment rather than therapy. They also said: 'Black people under pressure from social deprivation had the added burden of racism not only in their everyday life but also within the system they seek help. This leaves them to fight a double battle, sometimes without the help of family who cannot cope with the stigma of mental illness.' Dr Aggrey Burke, one of only two African Caribbean consultant psychiatrists in Britain, supported this belief, saying: 'Poverty in itself is most damaging. When you add racism it is a hurricane in terms of pressure.' This was a period when the label 'Big, Black and Dangerous' was being used frequently, spreading fear and loathing within certain sections of British society. Many of these cases, as the newspaper discovered, rarely fitted the stereotype and when it did it was invariably because they were prone to putting on excessive weight due to the side effects of their medication.

THE VOICE

London's First Black Newspaper!

1982 SOUVENIR CARNIVAL EDITION

GANG MAKES LIFE HELL FOR FAMILY

LIVING IN TERROR

LONDON BOROUGH YOUTH GAMES
See pages 26-27

32 POLICE officers are investigating incidents in which racist gangs made repeated attempt to burn down the house of a Pakistani family in Waltham Forest.

NON-STOP VIGIL

S. African "Justice": 6 witnesses in this trial (one a 15 year old girl) were beaten and given electric shocks. The three accused were hideously tortured for days on end.

Demonstrators outside South Africa House, Trafalgar Square.

WORLD-WIDE demonstrations have been launched for the release of three black South African freedom fighters who have been sentenced to death in Pretoria.

The three men — Anthony Tsotsobe, Johannes Shabangu and David Moise — have spent a year in Pretoria Prison's Death Row where they face hanging for high treason and other actions under South Africa's notorious security laws.

Their appeal against the death sentence is to be heard in Pretoria this week. Meanwhile, 196 British MPs of all political parties are pressing for the release of David Kitson a British trade unionist serving a 20 years prison sentence in South Africa.

The nightmare started on Thursday 12 August when a child of the Siddiq family of Lawrence Avenue was woken by the sound of a window breaking. As she called for her father, she saw smoke and fire coming from the hall.

Police and the fire brigade were called, but the fire was put out by the family before they arrived.

Since then the Siddiq family have been on guard with buckets of water ready in the hallway of their home.

The initial police response to the incident was described as "inadequate" by the Reverend Ron Waters, an officer of Waltham Forest Community Relations Council.

Rev. Waters was called in last Wednesday evening after a terrified Mr. Siddiq had reported the gathering of a large crowd of youths outside his house even as he was speaking by telephone to *The Voice*. As a result the Siddiq home was immediately given police protection and several arrests were subsequently made.

Detective Sergeant Read of Chingford police station later told *The Voice*: "We have detained nine people today in connection with the arson attacks and they are still being questioned. "We are very concerned indeed about this matter and every aspect of the case is being looked into. There are 32 officers involved in the investigation."

The Siddiq family have already been offered alternative accommodation by the Borough of Waltham Forest.

DYING ON THE DOLE

AS THE number of unemployed in Britain reaches an all time high of nearly 3,200,000 a survey claims that unemployed men are more than twice as likely to commit suicide and 40 per cent more vulnerable to cancer than their counterparts at work.

The survey has been conducted by Professor John Fox of the City University and Dr Peter Goldblatt of the Office of Population Censuses. Their findings show that the death risk for men aged 15 to 64 on the dole is 30 per cent greater than average.

Lord Scarman has estimated the rate of unemployment amongst blacks under 19 in

Brixton to be as high as 55 per cent.

In its annual report, Lambeth Council for Community Relations says that employment training programmes in Lambeth play a useful but limited role, and that the local authority and some businesses have started schemes which may yield more job opportunities. Otherwise the prospects are bleak.

Issue No. 4 Week ending 25 September, 1982

THE VOICE

London's First Black Newspaper!

Weekly **20p**

NO SWEAT!

Seeing eye to eye? Lloyd Coxsone with Cmdr Fairbairn, 'L' Division

A HIGH, bright sun worthy of the Caribbean blazed down on the Kennington Oval last Friday as Brixton West Indian CC met Brixton Police CC in their annual battle for the Leslie Walker Shield.

But there was no sweat (other than the little on the players' brows) no ill-feeling and certainly no trouble as the West Indian XI coasted to an easy victory over their opponents.

With, it seemed, at least half of the Frontline 'Possee' there to enjoy the match and add some distinctly West Indian banter to the proceedings it was a splendidly lighthearted affair. Even the purists were rewarded with the 226 runs and 13 wickets which distinguished it as a fine game of cricket.

Batting first, BWICC amassed 134-4 with Ken Robb stroking a sparkling 56 not out.

BPCC quickly lost four wickets before Chris Morley stopped the rot with 32. When he was out, caught Coxsone, bowled Owen Bows, the rout continued with the Police collapsing to 92-9.

The Voice says: Page 6

Inside VOICE

MUST our kids fail? centre pages

Have you seen this girl? page 2

UB 40 Competition See page 6

CALLING ALL READERS

If you have any trouble getting the Voice call **01-533 1321/6**

Issue 15 Week ending December 11, 1982

THE VOICE

London's First Black Newspaper

20p

FIRED

"BECAUSE I'M BLACK," says 22-year-old Sandra Luke.

Sandra had been working at John Howard of Brighton's fashion salon in the west end for just two months when she was asked to leave.

She had only recently left the London College of Fashion where she gained her diploma.

She was taken on for a week's trial as an illustrator and was asked to stay on. She negotiated a verbal agreement for her wages of £90 per week which would increase after a further trial period.

"When I first got there," she told *The Voice*, "I asked if they'd ever had a black person working there. They hadn't. The only black people working for the company were two young people who loaded the vans at the back of the shop.

"Part of my job was to sketch items for people but when I did that they kept me in another room so the customer wouldn't see me."

Sandra was told that her illustrations were totally satisfactory yet she noticed an advert had been placed in the Evening Standard for the job she was doing.

"I asked them what was happening and were they not satisfied with my work. They told me not to be silly, and let it go at that.

"The new girl they got was white and I noticed that there was an atmosphere in the shop.

"If I made a mistake they would make a lot more of it than if the white girl made a mistake."

Not long after that Sandra was called into the office and told that as production was down they would have to let her go. They told her they were working on a "last in, first out" basis.

When Sandra pointed out that she wasn't the last person employed and that the white girl was, the management pointed out that the white girl had more experience.

"Well, I don't see how they could have said that," Sandra said, "because they had to train the girl in the same things they had to train me in."

When *The Voice* tried to speak to the two directors of the company a woman said that as the directors were not expecting a call there was no way they would speak to the press.

Now Sandra, who is at present going through the CRE to demand justice is out of work and told *The Voice*;

"They got rid of me because I'm black. I think they were only using me to fill a gap — until they could get somebody white to work for them."

IT'S NOT ONLY HARDER TO FIND A JOB IF YOU'RE BLACK — IT'S HARDER TO KEEP IT

THE CHAMP

LAST WEEK in Taiwan, Britain captured the team championship at the World Karate Championships.

London's Jeoff Thompson (left) triumphed in the blue riband event, the heavyweight class, and it was no surprise when he visited *The Voice* to show us his medal.

Why?

Because Jeoff believes that *The Voice* is champion, just like him.

See page 27 for the full report.

Issue 20   Week ending January 22, 1983

THE VOICE

London's First Black Newspaper!

20p

VOICE talks to the Roach family

Page 5

Paul Worrell Memorial

PAN AFRICAN HISTORIAN TALKS TO THE VOICE *Page 9*

BOROUGH REPORT

BRENT

— looking to the future

Pages 14/15

CRICKET TOUR *Page 3*

Pages 18/19

ALL THE LATEST MUSIC ACTION

PLUS

Jeffrey Osborne

AND

Jackie Mitoo

THE BEST OF BLACK ARTS

COLIN ROACH TRAGEDY SPARKS REVOLT

DOORSTEP DEATH

Colin Roach.

"It was no suicide" claims mother

COLIN ROACH, a black man, aged 21, was found shot dead in the foyer of the Stoke Newington Police Station at 11.30pm, Wednesday, January 12. It is alleged that there were no witnesses on the scene when the death occurred.

Initially, the case was said to have been suicide but after a vast amount of scrutiny by the family and the black community, a demand for a full scale public inquiry is now being requested by the Hackney Legal Defence Committee.

Due to the conflicting reports by the police and the Media, and the dubious and suspicious circumstances surrounding the death; a number of crucial questions and issues have emerged, which further emphasise the mystery surrounding this tragedy.

The Voice has conducted a major investigation into the Colin Roach tragedy which reveals the following:

● Three conflicting police reports.
● The coroner's report.
● The Disturbances outside the station.
● The police crisis meeting.
● Councillor Dennis Twomey's version.
● The queries, issues and inconsistencies.

THE VOICE was the first newspaper to talk to Colin Roach's family and friends after the tragedy.

Twins, Joe and Jim Joseph had known Colin Roach for most of their lives and was with the family on the night of Colin's death.

Colin, Jim and Nester (a white man — friend of Colin and driver of the yellow Mercedes) were together on the night of Colins' death. Colin wanted to go to Stoke Newington to see his elder brother, Patrick and asked Nester to drop him. Nester agreed and dropped Colin off at the junction of Stoke Newington High Street (about 50 yards) from the police station and drove away up Stoke Newington High Street thereby passing the police station.

Jim told The Voice, "There was a delay of three hours before the police informed Mr

(Continued on page 3)

Pauline Roach (centre) and members of the family outside Stoke Newington police station.

INCONSISTENT POLICE BEHAVIOUR — Commander calls crisis meeting

● See page 3

Report by Gina Morley   Pics by Lloyd Jones

Got a problem? Write to our Agony Auntie

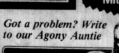

Dear Pas

Issue No. 100. Week ending August 18, 1984

THE VOICE

Britain's Best Black Newspaper!

30p weekly

BLACK GOLD

The outstanding achievements of black athletes caused a sensation at the Olympics. Sports Editor Richard Adeshiyan reports.

Tessa Sanderson   Evelyn Ashford   Carl Lewis   Daley Thompson

100 THIS WEEK

THE VOICE is 100 issues old this week and as part of our anniversary celebrations we donated a birthday cake to the New Testament Assembly children's summer project in Leyton, London. "We all read The Voice every week," said community leader, Pastor Lo Smith, "and we're really honoured to be chosen. I've never seen the children so excited!"

Our delightful photographer was regaled with a special rendition of 'Happy Birthday' courtesy of the lively youngsters.

Pastor Smith has been running a supplementary school in the day care centre for the past ten years. "I would like the children to become good citizens to help the young unemployed, but we need some sort of grant aid," she said.

"At present The New Testament Assembly Church runs its own fund raising through loans and support of the congregation.

However, the hard working pastor isn't just concerned with the welfare of the youth. She also runs a Friday lunch-over club for the elderly, supplemented by a meals-on-wheels service to the housebound.

"The Church should reach out to the community and help in many different ways, not just through prayer," said Pastor Smith.

THE worlds biggest ever sports jamboree is over and the phenomenal performances of black athletes will go down in history as one of the enduring features of the 23rd Olympiad.

The discipline, courage and determination needed to scale superhuman heights of endeavour were also necessary to combat a sinister threat from merchants of hate.

Los Angeles has been a virtual police state for the past two weeks after the Ku Klux Klan vowed to kill black athletes. There have been unconfirmed reports that an unnamed competitor narrowly missed serious injury when a letter bomb exploded.

Fearing a major catastrophe, police have been keeping a watch on known Klan activists after a mass influx of Klansmen into Los Angeles, a city with a black mayor and a large black population. Klansmen were also incensed that Ed Moses took the Olympic oath on behalf of all the competitors.

Despite the Klans threat to lynch 'black and yellow' athletes, the only hanging taking place at the Games was that of medals around the necks of proud athletes. Tom Bradley, Mayor of Los Angeles, commented that black sports stars graced the winners rostrum so frequently that it could have been their "second home".

See sports pages for Olympic Report.

Issue No. 158. W/E October 5, 1985

THE VOICE

Britain's Best Black Newspaper!

30p weekly

BRIXTON

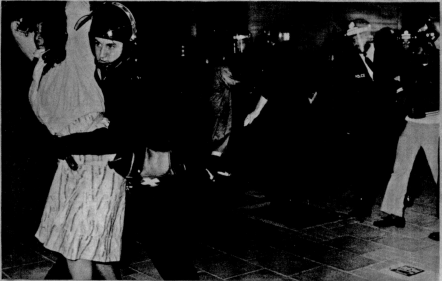

Pic by DAVE HOFFMAN

BURNS AGAIN

FULL STORY BEHIND THE RIOTING

Juliet Groce.

See pages 16 & 25

THE VOICE

Britain's Best Black Newspaper!

30p weekly

My Funny Valentine

....read the sizzling story of how four couples keep their love alive 365 days a year. See page 15

● Also look out for your Valentine Message on Page 25

Whoopi, Whoopi

...Goldberg is on the purple trail - how the Colour Purple is sweeping up all the prizes

★ MISSING STAR ... Who is looking for Five Star's Delroy?

● PLUS STEEL PULSE – Living the American Dream.

● COOL RULER VIDEO WINNERS INSIDE P.23

COPPERS PAY UP

Mum wins substantial damages

by April Ashley

A Sunday School teacher who was awarded £26,000 after being violently assaulted by police officers urged Britain's black community to follow her example and "get off their backsides and fight for their rights and principles."

46 year old mother of three Mrs Lora Lucas of Upland Road, Dulwich, South London said: "Many peo- ple said to me you can't fight against the police, but I believe you can. It was a hor- rible case and I was badly abused. But I believe in fighting to the death for what is right. I would do it all over again."

Continued on page 3

Smiling Winner... Mrs Lucas.

ASWAD
Still 'Bubbling'

Aswad once again proved themselves kings of British reg- gae by winning the title of Best British Reggae Band 1985.

At the 5th Official British Reggae Award presentations in West London's Hammersmith Palais last week, Aswad con- tinued their domination of British reggae. Not only were they voted top band, but their smash-hit single 'Bubbling' was voted the British reggae record of the year.

Photo by PATRICK FRIDAY

Jamaican High Commissioner Herbert Walker presents Aswad with the first of their two awards.

ISSUE No. 246. June 16, 1987

THE VOICE

Britain's Best Black Newspaper!

35p weekly

A NEW ERA

Will there be a black caucus at Westminster?

by Mark Harrison

Britain's new black MPs have hailed their historic wins as a new era in black political power.

Bernie Grant, Tottenham's new MP, predicted that "black people will be dancing in the streets", after hearing that Paul Boateng, Keith Vaz and Diane Abbott would join him as Britain's first black MPs since World War Two.

Hopes

The victorious four, all from the Labour Party, have high hopes that they can make the presence of the whole black community felt at Westminster.

Grant pledged they would extend black political activity by "keeping black concerns at the forefront of the political agenda".

Diane Abbott broke several barriers by becoming Britain's first black woman MP. As she won by a margin of 7,500 in Hackney North and Stoke Newington, she had this message for the black community:

"The black MPs need the support of all black people. We need to become the Westminster arm of a much wider political movement. It's not about personalities, it's about collective political advancement".

Caucus

Many observers predict that a black caucus of MPs will be formed. Keith Vaz, who trounced extreme right-winger Peter Bruinvels in Leicester East, and radical solicitor Paul Boateng, who won in Brent East, are expected to work closely with Grant and Abbott, to increase their political leverage.

Grant claimed they would "highlight the issues facing the black community". Abbott predicted: "we will come together and form common policies on issues like Africa, jobs and housing, and ensure that they are constantly aired."

Abbott is also highly confident that the white-dominated halls of Westminster will not neutralise their effectiveness. "We've come too far, gone through too much back biting and racist reporting. I for one, will not be intimidated".

Boateng — new face in commons

Vaz — beat right wing Tory

Grant — 'dancing in the streets'

Abbott — 'not be intimidated'

Although the newspaper often put the police under the microscope, the community also relied on the police to solve often shocking and disturbing Black stories happening on its 'own doorstep'. The newspaper carried regular reports on fatal stabbings and shootings, often at parties and clubs, and domestic murder and abuse. The reporting of a pregnant 16-year-old's fatal stabbing was particularly shocking, and the interviews with bereaved and grieving families revealed a blemish that would prove very hard to remove.

The story 'Black barrister stabbed', was just one of many that offered an unpalatable truth. 'I just hope they never come out of prison', a sobbing Julie Owusu told *The Voice* as two men were formally charged with the murder of her husband. 47-year-old Malik Owusu had been fatally stabbed in the chest just 20 yards from his Brixton flat after chasing two youths who had snatched a pendant worth £1,000 from a woman. The futility of his death was captured in the editorial comment, which remarked: 'Mr Owusu was one who chose to dedicate himself to improving the lot of fellow Black citizens by serving his community as a barrister. He had worked in a bank to pay his bills and studied long and hard, and was finally called to the Bar. Sadly, Malik Owusu was not to enjoy the fruits of his labour'. Conversely, the 1984 raid on Birmingham's famous Muhammad Ali Community Centre, was also hard to understand. Ten Black youths hurled missiles, wielded switch blades and brandished a gun as frightened occupants sheltered inside. James Hunte, the city's top Black politician said: 'The people who raided us don't have any understanding of what we are trying to do at the centre. I am shocked they are Black – they are a disgrace to the community'.

The Voice also exposed Britain's endemically racist housing policies. This was spotlighted in a two-page feature in 1982 titled 'Housing – it is time we helped ourselves.' The report said there was a fair amount of evidence to suggest that Black people were being placed in sub-standard housing and the situation was not improving. It also went on to add that local authorities had been accused of 'racist allocation practices' whereby Black people were dumped on run-down, predominantly white estates. As a result, groups of Black people took the initiative to form housing associations and co-operatives in an attempt to alleviate the problem, and the newspaper profiled some of these new organisations; Lacaye Housing Co-op, Umoja Housing Co-operative, Ujima Housing and CARIB Housing Association. The report, 'Housing rethink by councils', focused on a CRE investigation that found the housing departments of the Royal Borough of Chelsea and Kensington, Barnet and the GLC had all discriminated against people in the UK under the work permit provision of the Immigration Act. As a result all three bodies agreed to change their policies. Hackney was also exposed in a CRE report, which concluded that Black families received worse housing than white families in the borough. Camden, considered by many to be a liberal borough, was accused of 'racially discriminatory and sexist bias' practices in their housing transfer policies.

Racist housing policies were also exposed in Newham where Black families were placed in terrible sub-standard living conditions. A 1984 report, titled 'Newham slum shame – you wouldn't put a dog to live here', discovered a 52-year-old grandmother living in unimaginable conditions in a Stratford council home who had been battling council bureaucracy for seven years. The paper also revealed a 57-year-old disabled man living with his wife and two teenage children who had been on the council waiting list for nine years to be transferred from his damp three-storey Hackney flat. At this time the Black community's homes were also vulnerable to racist vandals. That year, *The Voice* revealed a group of thugs had smashed down the door of a woman's Barking home and sprayed the walls with racist slogans, slashed the furniture and clothes and poured bleach all over the carpet. She had also received threatening letters and horrifying phone calls since she had moved into the flat. The problem was highlighted in another of the paper's reports when Ian Mikado, MP for Bow and Poplar, criticised the police's lack of concern in these cases. In 1984 he and several London Labour MP's met with the Home Secretary to discuss the lack of police interest. There was no denying that housing and racist attacks were inextricably linked.

Unfortunately, the frequency of these cases did not ease as the 1990s arrived. In 1991 the Metropolitan Police's Annual Report revealed racial attacks had increased by a staggering 25 per cent, while the rate for solving these crimes had fallen. According to the Institute of Race Relations there had been over 70 racist murders since 1969, but the Metropolitan Police had only started recording racist murders in 1991. A *Voice* article on the report focused on the racist murder of 15-year-old Rolan Adams who was chased by a gang of 15 white youths and stabbed several times in Thamesmead, south-east London. Rolan's mother, Audrey, recounted that he was a talented musician who was due to play in a concert on the Saturday following his murder. The family's pain did not end there as they received death threats and racist abuse in the wake of their son's murder. Sadly, Rolan's shocking murder failed to capture national attention, but it did highlight the shocking racism that existed around the notorious Thamesmead estate and in parts of Eltham and Welling. Two years later, Stephen Lawrence was tragically murdered by a group of racist attackers not far from where Rolan was killed.

Thanks to the GLC, many Black voluntary groups received funding that helped to refresh grass roots activity. Many Black women's groups received a financial uplift along with the Black Gay and Lesbian community, which had requested GLC funding in 1982 to create a community centre. Their philosophy of self-help was illustrated by the work of London's East London Black Women's Organisation (ELBWO) and Moss Side's Abasindi Cooperative, which were profiled in one of *The Voice's* early issues. The abolishing of the GLC in 1986 would prove very damaging for many of these Black voluntary groups. Local councils also became the bastions of increasing community and political engagement with Black workers, groups and race relation units scrutinising injustices. Lewisham councillor Russell Profitt and North Kensington Labour councillor Ben Bousquet were prominent voices in the newspaper. The inimitable Bousquet, who arrived from St Lucia in his late teens, worked in Notting Hill with Claudia Jones who was about to launch the country's first immigrant newspaper, *West Indian Gazette*. He was also the subject of the first documentary on race when the BBC followed him around Brixton looking for a room.

The 1980s also saw an increasing number of Black politicians elected to positions of power. In 1982 Diane Abbott became the first Black woman to be elected to Westminster City Council, while Brent's Labour councillor Ambrozine Neil made a surprise defection to the Conservatives in 1984. But the real breakthrough came the following year, when the 41-year-old Bernie Grant became Britain's first Black council leader. *The Voice* celebrated his achievement with the headline: 'Bernie makes history.' The forming of the Labour Party Black

The '80s also saw a groundswell of support for the Labour Party as an increasing number of Black politicians were elected to high office

Sections, a caucus made up of African, Caribbean and Asian members in 1983 shook the party out of its complacency as the caucus felt Labour was taking the Black vote for granted. In the last issue before the 1987 general election, *The Voice's* front page declared, 'Vote Labour – why there is no other real choice,' which was backed up with an editorial titled, 'Why it has to be Labour.'

The following week the newspaper celebrated the political breakthrough of Diane Abbott in Hackney, Bernie Grant in Tottenham, Paul Boateng in Brent and Keith Vaz in Leicester, as the first elected Black members of parliament. The front-page headline read, 'A New Era – will there be a Black caucus in Westminster?', with Britain's new Black MPs hailing their historic wins as a new era in Black political power. In his victory speech Boateng, said triumphantly: 'Today Brent South, tomorrow Soweto.' Diane Abbott broke several barriers by becoming Britain's first Black female MP, winning by a 7,500 margin in Hackney North and Stoke Newington. Acknowledging her victory, she declared that they 'need the support of all Black people and that it was not about personalities, but collective political advancement.' Inside, *The Voice* editorial comment highlighted Black political progress and the prominence of race in the election. The article noted at the last election that 18 Black candidates were selected to stand for the four major political parties compared with 28 in 1987. This revolution had started in the town halls a decade earlier, when 37 Black candidates were fielded in the 1977 County Council elections, even though only four were elected. Yet in 1983, in a comparatively small place like Luton, 13 Black candidates were elected to the council. In 1986, Merle Amory and Linda Bellos were elected Britain's first Black women council leaders in Brent and

Lambeth respectively, emulating Grant's feat the previous year. Dorman Long would later take over from Amory.

For many, the 1987 election was considered a major break-through. Millard Scott of the Broadwater Farm Defence Campaign said: 'Previously, we have never had Black people in parliament to raise issues like police harassment, job discrimination. White MPs were always talking about the issues, but avoided doing anything about them.'

Marc Wadsworth, chair of the Labour Party Black Sections, said that the MPs would represent 'the views, demands and aspirations of Britain's Black communities'. Wadsworth would prove a sharp and wily political operator, co-founding the Anti-Racist Alliance, and became a prominent Black rights campaigner. In 1983, he had been appointed Thames Television's first Black reporter. This was also a period when Black workers were mobilising and found a platform in *The Voice*. The Society of Black Lawyers were taking the legal establishment to task, Black social workers also forged their own networks and the Federation of Black Housing Organisations, actively pushed Government to recognise the desperate Black housing issue.

This decade also saw the emergence of young Black community activists including Lee Jasper, a key member of the 1990 Trust; Simon Woolley, who was working with campaign group Charter 88; and David Weaver, co-founder of the National Black Caucus along with Jasper. They understood the Black political discourse needed energising, and brought over Nelson Mandela, not long after his release, and Black civil rights leaders such as Reverend Jesse Jackson and Reverend Al Sharpton.

The Voice also reported when Bill Morris was elected General Secretary of the Transport and General Workers' Union, becoming Britain's first Black leader of a major British trade

THE VOICE

Britains Best Black Newspaper! 48p

JANET JACKSON
How she fought the flab and won

RACE TO THE BAR
Will equal opportunities reach black lawyers

LARRY BLACKMON
Why Steel Pulse turned down Cameo role

BABY BEAUTIFUL AND TERRIFIC TODDLER '91 — NEXT WEEK MEET THE WINNERS

VOICE COMMENT

'I owe it all to you'

Bill Morris says a big thank you to Black Britain for their support in helping him make it to the top of Britains largest union.

Bills the boss

The election of Bill Morris as the new general secretary of the country's biggest union, the Transport and General Workers Union, is not only tremendous personal victory but probably the most significant ballot ever for the black community.

Morris's ability to understand the needs of his 1.2 million membership and his ceaseless work as the deputy general secretary for nearly five years has truly made him a man of the people and someone to be trusted.

For much too long the 165,000 black members of the TGWU have had no voice, and since its foundation in 1922 the union has been riddled with racism and prejudice. While Bill's election will not eradicate those problems overnight, there is at last light at the end of the tunnel.

Throughout the long campaign Bill stood on his record. He has also conducted himself impeccably, especially as the race issue threatened to overshadow his very high-profile campaign.

Too often when it comes to electing black officers there are cries of tokenism. But Bill Morris has proved beyond doubt that his dedication and hardwork, as well as his vision for a better and more representative union, make a mockery of the deepseated ignorance that has dogged black people in British society.

CELEBRATED American writer Maya Angelou has had to cut short her visit to Britain because of her mum's illness.

Despite her mother being poorly, Maya had honoured her promise to tour britain this year.

But 79-year-old Vivian Baxter's illness took a turn for the worse during her daughter's absence and Maya had to return to the States earlier than planned, postponing some of her UK dates.

It's not known what Ms Baxter is suffering from, and Maya is expected to complete her tour within the next few weeks.

For tour information call Virago on 071-383 5150.

Next week - NOW! features Maya Angelou.

Thank you Black Britain - that's what Bill Morris said loud and clear after being voted into the hot seat of Britain's biggest union last week.

Speaking exclusively to The Voice minutes after the landslide results were announced on Friday, a delighted Bill said: "I couldn't have done it without you.

He added: "The black community have been a tremendous support throughout my campaign and I want to take this opportunity to thank them. They made major contributions both in fund raising and morally."

Triumph

As general secretary of the two million member Transport and General Workers Union, Bill Morris will arguably be the most powerful black man in Europe.

He sees his victory as a triumph for meritocracy: "My election represents an endorsement of the pro-

By Lesley Thomas

gressive policies of our union. The members have demonstrated that colour or race are no barriers to anyone seeking to serve this union at the highest level."

And he pledged that equal opportunities would be one of his top priorities when he officially takes up the post next March.

"My victory shows that black people can succeed in Britain, but we need the opportunity to exercise our skills and our talents. But often we are not given those opportunities and our talents have been suppressed."

Bill, who beat his main
Continued on page 3

BILL MORRIS: Has a lot to smile about.

LOOKING FOR A JOB? Well look no further than JOB MARKET

In 1991 history was made when Bill Morris was elected general secretary of the UK's biggest Union, the Transport and General Workers Union

union. Herman Ouseley achieved an impressive hat-trick, becoming the first Black chief executive of the ILEA in 1988, then CEO of Lambeth Council in 1990 and finally the first Black executive chairman of the Commission for Racial Equality. Notably, Valerie Amos became Chief Executive of the Equal Opportunities Commission in 1989 while in 1988 John Roberts and Len Woodley had become the country's first Black QCs.

In 1991, 35-year-old Patricia Scotland would become Britain's first Black woman QC, while Reverend Wilfred Wood became Britain's first Black bishop and Reverend David Tonge became the first Black chaplain to the Queen. Gus John was Hackney's first Black Director of Education, while the country gained its first commercial Black radio station, Choice FM, co-founded by Neil Kenlock and Patrick Berry.

The newspaper's international coverage offered a window on the political and economic progress of Black America, and its extensive reports on Africa and the Caribbean helped create global awareness. However, the country that *The Voice* was perhaps most focused on was South Africa. When Nelson Mandela was released from prison in February 1990, *The Voice* ran a triumphant cover story with the headline, '"Free at Last" Mandela salutes a new dawn.' Inside, Mandela was pictured alongside his wife Winnie, both punching the air with a now iconic clench-fisted salute. It was a moment that sealed the approval of millions of viewers around the world. The newspaper devoted five pages to Mandela's release, and in the lead article Mandela restated his belief that the armed struggle must continue. 'I stand before you not as a prophet but as a humble servant,' he declared to hundreds of thousands assembled in the centre of Cape Town, who had waited over a quarter of a century to hear him speak.

He said: 'Comrades and fellow South Africans – I greet you all in the name of peace, democracy and freedom for all.' He stressed his unbroken resolve to rid his country of apartheid's evil, saying: 'I have fought against white domination and I have fought against Black domination. I cherish the ideals of democracy in a freed society in which all persons live in peace and harmony with equal opportunities.

'If needs be, it is an ideal for which I am prepared to die,' he pledged. 'The factors that necessitated the armed struggle still exist today. We have no option to continue.' But he added: 'We still hope for a climate conducive to negotiated settlement so there will no longer be a need for an armed struggle.'

Ironically, the visit of the charismatic Jesse Jackson also featured in that issue. Six years earlier, *The Voice* had reported how Jackson had stopped traffic on his visit to Brixton. On this occasion, Jackson arrived in the UK for a three-day visit on his way to South Africa. He was greeted with thunderous applause by 1,000-strong audience when he appeared at East London's Hackney Empire, and used the platform to address the issue of apartheid.

He said: 'By the sheer power of moral authority Nelson Mandela was the freest of men and he proved you cannot jail a man who is morally free.' In a voice cracking with emotion, he stated: 'Mandela's demands are not revolutionary but reasonable – he wants democracy.'

However, Jackson turned preacher when he appeared at North London's West Indian Cultural centre. The Reverend talked of Black people's rich history and passionately insisted they should define themselves as African:

We are not discoloured, or negro, or Black. It is not by our skin colour that we are defined, but by our heritage and our glorious roots. We are people shaped by history, culture and opportunities. We are not descendants of slaves, but of great people enslaved, who survived slavery against great odds. Let us teach our children not of their Blackness, brownness or yellowness, but of their Africaness. Tell our children those African pyramids and the sphinxes still stand, not on soul and rhythm, but on science. Sure we can sing well, but rhythms not all we got. Teach our children that failure is not a sin. We must aim high and work diligently, and when we do, no lie can deter us, no force can stop our will to be free.

A year later, US civil rights figure Reverend Al Sharpton arrived in the UK amidst controversy, but his visit confirmed the blossoming relationship that had developed between the two Black communities. The reverend visited *The Voice* offices and gave an exclusive interview. 'The media reaction was outrageous,' Sharpton said: 'To claim I'm more odious than murderers, rapists and thieves within the US, shows the racism of those who use the term.'

He added: 'The only interview I done with the British press before I came here was with *The Voice*. All of the things the rest of them said were based on their own imagination.'

'I read a lot of history and I have never read of anyone who tried to change society and was popular in their day. If I only read newspapers I may have thought of giving up, but the comfort for me is incidents like when I stopped off in Hackney to get some chicken. The kids in the store started dancing when they saw me – that's worth headlines.' *The Voice* also asked if his will impact renew efforts to gain equality for Britain's Black population.

Bernie Grant, the only MP to meet Sharpton, said: 'He has helped tremendously. He has shown the Black community the kind of militancy we need if we are going to get things done. He has made both Black and white people wake up.' The brutal slaughter of Rolan Adams was one of the main reasons for Sharpton's trip.

The education of young Black children was an issue that *The Voice* took very seriously. During this period an increasing number of Black children were being suspended, permanently excluded or classed as educationally subnormal. Terms such as 'difficult', 'problem kids' and 'maladjusted' became part of the lexicon. In reaction, *The Voice* devoted a weekly page to education issues and even gave Bernard Wilshire, Deputy of ILEA, a regular column 'Bernard's View'.

The release of the Swann Report in March 1985, which had been six years in making, effectively told the Black parents and their children what they already knew. *The Voice's* article on the report, headlined, 'Swann cites racism', stated that 'an education system designed for white children and stereotype perspectives of Black children was the main reasons for children of Afro-Caribbean background failing in schools.' It also described the worrying discrepancy that existed in the performance of African Caribbean children, compared with their white and Asian counterparts. A study of fifth-form examination results in an outer London borough found 22.7 per cent of white children were high achievers compared to 10.6 per cent of African Caribbean children. The Swann Committee also looked at the social and economic background in the West Indian community where 'there is a great deal of evidence that many minority groups are substantially more deprived than whites, and this must increase the significance of these factors.' The article said that the committee had rejected quite firmly the alleged low IQ of African-Caribbean children as cause for failure. IQ experts saw no significant differences in Black and white children. The report revealed racial prejudice inside schools as well as outside and said that 'society must root out discrimination by the white majority and must try to change the education system to allow for ethnic minorities to fulfil their true potential.'

The need for more Black teachers was also cited. However, the Caribbean Teachers' Association told *The Voice* that these were not new proposals. 'We have always argued for greater employment and promotion of Afro-Caribbean teachers,' said Chairman Henry Thomas. He continued: 'This report highlights one of the most important issues; recognition that our schools must serve the needs of a multi cultural society.' On the newspaper's education page, Elaine Foster's story provided the perfect antidote. Jamaican-born Foster, 37, had turned down career advice to work in a nursery and had now been appointed the first female Black head teacher of a Birmingham secondary school. She also became Birmingham's youngest secondary school head teacher when she took up a post at Handsworth Wood Girls' School. Several years after the findings of the Swann report, a 1991 *Voice* article revealed that one in eight African Caribbean people hold a degree or higher qualification, the same proportion as white people, according to a labour force survey. A 1991 report revealed Black women were achieving a staggering 16 per cent higher than their white counterparts. However a report by the CRE in 1989 found that it was much harder for Black graduates to gain employment than their white counterparts. At the time a *Voice* article explored how some parents were taking drastic action and sending their children back to the Caribbean. The headline read, 'Britain's not good enough for our kids.'

In one of the newspaper's early issues one story illustrated what was possible if opportunities were created. A front-page story, headlined, 'Brixton to Oxford', announced that 18-year-old Colin Douglas had been offered a place at Keble College, Oxford, to read Philosophy, Politics and Economics (PPE) as part of an agreement between the ILEA and the Universities of Oxford and Cambridge. Colin, a pupil at Tulse Hill School, represented his school at rugby, but felt he was not good enough and would do better concentrating on his studies. After receiving remedial coaching in reading and writing, through sheer determination, he achieved his goal. The ILEA scheme, designed for 'deprived areas' was a way of giving able students from London comprehensives a chance to study at Oxford or Cambridge. Asked what advice he had for other Black youngsters Colin said: 'It would be presumptuous of me as circumstances vary tremendously'. But he went on to say: 'Rather than trying to change any segment of the community, the system has to make sure it motivates more of those within'. He would appear in the newspaper nearly a decade later in the story at the launch of his book *West Indian Women at War*, which he co-authored with Ben Bousquet. Douglas said they came up with the idea after seeing the celebrations of the Second World War in 1989 and the role that West Indians played being completely ignored.

While many of Thatcher's policies hung like a millstone around the collective necks of the Black community, entrepreneurship offered a way out. The burgeoning hair care business was producing business people who were defying the odds, which was celebrated by *The Voice*. In 1984 the paper photographed businessman Tony Wade alongside his wife attending a 10 Downing Street reception, celebrating the country's best

Issue No. 75 Week ending February 25, 1984

THE VOICE

Britain's Best Black Newspaper!

30p weekly

INSIDE THIS WEEK

HOLLYWOOD'S FIRST BLACK MOVIE STAR
See pages 18/19

Have a go — says Tony

A SUCCESSFUL black businessman last week attended a Downing Street reception to celebrate the country's best entrepreneurs.

Tony Wade, one of the directors of hair and beauty products firm Dyke and Dryden, mat Mrs Thatcher at a Downing Street reception for the country's most successful entrepreneurs.

He told The Voice "What we have in common is that we both go for it. She is certainly a female to emulate and more people like her would certainly be a credit to what ever community they belong to. I don't go for all her policies but whatever her convictions she is sincere about them."

Mr Wade and his two partners, Dyke and Dryden, founded the small North London retail company promoting and distributing hair care products in 1965 which has now grown to the mammoth proportions of a wholesaling and retailing business in beauty aids.

The firm now employs hundreds of people selling its products to black communities across the world, with an annual turnover of more than £2 million.

Mr Wade admitted that the path to success has not been easy. "I have experienced all the problems that are well-known to a small black businessman but sheer determination and the will to succeed have enabled us to survive in these very difficult times."

Montserrat-born Mr Wade feels that Dyke and Dryden represents the aspirations and expectations of the black community.

"Black people starting in business must face the problem of proving that we are just as good as the next person. He stresses, "Establishing this proof is a hurdle but we mustn't let it become a handicap."

DJ in fatal knife attack

A grief-stricken mother spoke last week about the agonising decision to terminate her young son's life.

Twenty-two year old Hilbert Liverpool of Kimbolton Close, Lewisham, had been on a life-support machine at Lewisham Hospital for two days since he was brutally attacked on February 9.

Hilbert, a popular and well-liked DJ with the well-known local Spartacus sound system, was arranging with friends to take some equipment to the Paradise Garage Club in Lewisham when he was stabbed in the throat.

Bleeding profusely from a severed jugular vein, he was rushed by friends to Lewisham Hospital, where he was immediately put on a life-support system.

His mother, Victoria, a nursing assistant at Kingsley Old People's Home, Lewisham, first heard the tragic news from a work colleague.

"It was on Thursday, about 4.30, when someone rang to tell me to rush down to Lewisham Hospital. She said she thought Hilbert might be dead," said Victoria.

"When I arrived at the hospital, the doctors told me he was in a critical condition. His jugular vein had been cut so deeply that his brain was starved of oxygen."

Brain-death

Hospital staff told Mrs Liverpool that her son had suffered 'brain death' and that his breathing was being supported by artificial means.

"They told me that even if he recovered, he would be a vegetable," said Victoria, "but I would still have preferred that, knowing he was still alive, even if I had to do everything for him. That's why I sat there with him all night, hoping he would respond to me."

But after two days, the decision was taken to turn off the machine. "I was still hoping there would be a miracle," said a tearful Victoria, "but there was nothing more the doctors could do. They did their best."

Since the tragedy, Victoria, who has three teenage daughters, has had problems sleeping, despite being prescribed tranquillisers by her doctor. "I just feel so sick and confused inside," she said. "We were such a close family that it's hit everyone so hard, especially Mary, my youngest daughter. She and Hilbert were very close."

Many relatives, including the dead man's father, have arrived from the States since hearing the news. "My sister told me he broke down when he heard the news," said Victoria. "Even when he called me last week, he was too choked to speak."

Victoria explained that Hilbert was planning to visit his father in New York before the tragedy.

"Even now I can't believe he's dead," said Victoria. "He was such a loving and kind son. Maybe if he was a villain he'd still be alive today. People always seem to go after the quiet ones."

Mini-cab driver Robert Archer, 19, of Harriet Close, Greenwich, was taken into police custody shortly after the incident, and charged with Hilbert Liverpool's murder, at Greenwich Magistrates Court. He has been remanded in custody until February 24.

Sad mother Mrs Victoria Liverpool

Hilbert Liverpool

Mr and Mrs Wade outside No. 10 last week.

Picture by Asif Zubairy

The Voice *championed Black businesses from the launch of the newspaper*

entrepreneurs. Montserrat-born Wade, one of the directors of hair and beauty products firm Dyke and Dryden told *The Voice*: 'Black' people starting in business must face the problem of proving that we are just as good as the next person.' He added: 'Establishing this proof is a hurdle but we must not let it become a handicap.' The business, founded in 1965 by Len Dyke and Dudley Dryden as a small retail outfit, now employed hundreds of people selling his products all over the world and enjoyed a £2m turnover. However, it was predominantly Black women who would rise to the entrepreneurial challenge.

The burgeoning hair care industry received attention in an early issue of *The Voice*, which included a feature on 'a new growth industry.' The article reported there were now over 90 salons in London and the choice of products was expanding.

The article read: 'Black hair care is a competitive and cut-throat and, some would say an over-saturated market.' Popular hair fashions, reflecting the thinking of the times, have swung from the harsh straightening of the 1950s and 1960s through to the natural afro, which celebrated the late 1960s rise in Black consciousness, the American-imported curly perm, which has been the look of the 1980s together with more traditional African styles such as the canerow.

The early 1980s saw the industry truly established, and in 1984 16,000 people attended the Dyke and Dryden Afro Hair and Beauty Exhibition breaking all records to become one of the biggest Black events in the country to date.

Hairdresser Lorna St Clair was profiled in the newspaper's *'Voices'* section, a weekly spotlight on Black women achievers, confirmed an industry on the rise. St Clair who, along with her husband George, established the very successful St Clair's Hairdressing, was born in Jamaica and came to Britain in 1956. She left school with O Levels before working in a solicitor's office, but discovered her real passion was her hobby – hairdressing. She would meet and marry George St Clair, who had worked at the salon as an apprentice. The St Clairs bought the business when the owners decided to sell and Lorna went on to run a salon in Shepherd's Bush, while husband George ran a second in Marble Arch. Growing the business, presented an extra challenge, as she was also the mother to four children.

The Voice also featured the entrepreneurial journey of people finding success in the food industry. In 1987 the paper featured mother-of-two Dounne Moore, who claimed her concentrated 'Gramma's' hot pepper sauce specially blended with over 'twenty healing herbs and spices' was good for several ailments. She would be mentioned in *The Voice* again in 1990 when the hot sauce creator had made the finals of the Women Mean Business competition. The next year, Moore's sauce was being sold in 150 Tesco stores as well as 312 Safeway stores.

The 1988 article 'Delia's recipe for success' echoed Moore's story of drive and ambition. Mother-of-seven Delia Banks earned a stall in Harrod's food hall when she discovered there was no African food on offer in the department store. Moore, who ran Delia's Kitchen Afrika from her home in Dulwich, South London, imported food stuffs from all over Africa.

She told *The Voice*: 'I've found that my Egusi stew from Ghana has proved very popular with customers, and special recipes like the African curry and my coconut rice are also in demand.'

During this period Black businesses were really starting to get into their stride, but the realities of embarking on an entrepreneurial path presented challenges. *The Voice* spoke to clothes designer Darla-Jane Gilroy, 29, who faced a huge rate rise from £750 to over £5,000 on her boutique on Chelsea's King's Road.

'This is the most depressing New Year's present I could have had. It's like a bad joke,' said dejected Darla-Jane who already faced a rent rise of £12,000.

Black businesses during this period were really starting to get into their stride, but the realities of embarking on an entrepreneurial path presented challenges. In the mid-1980s *The Voice* spoke to clothes designer Darla-Jane Gilroy, 29, who faced a huge rate rise from £750 to over £5,000 on her boutique on Chelsea's King's Road. 'This is the most depressing New Year's present I could have had. It's like a bad joke,' said dejected Darla-Jane who already faced a rent rise of £12,000.

As a promising fashion student, Darla-Jane had famously featured as one of the 'Blitz Kids' in the video to David Bowie's iconic 1980 number one hit 'Ashes to Ashes'. She had secured the prized gig after Bowie had visited Soho's Blitz Club in the same year. During his visit, the club's celebrated host Steve Strange introduced her to Bowie and was offered a small sum to appear in the video. Darla Jane was dressed in her own Black design with white collar for the video shoot. She was considered one of the exciting emerging design talents alongside Bruce Oldfield and Joe Casely-Hayford.

Darla-Jane's mother, Guyanese-born Beryl Gilroy, was one of Britain's first Black head teachers and her pioneering work was captured in her 1976 book *Black Teacher*. Darla-Jane also boasts a celebrated sibling in Professor Paul Gilroy, one of the foremost theorists of race and racism working and teaching in the world today.

Interestingly, Brixton-born Bowie would appear in the newspaper giving the area a much welcomed boost. The newspaper's July 1983 story 'Bowie's backing Brixton' noted that he was performing a special charity concert at Hammersmith

Odeon for the Brixton Neighbourhood Community Association. At that event, he would meet its director Brixton stalwart Courtney Laws, a recognised activist and campaigner. Bowie told reporters: 'I left Brixton when I was still quite young, but that was enough to be affected by it. It left strong images in my mind. The idea of this charity show was to contribute something concrete to the Brixton community which has had its unfair share of heartache over the past few years.' Bowie donated £50,000 from the concert to the community association.

This was a generation in search of its own identity and on paper their journey should have offered little promise or hope. This generation, born mainly to Caribbean and African immigrants, and blessed with their parents resilience, refused to be beaten. Finally reading stories often identical to their own had an enormous psychological effect and was a realisation that they were not alone in their struggle. Harnessing this new found duality was essential in navigating life's twists and turns.

The landscape of international sport was inherently political in the 1980s – the diplomatic row over South African apartheid resulted in a number of high-profile sporting boycotts, while Black athletes were threatened with violence ahead of the 1984 Olympics in Los Angeles. Yet against this backdrop, a number of Black Brits fought to rise to the top of sport, and *The Voice* was on hand to document their journeys.

Javelin legend Tessa Sanderson secured her place as a sporting superstar when she became the first Black British woman to win an Olympic gold medal in 1984. Born in Jamaica, Sanderson was raised by her grandmother before following her Windrush Generation parents over to England when she was six years old. It was in Wolverhampton where her sense of purpose and love for sport was born. 'We slotted in with everything but one of the good things about having the parents we did was that they were really level-headed and taught us all about what to expect' she told *The Voice*.

Sanderson's PE teacher Barbara Richards introduced her to the javelin when she was just 14 and the sports star later joined Wolverhampton & Bilston Athletics Club. She won the first of eight British javelin titles in 1975, before making her Olympic debut in Montreal a year later, where she finished tenth. Sanderson would go on to compete at six Olympic games, but it was at her third, in Los Angeles in 1984, when she became the first and only British athlete to win an Olympic throwing event. *The Voice* celebrated her achievements on the front cover of its hundredth issue under the headline 'Black Gold', picturing Sanderson alongside sprinters Evelyn Ashford and Carl Lewis as well as decathlete Daley Thompson. Sanderson's victory was iconic, it broke down barriers and paved the way for other Black female athletes.

While he enjoyed success in the ring as a British and Commonwealth boxing champion, Michael Watson earned legendary status as a vocal disability campaigner. Emerging as a tough competitor in the 1980s, Watson defeated fellow Brit Nigel Benn to secure Commonwealth middleweight gold in 1989. But Watson was hungry for more. Months after his victory over Benn he told *The Voice*: 'I don't want to end up fighting for the World title known only as the guy who beat Nigel Benn. I want to be known as Michael Watson – a class boxer in his own right.'

Tragically, just two years later, Watson suffered a near-fatal brain injury during his 1991 WBO super middleweight title fight with Chris Eubank, an event that ended his boxing career. After spending 40 days in a medically induced coma, Michael defied the odds to make a miraculous comeback. His long road to recovery included numerous brain operations to remove a blood clot and a year in intensive care and rehabilitation. He spent six more years as a wheelchair user, slowly regaining the ability to walk, speak and write.

Michael has since become a vocal campaigner for disability sport, calling for improved disabled access to gyms and fitness centres, among other campaigns.

In 2003, he took on the London Marathon, using a walking stick to complete the 26.2-mile course over six days.

He told *The Voice*: 'When I crossed the finishing line, words couldn't explain how I felt. The moral support that I got from my fans, and people in general … I've never experienced anything like that in my life.' His incredible effort earned him a Spirit of London award, while the public support shown to him as he raised money for charity saw him dubbed the 'People's Champion.' In 2004, Watson was awarded an MBE for his services to disability sport and carried the Paralympics torch as part of 2012 London Olympic Games.

In the early 1980s, Barbados-born Roland Butcher broke boundaries as the first Black cricketer to represent England. Butcher moved to England at the age of 14, joined Middlesex in 1974 and was picked for two one-day internationals against Australia in 1980. That September, he won a place on the team's tour of the Caribbean. Ironically, Butcher made his debut in the Barbadian capital of Bridgetown.

Looking back on his career, Butcher told *The Voice*: 'That was the beginning of the motivation for many of the Black players in England who perhaps felt they would never get the opportunity to play.

'It certainly helped them and spurred them on. I feel very proud that I was the catalyst for that change. The numbers who have walked through that door have obviously motivated others as well. It needs to be spoken about.'

Acknowledging his place in history, Butcher said: 'I remember Viv Anderson and Laurie Cunningham were England's only Black international footballers at this time, but I think only later on, did I truly understand the significance of it.

'Back then I just wanted to play international cricket. Devon Malcolm spoke to me later and said I was an inspiration.'

However, Butcher attracted criticism from Bernie Grant in 1989 when he, along with fellow Black cricketer Phil DeFreitas, was announced as part of a 16-man team to tour South Africa. When it was reported at the time, each player was set to receive £100,000 from the South African apartheid government. Grant told *The Voice*: 'It is blood money and a massive propaganda coup for the South African government.' After the media backlash, both Butcher and DeFreitas withdrew from the tour.

Calm and likeable, it's clear to see why Butcher has always been regarded a key player in whatever team he was in. After retiring, he pursued business interests as well as coaching a variety of sides, including Tasmania and Bermuda.

Inducted into the National Football Museum Hall of Fame in 2021, England's first Black captain Paul Ince is well regarded as a trailblazer in combatting racial prejudice in sport. Born in Ilford, he was signed as an academy player for West Ham at the age of 14. Over his 21-year playing career he achieved 53 caps for England and a stint as captain during the 1993 tour of the United States.

After beginning his career with the Hammers, the club he grew up supporting, Ince soon cemented himself as a key member of one of the most successful Manchester United sides in the club's history, winning two Premier League titles, two FA

Cups and both the European Cup Winners' Cup and the Football League Cup. In a 1993 interview with *The Voice*, Ince said: 'I've been told to smile more often.

'But my attitude is that I'm better off getting stuck in than smiling. Football's a hard, competitive game and I haven't got time for that stuff.'

He went on to play for Inter Milan in the Serie A, making a UEFA Cup final, before returning home to play for Liverpool, Middlesbrough and Wolverhampton Wanderers.

Towards the end of his career, Ince featured as player-manager for Swindon Town and Macclesfield Town before making the successful transition to manager where he coached Milton Keynes Dons, Blackburn Rovers, Notts County, Blackpool and Reading.

Geoff Thompson is a former world karate champion who has gone on to become one of the country's most respected sports administrators and youth activists. Raised in Hackney, Thompson is a lifelong advocate of the role that education, sport and culture can play in improving the lives of young people. During a distinguished sporting career, he was the world heavyweight karate champion and world team karate champion between 1982 and 1986 and won more than 50 national and international titles. Following his retirement from competitive sport, he spoke out against British karate, telling *The Voice* in 1988: 'They didn't give a toss whether you were alive or dead until a win was needed on the square.'

Following his retirement from competitive sport, he established himself as an influential sports politician and administrator, taking on numerous public and private sector appointments with the aim of promoting equality, diversity and inclusion at all levels of society. When he became chair at the University of East London, he underpinned his passion when he said: 'My life has been dedicated to unlocking young people's potential and challenging injustice.' Geoff is the founder of the Youth Charter, which marked three decades of hard work in March 2022. This international charity and United Nations NGO maintains the same drive and focus that the organisation had when it was launched.

Geoff says that sport has given him everything. He told *The Voice*:

> My life has been about overcoming adversity. Challenges have been placed before me. I'm still fighting those barriers. I'm still ignored. I'm still described as quirky and strange.
>
> I'm comfortable with that. I'm comfortable in my skin. I want all young people who look like me to get to that point.
>
> I will always push the boundaries and look to raise the bar of excellence.

The hypnotic Bob Marley and the Wailers 'Concrete Jungle' from their critically acclaimed 1973 debut *Catch A Fire* album provided a soundtrack to urban Black life and its poignancy registered with a 1980s generation starting to move to its own beat. Reggae's spiritual message, rooted in the tenets of Rastafarianism, would also resonate with several young home-grown Black British groups. Birmingham's Steel Pulse, and London's Aswad and Misty in Roots, all collectively helped evolve roots reggae outside Jamaica.

In 1982 when Birmingham group Musical Youth hit number one in the UK charts with their single 'Pass the Dutchie', *The*

The Voice *celebrated when reggae band Musical Youth topped the UK charts in 1982*

Voice hailed them 'the group of the 1980s' and 'Britain's answer to the Jacksons.' The newspaper was already one step ahead and had received permission from their record label MCA to publish their cartoon adventures, which appeared in the third issue of the newspaper. Brixton's Jamaican-born dub poet Linton Kwesi Johnson was also a frequent presence in the newspaper and his work articulated the thoughts of many disenfranchised Black youth. Ironically, his interview, which dubbed him the 'Brixton Bard', would appear in the same issue that also featured the Brixton disturbances splashed on its front page. Conversely, Smiley Culture's 1984 hit 'Mr Police Officer' would show reggae's humorous side and, although very tongue-in-cheek, its lyrics brilliantly role-played the relationship and exchanges Black youngsters were having with the police.

The newspaper had recognised this cultural rebirth very early on and lyrics of Bob and Marcia's 1970 hit 'Young, Gifted and Black' aptly conveyed a newfound optimism in the 1980s. Jazzie B's soul collective, Soul II Soul, would also symbolise this movement, playing their role in reimagining this period of exploration. Music, theatre and fashion offered a welcome cultural sunburst, which helped disperse the dark clouds often attached to daily life. The newspaper's music pages also championed reggae's Lovers' Rock, an emerging and distinctive British sound, and regularly featured rising singers such as Janet Kay, Carroll Thompson, Jean Adebambo, Louisa Mark, Sylvia Tella and Donna Rhoden.

Fittingly, both Thompson and Kay were interviewed in the first year of *The Voice*. Thompson's popularity earned him a profile in the 'Voices' section in 1982, and like Lorna St Clair, she would also turn her hobby into a career. She said: 'I always enjoyed singing in church, it was a natural progression to team up with other musicians.' After graduating from Hitchin College with a degree in Business Studies, she worked as an accounts trainee before deciding to pursue a singing career. Her singles 'Simply in Love' and 'Hopelessly in Love' both became chart-toppers and established her internationally. Several months later the interview, 'No problems for Janet,' looked at how Kay was successfully combining a singing and acting career. She talked about cutting her first record while still at secretarial college and said: 'It was simply a matter of being in the right place at the right time.' 'Loving You' would make a big impact on the reggae charts but did not make her a household name. After taking a succession of secretarial jobs, her second record 'Silly Games' proved a huge hit, but she really wanted to go into acting. She met actor Victor Romero Evans by chance at the opening of a record shop and he passed on her details to the director of *Mama Dragon*, securing her first audition and role. She would later get involved with Black Theatre Co-op, which came up with the concept of Channel 4's 'No Problem.'

The Voice also celebrated Black beauty in all its forms. Miss Black UK, Miss Jamaica UK, along with Mr Supercool, Mr Batchelor, and *The Voice*-sponsored Classy Couples, all offered Black models a welcome platform. The paper also created its own 'Baby Beautiful and Toddler' competition with sponsorship from high street retailers Mothercare and C&A. The fusing of fashion, music, beauty and hair care created fresh opportunities, and was epitomised by young Black talent taking their first tentative steps into the fashion world. In October 1982 they carried a fashion spread showcasing the talents of Reginald Knight, Ethney Charles and Clariscia Gill, three young designers who had recently graduated from the prestigious London College of Fashion.

23-year-old Gill's stylish Black dress design made the front page and when she was interviewed in *The Voice*, it was clear she was looking forward to a promising career.

She said: 'I have always craved independence and after leaving fashion college worked for Berman's and Nathan's, the theatrical and film costumiers. It was very hard work – but the experience I got was tremendous. I worked on *Superman* and *Star Wars*.' She later took out a bank loan to start her own business. She said: 'At times I felt like packing it all in, but I always knew it would be worthwhile in the end.' Her designs had already been used in an Avon brochure, she had been interviewed by the BBC and was profiled in *Black Beauty* and *Hair* magazine.

The newspaper was also a huge supporter of the Black church and recognised the valuable contribution of gospel music. Talented gospel artists such as Paul Johnson, Lavine Hudson and Mica Paris, who had made her name with Spirit of Watts Gospel Choir, before crossing over to secular music, often made the headlines. *The Voice* also teamed up with Capital FM to present a live concert featuring legendary US singer Al Green. The success of 19-year-old Paris was particularly rewarding for the newspaper as it had followed and supported her career from the very beginning. She hit the front page in 1988 when her single 'My One Temptation' broke the Top 10, selling 100,000 copies.

But Mica Paris was not the only young performer who was championed by *The Voice* from the beginning. In 1982 10-year-old Scott Sherrin made the front page when he was cast as Fizzy in the stage musical *Bugsy Malone*. Sherrin, from Hackney, was an accomplished singer, dancer and athlete had appeared in the *Minipops* TV series as well as adverts on television ranging from Steradent to Smarties. *The Voice* wondered if he was feeling

MP TAKES UP CASE OF PRISON'S FORGOTTEN MAN

POLICE IGNORE BLACK OPINION

Black people's expertise on race matters is still being ignored, according to a new report slamming their lack of involvement in police training.

Greater London Action for Racial Equality (GLARE) were incensed about the blatant lack of collaboration with black people in police training and their new report — Race Issues in Police training has slammed the force for their insensitivity.

David Dibosa, GLARE research and campaigns officer, said: "The police must get right away from their persistent and narrow view of training as being about the background and culture of black peoples."

He continued: "Training is about police facing their own problems in their relationship with black communities. If they are to find effective solutions they must seriously bring black people right into the police training process."

There are ten recommendations in the report, including a proposal to re-select instructors so that only people sympathetic to the promotion of racial equality are selected. It also recommends the setting up of an advisory group drawn from the black community to help the police devise the course and evaluate its success.

RADIO STATION FINED FOR ANTI-SADDAM OUTPUT

A community radio station has been disciplined over its Gulf War broadcasts by the Radio Authority.

Ironically, Bradford City Radio (BCR) was fined £2,500 after it cancelled its music programme in order to counteract pro-Saddam 'propaganda' that was broadcast on four Muslim pirate radio stations.

The pirates, repeating Baghdad Radio messages, had been advocating a 'jihad' (holy war) against British and American "imperialist targets", trying to incite British Muslims to civil disorder.

"It got to a point where we had to do something," said Pervez Akhtor, Brad-

ford City Radio's chief executive, and by "providing accurate information with an establishment point of view, we wanted to protect the good name of our Muslims".

Bradford City Radio the first independent radio station to be fined for breach of 'promise of performance' said it had not meant to offend its audience.

Akhtar said: "I believe we were instrumental in allaying Muslim fears about the war rather than inflaming passions".

SINITTA: Animal lover.

Sinitta urges animal Remembrance Day

PINTSIZED popstar Sinitta will help highlight the plight of laboratory animals with the National Anti-Vivisection Society by calling for a national black armband Day of Remembrance for the creatures.

Sinitta, who is patron of the youth branch of the 100-year-old society will also sing two of her new songs at the end of a rally to be held in London.

Anti-Vivisectionists want to abolish the laws which allow experiments on live animals while they are alive.

"We have to show that vivisection doesn't work, that artificial disease grows differently in animals, explained Jan Creamer, Director of the National Anti-Vivisection Society.

The Anti-Vivisectionists who want to use computer technology and tissue cultures instead of animals plan their demo for April 24.

Release campaign hots up

An MP has slammed the continued imprisonment of an ailing 72-year-old man as "judicial vindictiveness".

Now Tony Lloyd has pledged to draw Parliament's attention to Angela Howard's plight which was highlighted in The Voice last month (March 26).

"It's sheer judicial vindictiveness that these officials are refusing to let Mr Howard out," blasted the Manchester MP.

"He is a frail old man who couldn't possibly be a physical danger to society, and has in fact been recommended for release by the governor at his last prison."

Tony Lloyd

Risk

Howard has languished in prison since 1974 after being convicted for the murder of his common law wife.

He has always protested his innocence but has already served seven years longer than the average ten years done by similar

category prisoners. By the time his next parole comes up, he will have served 20 years.

But the Home Office's Life Sentence Review Section, continue to insist that the poorly, 5 st Guyanian is a "risk to society".

Now community leaders and residents in Manchester's Moss Side, where Howard lived, are

Angela Rumbold

adding their results to the campaign for his release.

Howard's long-time friend, newsagent Ras Finn, said he had been mandated by requests from customers who were "shocked" by the prisoner's plight and wanted to know more about the case.

And Bishop Ronni Slake, of the local African Methodist Evangelical Church, said: "We're surprised to hear of this hidden injustice. I would certainly be interested in a public meeting to discuss a plan of action."

Disbelief

Local councillors label Sram and Vince Young have also pledged support and plan to hold a public meeting. "My initial reaction was one of disbelief. We are going to try and organise a petition for presentation to the Home Secretary," said Cllr Sram.

The well known 'rough justice' campaigner, James Stevenson, who has twice

visited Howard in Bristol Prison, said he was "very encouraged" by the interest the Moss Side community has taken in the case.

"This guy is black and he's challenged the system — that's why the Home Office don't want to release him.

"If we make this an election issue and refuse to vote for a government which allows its Home Office to behave in such a disgusting manner, then perhaps they'll listen."

Mr Lloyd, who represents Stretford for Labour pledged that he would seek a meeting with the Minister for Prisons, Angela Rumbold, and raise questions in Parliament if the matter wasn't resolved.

POLL BATTLE KICKS OFF

The heat is on for the battle of the town halls as the major political parties prepare for local elections on May 2.

More than 12,000 seats are being contested in what is being seen as the most crucial poll in recent political history.

The Tories are hoping to gauge how the public feel about the hybrid poll tax and the new Prime Minister in what could turn out to be a practice run for a June general election.

Meanwhile, black Britons are being urged to use their right to vote. Shock figures released last week showed that hundreds of thousands of people have dropped off the electoral register. In the south London Borough of Lambeth, for example, a phenomenal 7,718 people fell from the roll in the past year alone possibly in an attempt to avoid paying the poll tax.

And those who are registered don't even bother to take the opportunity to vote. At the last local elections there, only 39 per cent of those eligible took part.

MP Bernie Grant says it is crucial that black people exercise their rights. "If democracy is to work," he says, "it must work for all people and we owe it to ourselves and our children to ensure that it works for the black communities in Britain."

What's on offer

Labour

Neil Kinnock's announcement that Labour's intention was to cut the average household bill by £140 with the 'fair rates' system left Tory chairman Chris Patten 'gobsmacked'.

The poll tax replacement would be based on the old rates system so people with large houses will probably lose out. But, says shadow environment secretary Brian Gould, seven out of ten people would be better off under their system.

Labour have also promised to impose a 'quality commission' on local authorities to make sure council workers do their jobs properly.

Tories

There were few surprises in the Conservatives' local election manifesto. Michael Heseltine, the Environment Secretary, said that voters would be delighted with details of their poll tax replacement — which Mr Kinnock dubbed "Son of the poll tax".

But at the launch of their campaign last week Mr Heseltine said the details of the new tax were not quite ready. "We shall publish the details during the course of the campaign," he said. "It will be a popular announcement because the proposals in it will be seen to be fair."

The campaign will concentrate on the fact that Labour councils spend more.

Chris Patten said that the price of electing a Labour councillor rather than a Tory would be an extra £201,460.

Liberal Democrats

Like everyone else, Paddy Ashdown wants to introduce a local tax that is fair and easy to collect.

The Liberal Democrats plan to take away the secrecy that surrounds local government decision-making by introducing a public question time at council meetings and bringing in consumer panels.

Still pushing for electoral reform, the party's manifesto proposes the introduction of proportional representation at local elections.

IDRIS ELBA: Poised for success.

IDRIS BECOMES TOP GUY

Lucky dancer Idris Elba was chosen from over 2,000 youngsters to join a top class musical production.

The 18-year-old of East Ham, east London, was one of only 22 people chosen to take part in the National Youth Music Theatre's production of Guy and Dolls which will be taken to festivals in Japan and Edinburgh.

After a day of gruelling auditions, Idris told The Voice: "They were the hardest

auditions I've ever been to. I couldn't believe it when they chose me out of all those people."

The multi-talented performer also sings and acts and could be chosen for any one of the production's plum roles. "I don't know which part I've got yet but I'm really looking forward to rehearsals which start next month.

Idris will have to take a three-month break from his course in performing arts at Barking Technical College to tour with the show and is looking for sponsors to cover his expenses.

In 1991 The Voice *interviewed an unknown 18-year-old actor called Idris Elba, who had just won a role in the National Youth Musical Theatre's production of Guys and Dolls*

nervous, and replied he did, but declared: 'Once you get on stage, you never want to come off.'

The Voice also celebrated the achievements of Tanya Elliot and Evan Williams when they secured places at the Royal Ballet School, following in the footsteps of just a handful of Black dancers. Elliot, 11, from Ruislip, Middlesex, competed against some of the finest dancers from all over the world to gain a place at the Royal Ballet School on junior level. Meanwhile 16-year-old Evan, from the Stonebridge estate in North London, auditioned and was accepted at three dance schools: Ballet Rambert, Contemporary Dance School and Royal Ballet.

Dance would also launch the career of one of Britain's acting superstars. In 1991, *The Voice* reported that 18-year-old Idris Elba, from East Ham, was chosen from 2,000 youngsters to join the National Youth Musical Theatre's production of *Guys and Dolls*. After a day of gruelling auditions, he told *The Voice*: 'They were the hardest auditions I had ever been to. I couldn't believe it when they chose me out of all those people.' Idris would have to take three months out from his course in performing arts at Barking Technical College to go on the tour.

During the late 1980s and early 1990s young, independently minded Black audiences flocked to the thriving comedy and variety circuit, and *The Voice* also witnessed Black theatre punching well above it weight, even though it was severely cash-strapped. A copy of a report 'Black Theatres in England', commissioned by the Arts Council, was leaked to the newspaper in 1991. In it Dr Elizabeth Clarke wrote:

Eight weeks of trekking through London's inner city streets, grimy community centres and council estates in pursuit of Black theatre merely lends visual proof to yet another epic of inadequate funding, understaffing, meagre resources being stretched to superhuman ends, offices doubling up as living rooms ...I finished the report totally dazed at the near pathological tenacity with which Black theatre still manages to hold on and function.

Theatre groups such as Talawa, Temba, and Black Theatre Co-up were not only producing talented stage actors, but many would make a successful move into television. Channel 4's *No Problem!* along with *Desmond's* were joined by BBC's *The Real McCoy* in mainstreaming Black talent. In addition, the collectives of the all-female BiBi Crew and all-male outfit, Posse, proved equally popular in the early 1990s. Hackney Empire's 291 Club was a variety show that encapsulated this new energy, engaging predominantly Black audiences. The winner of each final was flown out to New York to take part in Showtime at the Apollo, the event that inspired the UK show. *The Voice* charted the show's meteoric rise in a two-page feature, headlined: 'Laugh, I nearly died!

However, while acknowledging its success, 291 co-ordinator Beverly Randall said that they had relied, 'entirely on the goodwill of *The Voice* and *Time Out* who have sponsored the event all the way, and LWT who have first option to televise the show and sponsored is in the second season.'

Chris Amoo of the soul group the Real Thing showed that Black people could achieve in unexpected places, and the newspaper gleefully announced his dog, Viscount Grant, had been crowned 'Supreme Champion' at Cruft's Dog Show, with Viscount beating around 14,000 other dogs.

The decade was also memorable for well-known personalities' visits to *The Voice's* offices. In 1986, US actor and tap-dancing star Gregory Hines was snapped entering the newspaper's Bow Road offices clutching his copy of *The Voice*, alongside the headline 'Hines' surprise!'

Forty issues in, *The Voice* changed its masthead, proclaiming itself to be 'Britain's Best Black Newspaper' rather than 'London's First Black Newspaper'. In November 1987, the newspaper moved from Bow in East London to Brixton's Coldharbour Lane, where it was truly in the cultural mix. While they were moving in, others were moving out and the neighbourhood's perceived notoriety was now giving way to an emerging prosperity. A year after the move, *The Voice* published a feature with the headline, 'Goodbye Brixton, hello Kingston,' reflecting the number of Black Britons who were cashing in on the inner-city property boom and moving to the Caribbean or the outskirts of London. The piece cites one Brixton couple who had bought a rundown council house for £14,000 six years ago and now their five-bedroom semi was valued at £165,000. It seemed somewhat ironic that in the same year *The Voice*, along with Lambeth Council and the South London Press, would produce a 46-page booklet celebrating the fortieth anniversary of the arrival of the Windrush Generation.

As the decade went on, the newspaper became more assured, introducing colour to its pages and posting an officially audited circulation. The newspaper used its influence to support initiatives and launch campaigns. In the late 1980s the newspaper helped raise £15,000 with the support of celebrities and readers, to send three-year-old, Ben Lindsay, who has cerebral palsy to the world-renowned Peto Clinic in Hungary for treatment.

The Voice launched a 'Stamp Out Knives' campaign in support of the Met Police's 'Amnesty for Knives' initiative, and also got behind an anti-drugs campaign targeting the evils of cocaine. It regularly ran fostering and adoption campaigns, and fundraising campaigns addressing the plight of those with sickle cell disease. Lenny Henry's Comic Relief also received a boost when the newspaper asked readers, Black businesses and advertisers to donate to help famine-hit Ethiopia, Sudan and Somalia. In the late 1980s *The Voice*, in association with the Jamaican Information Service (JIS), introduced the Marcus Garvey Scholarship Award to mark the centenary of his birth. They were also early sponsors of Flip Fraser's successful stage musical *Black Heroes in the Hall of Fame*, which entertained and educated Black audiences nationally and internationally. Additionally, *The Voice's* 'Search for Star' became the country's biggest Black talent competition.

By the early 1990s the newspaper had built a rapport with leading Black personalities on both sides of the Atlantic. They were often the smiling faces, helping to lift the gloom. *The Voice* was in Birmingham in 1984 when Muhammad Ali visited the city to check on the progress of the city's Black community centre, which was named after him. An impressive roster of Black British talent were featured in the newspaper, including top television newsreader Trevor McDonald, comedian Lenny Henry and the multi-talented Floella Benjamin, proving that the newspaper's content could mix it up with the mainstream. The interview with ex-footballer Justin Fashanu in the early 1990s, where he spoke out about being the first openly gay football player. It was one of the rare occasions that a Black personality had spoken so candidly to a Black newspaper.

By the late 1980s and early 1990s, the newspaper was now recognised as a valuable 'training academy' for young Black journalists. The appalling headline stories, which had become a staple of the early years, had not gone away, but the editorial mix was far more balanced. More importantly, its nuanced

THE VOICE

Britain's Best Black Newspaper! 46p

WHO STOLE THE SOUL?
Public Enemy asked the question now get ready for some answers

THE RETURN OF THE TEENIES
Another Bad Creation are the new kids on the block

Let your fingers do the walking in your BIGGER, BETTER, JOBMARKET

'THE TOUGHEST TIME OF MY LIFE'

Gay soccer star Justin Fashanu speaks out

Soccer star Justin Fashanu has spoken out for the first time about the fears and heart-aches that have dogged him since he 'came out'.

In an exclusive interview with The Voice, Fashanu, admitted that the last six months have been one of the toughest periods in his life. He has had to:

● Battle with soccer bosses determined to keep him out of the game forever;

● Face a stone wall of silence from his famous brothers;

● Endure mental anguish as he tries to reconcile his

By Diran Adebayo

homosexuality with his strong Christian beliefs.

Responsibility

"I am afraid every day, every minute. But when you decide to come out, you have to take on the responsibility," said Fashanu.

Although Fashanu received a fee for his original story in The Sun newspaper, he says he was offered "more money

from somebody not to do it".

But, after a gay friend of Fashanu's committed suicide by throwing himself off the balcony of a hotel where he was staying, the soccer star decided to go public.

"There are so many gay kids who have no hope. I wanted to be their role model," he said.

For the full story, turn to pages 12 and 13.

Fashanu: Battled with soccer bosses

WAITING TO BE HAMMERED!

WHY are 13 year-old Vanya Rasburn and 12-year-old Andrea Harriot looking so happy? And possibly a bit nervous?

Because the two lucky youngsters were winners of The Voice's 'Meet MC Hammer' competition and here they are just minutes before meeting their hero.

Backstage at Wembley Arena the main man was waiting for them in a room stuffed with food and champers. And, of course, we had a photographer standing by to capture the momentous occasion. What does it feel like to almost faint at the most crucial moment of your life? Read the whole story inside NOW!

Government robs OAPs

Thousands of people who retired to the Caribbean have had millions of pounds-worth of pensions held back by penny-pinching Government officials.

For many of the elderly, who have often worked in the hardest and lowest-paid jobs, money has been frozen from the day they left for home.

Only those returning to the Caribbean countries of Bermuda and Jamaica receive pension increases in line with Britain. That leaves another 5,000 elderly people every year with pensions whose value will whittle away.

Carlton Jacobs, President of the Antigua and Barbuda Association, intends to retire to Antigua soon and has taken the matter up with his High Commission.

He hit out: "This is daylight robbery. Ten years after retirement with inflation as it is these days, pensions will probably be halved.

"I've worked all my life and paid my national insurance contributions. What you pay is supposed to be what you get," said Mr Jacobs, who was recently made redundant by British Telecom.

MP Bernie Grant has raised the matter in Parliament only to be told that there were no plans for similar arrangements to be made with other Caribbean countries.

In an exclusive interview with The Voice *in 1991, Britain's first openly gay footballer Justin Fashanu described the difficulties he had faced since coming out*

approach had offered a generation a rare voice and in the process infused mainstream society with a fresh understanding of contemporary Black Britain. The newspaper had survived the Thatcher years and, in 1990, Brixton was once again the focus of attention, when John Major, one of its famous sons, was elected Prime Minister.

The ground had been thoroughly prepared for the next decade and *The Voice* could proudly claim it had helped to sow the early seeds of multicultural Britain. By the early 1990s, the green shoots were evident, but there was still a very long way to go. In truth, Britain's Black communities were still no closer to escaping the kind of 'Concrete Jungle' that Bob Marley and the Wailers had sung about almost two decades before. But the strength and resilience of Britain's Black communities, so evident in the pages of the newspaper, chimed with the words of Maya Angelou's empowering poem 'Still I Rise', offering an optimistic rallying cry for a new generation. 'I Rise, I Rise, I Rise'.

1993–2002
The Black British middle class in 100 letters

By Dotun Adebayo

In the 1993 New Year's edition of *The Voice*, 1992 was summed up as 'downhill most of the way' with inflation hitting Black Brits hard, causing thousands of job losses and home repossessions. But in this second decade of the paper there was every reason for optimism. Things, we believed, could only get better. The paper had celebrated its tenth anniversary in the autumn of 1992 with a star-studded dinner and dance at a top West End hotel. It was an event that set down a firm marker for Black Britain and the new decade of the paper.

This is who we are. This is where we belong. At the very top.

Linford Christie had just won Olympic gold. Lennox Lewis was the new world heavyweight champion. Trevor McDonald was the *News at Ten* anchor. Chrystal Rose was the latest chat show host. Rianna Scipio was everybody's favourite TV weather girl. In parliament, Diane Abbott and Bernie Grant were holding power to account on behalf of Black Britons.

Upward social mobility was the order of the day. 'Buppies' was the new buzz word that described of the Black version of the young upwardly mobile white middle classes (yuppies). Buppies were the opposite of 'ragamuffins', a catchall phrase to describe members of the Black community who were not upwardly mobile in the traditional sense and displayed an ostentatious 'street' lifestyle with a soundtrack to go with it – dancehall or 'ragga'. Ragga contained what a buppie would describe as dubious lyrical content that denigrates women. It was an age of ragga music, ragga style/fashion and ragga philosophy that the Black middle classes found themselves in – a diametrically opposite way of life to theirs. This was reflected in the letters page of *The Voice* – journalists know that the contents of the letters page is how a publisher can gauge who its readership is and what matters to them. In the 1990s *The Voice's* letters page became a battleground for the heart and soul of the Black British mindset.

'Let's end the slackness,' one reader, Diane, urged:

Being of Jamaican parentage I have a lot of pride in my heritage. My complaint is that I see my culture, morals and principles being eroded by the onslaught of slackness. In all walks of life there is deviant behaviour. The women who appeared on the television programme (BBC 2's *Def II*) suggested this was part and parcel of Jamaican life. Men's attitudes are shaped on what we as women and mothers show them. Men love dancehall music as much as these women do. This does not, as far as I'm aware, persuade men to 'skin out' as these women feel the need to do at every given opportunity. I'm not saying it is disgusting to dress provocatively, but there is a distinct line between what is acceptable and what is not. There are plenty of women who do not 'underdress' as much as others, but even condoning such degradation is bad. Slackness both in dress and music should be censored. As a mother of a daughter, I shall do everything possible to make sure she doesn't end up like any of the women featured on the programme. I am a lover of heavy bass-line reggae music but feel I have a moral duty to speak out against the rotten apples in the barrel.

On many occasions, especially when there are so many versions of the same backing track, I have been attracted to the music and caught out by slack lyrics. 'Eye Nuh See' by Simpleton springs to mind. I consider it degrading to hear a record like this goading me and other women to 'skin out' for male sexual gratification. I feel the way they danced was simply a display of their sexual prowess to men looking for agile bed partners. I'm sure the majority of young men coming through the dancehall circuit have witnessed the carryings on and are keen not to be associated with these 'sheep'. If sounds stopped promoting the slackness people would not request to hear them. There are those who want to hear the dancehall beat – but without the slackness.

In a similar vein, while Maxi Priest was top of the British musical tree at the beginning of 1993, his collaboration with ragga don Shabba Ranks didn't go down too well among the most genteel of Black people. This letter echoes the changing view of the Black community in Britain. It was now safe to air your disapproval of the top-ranking musical artists and to express your disapproval:

I must protest about Channel Four's *The Word* (programme), which (featured) Shabba Ranks and his disgusting video.

I felt shocked and embarrassed that he was allowed to go on national television in front of millions of viewers with his limited vocabulary, which revolved around sex.

Any self-respecting Black-minded person could see that Mr Ranks' respect for Black women is non-existent. Somebody needs to tell Ranks that the status of Black women has improved since the days of slavery, we are no longer slave machines. His music is oppressive and disrespectful to the Black woman.

It seems that with the death of Bob Marley reggae music has died.

The Voice's job market pages, a mainstay of the paper's success and a hallmark of the Black British community were now as likely to be filled with professional and executive appointments as they were with public sector and community vacancy adverts.

On the surface, it looked like Black Brits were now mainstream and that the barriers to achievement, at least in the labour market, had been lifted, and for those companies which transgressed, there were now laws to punish them.

But the first news stories of 1993 suggested there were still some broad structural constraints to an equitable Britain. *The Voice* reported that car repair chain Kwik-Fit had to pay 40-year-old Robert Young £10,000 after he took the company to industrial tribunal after being subjected to a year and half of racial harassment at the hands of his bosses while he managed the Wandsworth branch. The London Underground had to pay out £80,000 after it was discovered it was paying long-serving Black managers less than their white colleagues.

This man is part of a small minority.

He's a Royal Navy Officer.

The Royal Navy is an equal opportunities employer.

If you think you're equal to the opportunities, get in touch. Call us on 0345 300 123 or fill in the coupon.

The Royal Navy is looking for men and women to fill vacancies. Contact your local Jobcentre or send to: The Royal Navy and Royal Marines Careers Service, Dept (AH50650), FREEPOST 4335, Bristol BS1 3YX. No stamp needed. http://www.open.gov.uk/navy/rnhm.htm

NAME (Mr, Mrs, Miss)

ADDRESS

POSTCODE   DATE OF BIRTH

TELEPHONE

We are equal opportunity employers under the Race Relations Act and welcome enquiries and applications from all ethnic groups.

ROYAL NAVY

Join the Navy and see the world. Differently.

The Voice's jobs pages were filled with professional appointments as well as public sector and community vacancies

It was not the rest of the country that was being urged to '*Say No*' to the new Asylum and Immigration Bill being debated through parliament. It was all about the Black community and their loved ones and their need to oppose it. The underlying context of this was that, despite the achievements and progress of the last ten years, life was not altogether rosy for the community at large. Indeed, it was still an unmitigated struggle for many if not most people of African and Caribbean heritage in the UK simply because of the colour of their skin.

Even as *The Voice* championed the 'new Britain' of Black achievement and aspiration, it would keep one eye on 'ye olde unreconstructed Britain' and the need to call it out and, when necessary, call upon the spirit of resistance that had seen us get up, stand up and fight for our rights, even though it was nearly half a century since the Windrush Generation landed in Britain. It was a dichotomy that every Black Brit had to navigate their way through, whether you were rich or poor. No matter how much we believed that we had been accepted and become part of the mainstream, no matter whether we stayed in our inner-city neighbourhoods or moved to new pastures because of our economic circumstances, we were never more than one incident away from being second-class citizens.

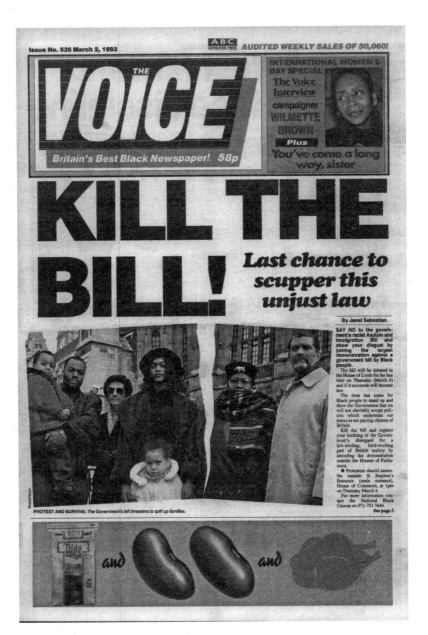

Issue No. 538 March 2, 1993

ABC CONSUMER PRESS **AUDITED WEEKLY SALES OF 50,060!**

THE VOICE

Britain's Best Black Newspaper! 58p

INTERNATIONAL WOMEN'S DAY SPECIAL

The Voice Interview campaigner **WILMETTE BROWN**

Plus

You've come a long way, sister

KILL THE BILL!

Last chance to scupper this unjust law

By Janet Sebastian

SAY NO to the government's racist Asylum and Immigration Bill and show your disgust by joining the largest demonstration against a government bill by Black people.

The bill will be debated in the House of Lords for the last time on Thursday (March 4) and if it succeeds will become law.

The time has come for Black people to stand up and show the Government that we will not slavishly accept policies which undermine our status as tax paying citizens of Britain.

Kill the bill and register your loathing of the Government's disregard for a law-abiding, hard-working part of British society by attending the demonstration outside the Houses of Parliament.

● Protesters should assemble outside St Stephen's Entrance (main entrance), House of Commons, at 1pm on Thursday March 4.

For more information contact the National Black Caucus on 071-721 7646.
See page 3

PROTEST AND SURVIVE: *The Government's bill threatens to split up families.*

Tilda and and

At the start of the decade The Voice *campaigned against the government's 1983 Asylum and Immigration Bill*

The Voice was not mincing its words when it came to immigration. 'We're here to stay' was the editor's comment in the March 2 issue:

> If the Government's racist Asylum and Immigration Bill goes through, it will adversely affect the majority of Black people in Britain ... An immigration official who rolls out of bed on the wrong side can take an unreasonable dislike to a visitor who will be removed from these shores without the opportunity to appeal against the decision – or even be given a reason as to why the decision has been made ... Black Britons have to stand up and be heard. We have to now show the Government that ... We have every right to be here. This country is our home and our families have every right to come and visit without fear that at the first port of call ... a stroke of a pen can make us undesirables.

An international conference of the Society of Black Lawyers was coincidentally being held in London at the time. On her way to the event, 38-year old Margret Jackson, who had flown from the Caribbean to attend, was horrified when she was stopped on suspicion of being a drugs smuggler.

'It was the most degrading thing that has ever happened to me,' she told *The Voice*. 'I showed them my business card and explained why I was here but they just didn't believe me.' After a Society of Black Lawyers-backed protest, she eventually received an apology from the government, but no amount of 'sorry' could take away the nagging feeling that every Black person in Britain is constantly under suspicion of being a drug dealer or drugs smuggler. No matter who or what they are. This balancing act of being both a campaigning paper fighting for the rights of Black Brits and being an aspirational publication that reflects and promotes social mobility was a tricky one. Not least in London.

It was to the capital that the nation's Black youth in particular flocked for opportunity. London was arguably the Black capital of Britain. *The Voice's* young staff of mostly graduates, like many of its readers, had come from as far afield as Sheffield, Cardiff, Manchester and Wolverhampton. It was in London that most of the papers 53,000 audited sales were to be found. It was in London that the great and the good of the Black community gathered with increasing regularity for balls at the Hilton or Dorchester Hotel. It was also in London that the Black British aesthetic was being defined and formulated. In 1993, this meant the letter 'X' was added to everything. An 'X' on your baseball cap. An 'X' on your jacket and an 'X' on your baggy jeans. All in anticipation of the much-hyped Malcolm X biopic by director Spike Lee. It meant a visit to the annual Afro Hair and Beauty Show, which was at this point in its eleventh year. The show, which billed itself as Europe's premier exhibition for the Black hair and beauty industries, was the same age as *The Voice* and their success went almost hand in hand.

The show was one of the highlights of the Black calendar, but just like *The Voice*, it was borne out of the frustration that Black women felt about the mainstream markets not catering for their needs. The event put the glamour into being young and Black and upwardly mobile in a Britain that was never far from being unglamorously frustrating for young Black and upwardly mobile citizens.

Most importantly, London was where Brixton was. Brixton was the true centre of Black Britain. Brixton was the physical and spiritual home of postwar immigrants from the Caribbean.

In fact, *The Voice's* Brixton offices were right next door to the dole office that the boatload of men who had arrived on *Windrush* in June 1948 had gone to look for the work they had heard was in abundance in the 'motherland'. In 1993, there was already talk of a Brixton renaissance on the pages of *The Voice*. It would be a literary revolution, like Harlem had experienced in the 1920s and 1930s, spearheaded by my publishing company The X Press, which was already the biggest Black-interest publishing company in the country after just six months. The X Press's debut novel had been a runaway bestseller and had spurred many other writers to take up the pen. It may not have been a renaissance just yet but there was gentrification going on in the London postcodes of SW2 and SW9. 'Brixton riot' was now the name of a popular cocktail at the rum bar opposite the tube station. A Russian-speaking Black woman was the local mayor, and even the 'bad bwoys in da hood' were reading Victor Headley's *Yardie*.

Of course, there was life outside London, and *The Voice* did more than any other newspaper to map the cities where Black British life existed beyond the capital. So much so that editions of the paper featuring the communities of Moss Side Liverpool Leicester and Leeds have become historical documents.

The Voice's special correspondent Mike Best went to Chapeltown in Leeds at the beginning of 1993 to find the highest concentration of Black people anywhere in West Yorkshire, even though the Black population was only 10,815. Most people from the Caribbean islands of St Kitts and Nevis, and Best discovered that in two particular wards, Chapel Allerton and Harehills, an incredible seven out of every ten homes were owned by Black residents. This article also featured the only Black barrister in Yorkshire, Stephen Bedeau. But he also reported that the unemployment rate in the community was an alarming 30 per cent.

In lieu of work, the younger generation gathered in the 'front-line', a fabled stretch of road in every Black community in the country where those grasping at the bottom of the occupational ladder, thwarted by structural racism, could vent their frustrations. In Brixton it was Railton Road, Tottenham had Broadwater Farm) and Stoke Newington had Sandringham Road. The Leeds frontline was on Chapeltown Road, in the heart of the community, where in the summer of 1981 an estimated 400 youths vented their frustrations and anger in a night of rioting that resulted in 70 arrests. To the upwardly mobile young Black men and women living 200 miles away in the capital, the problems of the Black community of Leeds seemed like a throwback to their parents' generation. For the unemployed youth of Chapeltown reading the pages of *The Voice* in the West Indian Centre, the upwardly mobile concerns of their counterparts in London must have seemed like an existential pre-occupation too far.

Perhaps not surprisingly, the different communities did not always see eye to eye. The Moss Side community in Manchester, for example, were divided as to what good boxing champ Chris Eubank could do on his mission to stop the gang violence in Manchester after the shooting of a young boy. Indeed, his visit there after the killing of 14-year-old 'Benjl' Stanley was greeted with scorn by some.

'Chris is just what Moss Side needs', wrote *a The Voice* reader Sean who argued that the boxer should have been welcomed with open arms:

Nothing irks me more than those individuals who relish the wanton assaults on people's characters, especially

While upwardly mobile 'buppies' became more prevalent in the '90s, tensions still existed in areas such as in Manchester's Moss Side

when their guns are aimed at young Black achievers. My wrath was unleashed after I read an article in *The Voice* which suggested that some members of the community and the Church had not welcomed the visit by world boxing champion Chris Eubank to Moss Side. The story mentioned one of the community's exemplary figures, Father Phil Sumner, priest of St Wilfred's Church and governor of two local schools. Eubank's mission to the area to inspire peace between the warring factions was rebuffed by Father Summer and others. Father Sumner, who was a friend of the deceased, argued that: 'Chris Eubank is not the kind of role model we need.' As the guns continue to blaze in the stricken Manchester area, the dead are mourned and the sirens wail. In the meantime, people squabble over the non-issue of who is qualified to be a role-model for Moss Side's youngsters . . . I say disrespect is no virtue.

To be or not to be a 'buppie' was nevertheless an important consideration for the ever-increasing numbers of young graduates who seemed to be achieving parity with their white counterparts and whose degrees set them apart from their parents' generation. Not just professionally but also intellectually, and the reading material for an upwardly mobile Black person should surely reflect that.

This letter from *The Voice* reader Vanessa, titled 'Variety is the spice of life', was a typical old versus new conundrum of the upwardly mobile's reading list:

My message to Lorren McKellar (Viewpoint, *The Voice*) is a simple one – 'chill out woman.'

So, she didn't enjoy Naomi King's *OPP* or Victor Headley's *Yardie*. Well neither did I (they're not the type of books I usually read), but surely the great thing here is that Black readers have more to choose from? It's all very well to sing the praises of Chinua Achebe and Ben Okri (no disrespect intended), but the Black population needs its own Jackie Collins and James Hadley Chase too. Crass perhaps but the point is that everyone is catered for. It's the same with Black movies: *Mo, Money* was not *Boyz 'N' the Hood*, but variety is the spice of life and some people just want to be entertained. There are plenty of writers exploring the psychology of Black men and women, and Black culture is so diverse that there is a huge untapped pool waiting to be discovered. I say more power to Ms King. As for white people assuming that we are all drug takers and gun runners, well I don't have time for preconceived notions. I just go ahead and over achieve.

One of the book publishers also responded to the criticism:

The X Press way to popular writing, it seems that Loreen McKellar has misunderstood certain statements I made in a recent interview with *The Voice*. She confuses my expression 'intelligentsia' with the word intelligent. When I said The X Press was not appealing to the intelligentsia, I was referring to those intellectual snobs whose narrow-minded, 'politically correct' perspectives prevent them from appreciating anything that is labelled 'popularist'. The fact that writers such as Ben Okri have limited 'popular appeal' in the Black (and White) community is not a criticism of Mr Okri's work. It is an indication that there is clearly a demand for books that are reflective of things happening in Black Britain today.

Just because Mr Okri's books are· not in as many Black homes as Terry McMillan's or Victor Headley's, it can hardly be understood to mean that Black people do not read or are not intelligent, as Ms McKellar seems to infer.

The transformation from community of struggle to community of aspiration that was so evident in the capital was riven with existential challenges and a lot of soul searching on questions of identity. Despite the economic differences in the community, we still apparently moved as a pack. One Black person represented all other Black people, and those who had succeeded didn't want to be brought down by old thinking. So, the questions posed included: Who are we? What are we? Where are we supposed to be – intellectually and otherwise? Which way should we vote in an election? And is a 'buppie' a credit to the community or a token, a careerist, or even worse – a sell-out who accepts the status quo and has been creamed off into a fat-salaried position to keep them quiet and by so doing divides and weakens the Black community? Is it even possible to be Black and middle class in 1993 Britain?

The Birmingham reggae emcee Macka B in his 'Buppie Culture' tune, questioned the racial consciousness of well-to-do Black people as they pulled away economically from their African/Caribbean counterparts. What he wanted to know was whether they were more inclined to think of themselves in terms of their Blackness or in terms of their upward mobility.

You have good buppie and you have bad buppie
Good buppie them irie
Dem help out in the community
Dem nuh look down 'pon anybody
But the bad buppie dem nuh ready
Gwan like dem better than everybody
Dem nuh go a club where dem let in natty . . .

The last line in particular was a bone of contention. Were we not all 'proud to be Black' as Crucial Robbie had insisted on his hit single of the same name. Or were class and racial pride in constant conflict with racial excess baggage?

Reader Elizabeth from Cleveland took issue with a quote from world heavyweight champion boxer Larry Holmes: 'I'm not Black anymore. I was Black when I was poor.' In a letter she wrote:

I fail to see where racial pride comes in when changing your colour is directly related to changing your financial status. This argument cheapens the meaning of our rich Black heritage and culture. It also begs the question: if Mr Holmes is no longer Black, what is he? It strikes me that this is the kind of logic that results from race fatigue.

As some members of the Black community became more affluent, they also found themselves conflicted in relation to the much wider Black community for whom upward mobility was still very much a pipe dream. Was the buppie then a racial fraction of the British middle class, or a class fraction of a racial group? They lived lifestyles commensurate with their new - found wealth and status, but lifestyles that were invariably one step away from being affordable for the majority of Black Brits who made up 'the community.' They followed the white flight out of the run-down urban environment that Black immigrants had populated since the Windrush Generation. By 1993, Black middle-class 'colonies' were emerging on the edge of the inner cities, where buppie enclaves were transforming Britain's green and pleasant suburbs into symbols of Black success. Middle-class African Americans had their Sugar Hills and their Baldwin Hills. Their UK counterparts had Croydon and Streatham (or St. Reatham as local buppies prefer to call it) in South London. Birmingham buppies had Small Heath and Black middle-class Mancs were pushing to the edges of Didsbury and Chorlton. These plush neighbourhoods were new frontiers for the middle classes in Black Britain as far away from the 'frontline' experience of the traditionally Black neighbourhoods as it was possible to get.

It is important to note that buppies were not, however, fleeing the Black experience. On the contrary, in these new communities there was a togetherness among the Black middle classes. There was strength in numbers. They shared similar interests, socialised with one another and were equally attuned to the mantra of education, education, education.

But they also still shared the experience of discrimination with their counterparts in the inner cities. In one letter a woman from Milton Keynes wrote:

With reference to Ms Saunders' letter about racism in education, I would like to point out that racism is all around us, but by blaming it for not getting her degree she is conceding victory to the racists.

Black people in higher education do have to work harder than our white counterparts, but what's new? We can allow racism to defeat us or we can rise above it.

I attended institutes of higher education and obtained my degree. Having that degree hasn't made life easy but it has helped to the extent that I can say it was well worth the years of sacrifice, hard work and dedication.

To all those out there considering higher educa- tion, I have one piece of advice: go for it. If you do encounter racism, just think which outcome would be a kick in the teeth for the racist – you dropping out and failing your degree or you walking up to the rostrum, head held high, to collect your certificate.

Ms A.B Bsc Hons, Milton Keynes, Bedfordshire

When it came to socialising, many buppies still had one foot in the roots and culture of their background and still went back to traditional bars and clubs in the inner-city neighbourhoods they had moved away from. After all, that was still where the vibe they were looking for was. Others eschewed the old neigh- bourhood raves and now went uptown for their weekend entertainment. Although there were still unofficial colour bars in many white venues, if you looked the part of a buppie, wore the right clothes and appeared unthreatening to the bouncers, you had an increasingly good chance of getting through the doors. Not always, but venues that once deemed themselves out of bounds to Black customers were now opening their doors to this new-found wealth. Definitely no dreadlocks though.

Black promoters soon saw the gap in the market and quickly filled in the void for non-discriminatory entertainment that could bring buppies and ragamuffins together under one musical groove – usually soul with a little bit of reggae or vice versa. A handful of mainly Black-owned venues like the legendary Night Moves in Shoreditch were established to cater for that intersection between the Black haves and haves-not. Did the Black middle classes have more in common with the white middle classes than they did with the Black working classes? Was this confirmation of Karl Marx's prediction that race, nationality and ethnicity would become increasingly irrelevant as principles of group formation and collective identity would centre around class?

This letter published in *The Voice* at the beginning of January 1993 reflected the earliest discussions among Black Brits regarding what today would be termed as 'cultural appropriation':

I feel I have to write in response to those people who claim David Rodigan is the 'oppressor'.

It is clear they are not only ignorant but also backward in their way of thinking. We are in the 1990s, not Medieval times, and I believe we should not be concerned about whether a Black or a White person is playing Black music.

At the end of the day, Rodigan is a DJ who is not only doing a very good job, but also contributing much to Black music, which counts for a lot.

I was pleased to see the article on him in *The Voice* (December 1). It certainly was not a 'waste of space' as one reader claimed, but enjoyable to read.

From listening to his shows, it is clear he is someone who is doing the job through sheer love of music and it is this he wants to share with other people. All I can say is I hope he keeps up the good work.

Jacquie, London, SE5

When it came to class, the fledgling Society of Black Lawyers had a membership that was the epitome of buppie but a leadership, under Peter Herbert QC, that was as radical as anything the profession had seen. They were the 'good buppies' that Macka B had rapped about. In demanding multi racial juries as standard, even if it meant you had to transport Black people from one area to another to achieve this, and that uncorroborated confessions to policemen should not be accepted by courts, they were certainly not the 'good guys' that MP Sir George Young urged the government to support. He warned ominously: 'We've got to back the good "guys," the sensible, moderate, responsible leaders of the ethnic groups ... If they are seen to deliver, to get financial support from central government for urban projects then it reinforces their standing and credibility in the community. If they don't deliver, people will turn to the militants.'

Even the Church of England, regarded by many as an unwelcoming place of worship for Black churchgoers, was beginning to stretch its hands of fellowship out to Britain's Caribbean communities, much of which had built up its own congregations in schools, community centres and even front living rooms, out of frustration from the way they were shunned by the Anglican faith for the decades since the Windrush Generation.

Among England's 43 Anglican bishops, stood alone Black face, *The Voice*'s long-serving religious correspondent Marcia Dixon observed in her 'Soul Stirrings' page in 1993. Eight years earlier Barbadian-born Wilfred Wood was appointed Bishop of Croydon, presiding over 122 churches. At a stroke, this admirer of Malcolm X and Martin Luther King Jr became one of the most powerful clergymen in the country. He was a social activist who protested against apartheid and was broadly behind the struggles of Black people in Britain.

In the rest of the paper, people were reading about a two-year jail term for a 'cashanova' who had seduced over 100 women and emptied their bank accounts, a Black undercover policeman who wore a dreadlocks wig to foil a drugs deal, and the ironic news that former apartheid cabinet minister in South Africa, Dr Piet Koornhof, had fathered a child with his Black secretary.

When it came to TV presenters, hyperactive 26-year-old Norman Anderson, also known as Normski, was not everyone's cup of tea. But when the normally conventional BBC took him on as the hype man for their 'urban' programme *Dance Energy*, it opened the way up for so many others to follow without being strait jacketed by the otherwise received pronunciation of the BBC's other presenters. He spoke his own version of 'street' talk and came with his own version of street hype complete with baby dreadlocks, bullet-hole jeans and a catchphrase: 'RESPECK'. His formula was highly effective and an obvious winner with the viewer, but it would not last the decade. Channel 4's *Desmond's* had staying power on the other hand. Launched in 1989 it became the nation's best-loved sitcom and won the accolades and gongs to boot with the unforgettable Norman Beaton in the lead role. In sport Oliver Skeete became Britain's first Black showjumper, in business Equinox management consultancy was advising companies worldwide, and in politics there was a line of Black parliamentary candidates awaiting their turn on the Tories side.

Things, one could argue, had never seemed rosier for the Black British community. Until April 22 1993 when in South London, in the most callous way, the whole of Black Britain was reminded that no matter how far up the social ladder Black people climbed, Britain was still a killing field of our children.

The Voice *closely followed the campaigning work of Doreen and Neville Lawrence after their son Stephen was killed in 1993*

The Voice's comment piece on April 27 read:

> Once again, a young Black man's life has been taken for
> no other reason than the colour of his skin.
>
> Eighteen-year-old Stephen Lawrence was savagely
> stabbed to death by odious racist thugs as he walked
> along the street with a friend. This is the third racist slay-
> ing of a young Black man in the area in recent years.
>
> Black people and children are being murdered while
> the government stands aside and does nothing.
>
> It is now crucial for the community to mobilise and
> let the government know we will not be as lambs to the
> slaughter. It is also the responsibility of each member of
> the Black community to lobby their local MPs, march
> to parliament and let the government know of the dis-
> content running through Black Britain ...'

Stephen Lawrence was waiting at a bus stop in Eltham when he
was murdered by a baying mob of white racists. It was to *The
Voice* newspaper that Stephen's parents turned in their moments
of grief when the authorities, chief among them the police, had
let them down. Looking back through that issue of *The Voice* is
the most haunting of experiences. Because now we know the
full horror of the murder. We know the full extent to which his
parents were let down, and we know the full impact that this
murder would have on race relations throughout the entire
country. But we didn't know then. We couldn't know the
unforetold consequences. We couldn't know that it would take
many years for anybody to be prosecuted for the crime and that
most of the perpetrators would get away with murder. We
couldn't know that the murder would have profound

consequences on the Black community. On our Blackness, our Britishness and our place in this country.

The Voice's front-page headline, 'Murdered for being Black', was truly shocking. It was not, however, the first time. The Black community knew only too well. Rolan Adams, a 15-year-old boy had been murdered just two years earlier for simply being Black and in the wrong place at the wrong time.

'It doesn't take a genius to see that it was a racial murder,' Stephen Lawrence's father Neville told the paper. '[Stephen] was chased down the road by about six white youths for no other reason than he was Black.'

Crucially, the police didn't want to see it like that to begin with.

They may not have wanted to talk about it but 'murdered for being Black' was a narrative that went all the way back to the murder of Kelso Cochrane on the streets of West London back in 1958. Nobody was ever convicted of that crime. In the 35 years between Stephen's and Kelso's murders, there had been several instances in which 'murdered for being Black' could have been a headline. Yet, there was something different about this murder that would later, much later, start to sink in and shock the entire nation. There was something about the circumstances. There was something about this young man's background and the failure of the police to investigate in those first crucial hours. In *The Voice* front-page article, there was something in that opening paragraph that would resonate right across the country. Stephen Lawrence would forever be 'the Black teenager' who was murdered by a gang of white thugs.

Like any teenager, he had a full life ahead of him that would never be realised. Stephen Lawrence could have been any Black parent's teenage son. Every Black parent knew that. But there was something more. Something about the dignity with which his heartbroken parents searched for justice, while trying to make sense of the unimaginable, that resonated across the races. You saw and felt their pain.

Doreen and Neville Lawrence's campaign would touch the hearts of everyone they came across. They were the aspiration – an upwardly mobile Black family. The 'every family'. A close-knit family. Stephen's brother Stewart had celebrated his sixteenth birthday just the previous week. The full effect of the murder was yet still to be seen on his sister Georgina. His mother Doreen, a teacher, was too distressed to talk about what happened. The father, a self-made painter and decorator, ran his own business successfully, despite the recession. The children studied hard in pursuit of their dreams. Stephen dreamed of being an architect. In many ways, they were the ideal Black middle-class family and yet, despite their audacity of hope that if you worked hard you would make it, their son was taken away from them while studying for his A levels, by people who never knew him and never cared.

The resonance was not lost on any Black person in this country. You could be as upwardly mobile as you like, but the price of being Black in a racist society would always hang over your head. Every day. Every hour of the day. That was the conclusion the authorities were still denying.

The Voice came out on Tuesday, five days after the attack. While the police were now acknowledging that it was 'a completely unprovoked attack', they had missed the crucial time period of investigation because they had initially treated it as a gang fight or a drug-related incident. Why? Because Stephen Lawrence was Black.

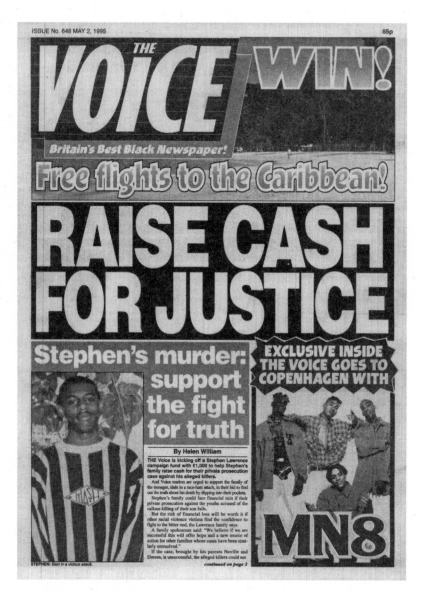

ISSUE No. 648 MAY 2, 1995

65p

THE VOICE

WIN!

Britain's Best Black Newspaper!

Free flights to the Caribbean!

RAISE CASH FOR JUSTICE

Stephen's murder: support the fight for truth

By Helen William

THE Voice is kicking off a Stephen Lawrence campaign fund with £1,000 to help Stephen's family raise cash for their private prosecution case against his alleged killers.

And Voice readers are urged to support the family of the teenager, slain in a race-hate attack, in their bid to find out the truth about his death by dipping into their pockets.

Stephen's family could face financial ruin if their private prosecution against the youths accused of the callous killing of their son fails.

But the risk of financial loss will be worth it if other racial violence victims find the confidence to fight to the bitter end, the Lawrence family says.

A family spokesman said: "We believe if we are successful this will offer hope and a new source of action for other families whose cases have been similarly unresolved."

If the case, brought by his parents Neville and Doreen, is unsuccessful, the alleged killers could sue

continued on page 2

STEPHEN: *Slain in a vicious attack.*

EXCLUSIVE INSIDE THE VOICE GOES TO COPENHAGEN WITH

MN8

In 1994 The Voice *donated £1,000 to help the Lawrences raise money to mount a private prosecution against his alleged killers*

ABC
CONSUMER PRESS

AUDITED WEEKLY SALES OF 49,558!

THE VOICE

Britain's Best Black Newspaper! 54p

NEWS SPECIAL

The final stage of the Asylum and Immigration Bill is to be debated in the House of Lords on January 11. How will it affect you? Find out and make your voice heard . SAY NO to the bill. For the full story see pages 4 & 5

Say NO

 Cut here and display to show your support

 *and*

ABC CONSUMER PRESS — AUDITED WEEKLY SALES OF 50,060!

THE VOICE

Britain's Best Black Newspaper! 58p

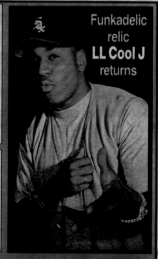

Funkadelic relic
LL Cool J
returns

The hunk of
Westbeach
Ricco Ross

The race is on for
BABY BEAUTIFUL '93
sponsored by the
makers of
MARMITE
YEAST EXTRACT
See inside for details

The Voice Interview
Controversial US author
EDDY L HARRIS

'BABY' BROWN SNOOZED HIS WAY THROUGH JAIL

The godfather of soul, James Brown, slept his way through prison.

Brown, who served an 18-month stretch in 1990 for a traffic offence, admitted that the only way he could overcome the frustration of being locked up was to sleep.

"When I went to jail I slept for three months. I was tired, tired - a man in his late fifties goes in there after doing what I did everyday. I slept like a baby," he confided.

MURDERED FOR BEING BLACK

Dead boy's father demands death penalty for killers

THE FATHER of a Black teenager who was killed by a gang of White thugs has called for the return of capital punishment for the racist knifemen.

Still in shock after the pointless murder of his son in a vicious knife attack in Eltham, south east London, Neville Lawrence said: "I think that they should bring back hanging for something like this. It is just a senseless murder.

"It doesn't take a genius to see that it was a racial murder. He was chased down the street by about six White youths for no other reason than he was Black."

Last Thursday (April 22)

EXCLUSIVE

By Helen William

Stephen Lawrence, 18, was stabbed to death in what police described as "a completely unprovoked attack" as he waited by a bus stop with a schoolfriend. It was about 10.40pm and he was returning

(continued on page 3)

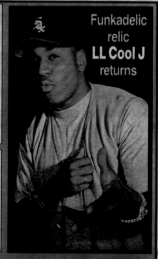

STEPHEN: Hounded to his death.

ISSUE No. 656 JUNE 20, 1995

65p

THE VOICE

Britain's Best Black Newspaper!

This woman died after police officers shackled her and gagged her with 13 feet of tape.

Joy Gardner has been sent to her grave.

None of the officers has been sent to jail.

So WHO is responsible for her death?

NO PEACE FOR JOY

ISSUE No. 651 MAY 16, 1995

65p

THE VOICE

Britain's Best Black Newspaper!

First victim of the new police baton

THIS man's family suffered the agony of watching him become the twentieth Black person in the past decade to die after being taken into police custody and pleaded: "How many more?"

By Ainsley Okoro

Brian Douglas, 33, and a friend were stopped for a minor motoring offence by two PCs armed with new American-style 2ft long batons.

However, a scuffle broke out during the arrest - and he was later rushed to hospital with a fractured skull.

But he was kept for 15 hours in a police cell before being taken there. Police surgeons examined him four times while he was detained - but failed to spot his injuries.

Last year, police surgeons themselves warned that badly-trained members of their profession were putting detainees' lives at risk.

A post-mortem showed up the fracture, but police said there was as yet no proof that the injury killed him. Further tests are due next month.

Brutality

Now his family and civil rights campaigners are demanding tough government

(Continued on page 5)

HOW MANY MORE, MR MAJOR?

65p

THE VOICE

Britain's Best Black Newspaper!

News special - the Met in crisis

IF THIS MAN WERE BLACK ...

MET Police Chief Sir Paul Condon attacks The Voice as "inflammatory and irresponsible" - merely for demanding the truth about Black deaths in custody.

Which is why today we feel we must rebut his ill-founded charges in the strongest terms.

For his claims are not just a slur on The Voice - which, after all, is *your* paper. When he accuses us of "fuelling discontent" he inadvertently attacks the whole Black community.

If he really wants to understand our frustrations he might stop to consider that had he really been a Black Londoner he would be:

● Three times more likely than White youths to be mugged. Just 1 per cent of all White people - but 3 per cent of Black and Asian people - are victims. (British Crime Survey/ Home Office).

● Twice as likely to be burgled. Six per cent of White people - but 12 per cent of Black people - suffer break-ins. (British Crime Survey/Home Office).

● Five times more likely to be stopped by police. One in seven Black Londoners are apprehended - but just one in 32 White people. (Scotland Yard).

● Three times more likely than White people to be

(Continued on page 2)

DU'AINE'S 400m RICE

Tilda EASYCOOK LONG GRAIN RICE

PRODUCE OF THE USA

THE VOICE

BRITAIN'S **BEST** BLACK PAPER

ISSUE No. 845 FEBRUARY 22, 1999   65p

> **"When my son was killed I genuinely believed that those responsible would be caught and be punished for their crime. I waited patiently for this to happen, but it did not.**
>
> **"I suppose at the time I secretly knew that this would never happen because my son was Black, but I still hoped for justice."**
>
> *Doreen Lawrence, to the Stephen Lawrence Inquiry*

NOW CHANGE MUST COME

SEE LAWRENCE INQUIRY SPECIAL (CENTRE PAGES)

PART TWO OF TYSON SPECIAL
SEE NEWS FEATURE

Exclusive interview with Grammy
Award nominee LAURYN HILL

THE VOICE

BRITAIN'S *BEST* BLACK PAPER

ISSUE No. 903 APRIL 10, 2000   75p

JAMIE FOX

on working with Al Pacino and clashing with LL Cool J in his new movie

OUT NEXT WEEK YOUR woman2woman SUPPLEMENT

WIN a week in Gambia

for the Homecoming Festival

PLUS £50 to give away

SEE DETAILS INSIDE

▶ **VISIT OUR WEBSITE NOW AT www.voice-online.co.uk**

BERNIE GRANT IS DEAD

Tributes pour in as Britain mourns champion of justice

THE world of British politics is in mourning following the death of Tottenham MP Bernie Grant, the black community's most senior and respected politician, at the weekend. He suffered a fatal heart attack.

The Prime Minister and other senior politicians led the tributes to the Tottenham Labour MP who died aged 56 in the

By Paul Macey and Tony Sewell

Middlesex Hospital, north London in the early hours of Saturday morning.

Speaking only hours after learning of the news a stunned Tony Blair said: "Although I know Bernie had health problems, his death is a dreadful shock, and my thoughts and

prayers are with his family. He was someone for whom I had immense respect and affection. He was a dedicated and diligent constituency MP who worked tirelessly for the less well off. His commitment to social justice was unwavering and he also made a powerful contribution to development issues."

The Prime Minister also spoke

Continued on page 4

LOOKING FOR A JOB? LOOK INSIDE! PAGES AND PAGES FOR YOU

THE VOICE

BRITAIN'S *BEST* BLACK PAPER

ISSUE No. 937 DECEMBER 4, 2000   75p

MONTSERRAT – Emerald Isle on the mend SEE PAGES 14-15

BRIGHT SPARK: *Murdered Damilola.*

DAMILOLA, WE FAILED YOU

Tragic boy's lonely death rocks a community which has lost its heart

COMMENT

THE chilling image of a frightened 10-year-old black youth, viciously attacked, knifed and left to bleed to death on a grimy staircase in a south London estate, has stunned the entire nation.

Little Damilola Taylor who had complained to his mum, Gloria, of being bullied at Oliver Goldsmith Primary School, bled to death after being stabbed in the leg.

Responsibility

With the investigation only just begun, we do not yet know if there is any link with alleged bullying. Graphic images and accounts of the tragedy cannot have escaped the attention of

black parents. Many sent messages of condolence to Damilola's grieving family.

But this sad event has now presented them with a harsh wake up call. The black community must stand up and accept responsibility for what happened to Damilola.

The stark image of a little boy collapsing on the stairs and gasping his last as the life drained from him while residents passed by without offering help, speaks volumes. An 'every man for himself attitude' has taken over our community.

Those who did stop to try to lend a hand must be commended, at least they have not forgotten

Continued on page 5

TRIBUTE: *Flowers and gifts mark the spot where Damilola died.*   Pic: Colin Patterson

Neville Lawrence, did not hold back. To *The Voice*, he spelled out the full horror of the attack: '[Stephen] had many wounds ... It seems he was hit with some sort of iron pipe, stabbed in the heart ... and a horrific stab wound in the neck.'

'There have been too many murders in the same [area] ... People are not going to stand and just watch their young, prosperous kids go down the drain like that any more. It's too much to ask,' said Mr Lawrence. Since the murder of Rolan Adams in chillingly similar circumstances in February 1991, Stephen had been warned of the risks. 'But no one's child should be a prisoner in their own home because of violent thugs,' Neville Lawrence added. Rolan Adams's father, Richard, was one of the early supporters of the Lawrence family. He was shocked but not surprised by this latest murder on the same streets.

He told *The Voice*:

If Black people don't take hold of the reigns in this situation, Black boys will continue to be murdered. The white community don't have to do anything because it is not happening to them. We've got to start laying down our own deterrents if the Government and the police refuse to. When the Crown Prosecution Service fails to prosecute racist murderers and attackers, (we) should take out private cases.

Labour MP Bernie Grant called on the Black community to ensure that Stephen Lawrence's murder is the last race killing: 'We will not allow our young people to (be murdered),' he told *The Voice*. 'Our community is entitled to defend itself in law. If the police won't defend us, we must defend ourselves.'

He was backed up by angry calls from Anti-Racist Alliance (ARA) that pointed out that the area where Stephen was murdered was notorious for racist attacks on young Black men and renewed its call on the authorities to close down the racist British National Party office in nearby Welling.

'The Greenwich area has become the racist murder capital of Britain. Bexley Council should use their planning powers to close down the Nazi bunker which is clearly spreading race hate among the local population,' the ARA said.

At this point, Stephen Lawrence's murder was barely covered in the daily newspapers or the main news bulletins on radio and television. *The Voice*, however, was determined to keep this murder on the front page. 'You just don't give a damn,' was the headline in the paper three weeks later.

The irony was not lost on a distraught Neville Lawrence that it took Nelson Mandela to visit the UK in support of his family for the rest of the British media to take the murder of his son seriously.

He accused the government of remaining silent and indifferent to his son's killing:

The Prime Minister, the Queen and other members of the establishment have turned a blind eye to the murder.

[Mandela] is showing us and the Black kids in Britain that he is interested in what happens to us. But the complete lack of interest from the Prime Minister and people in this country who can do something about this tragedy tells us that a Black life is not valued.

If this had been the death of a white child who had been killed by six Black youths, there would have

THE VOICE

Britain's Best Black Newspaper!

DEVASTATED

... but Stephen's parents thank their supporters

EXCLUSIVE
By Helen William

THE devastated parents of murdered teenager Stephen Lawrence have said thank you for all the support they received which enabled them to mount a private prosecution against youths accused - and sensationally cleared - of his killing.

Much of Neville and Doreen Lawrence's lives since Stephen's racist murder three years ago has come to a standstill. The anti-racism campaigning which helped to keep them sane will be put on the back burner for the next week. Instead they try to come to terms with the fact that three White youths walked free from the Old Bailey last week - cleared of their son's murder.

Mr Lawrence said: "We would just like to thank everyone for their support over the past three years - it has been greatly appreciated. We have had a lot of support from people, responsible people both Black and White, and we appreciate it."

Difficult

The most difficult task ahead of them at present will be trying to get back to normal with their remaining children Stuart, 19, and Georgina, 14.

"We have to spend some time now with our children," said Mr Lawrence. "We will spend the next week just trying to decide what is going on with the campaign and speaking to our legal team."

The Lawrences have poured a lot of faith and patience into the belief

(Continued on page 3)

STEPHEN: Who murdered him?

MR & MRS LAWRENCE: Dignified in defeat.

Three years after Stephen's death, three youths accused were cleared of his murder

been public outrage and it would have been headline news,' said Stephen's mother Doreen. 'It just goes to show that people from abroad are more concerned about the death of Black children than the Prime Minister of our own country, the Queen and all the ministers.

The Voice commented:

A Black child is murdered on the streets of London by racist thugs but the silence from the establishment is deafening.

The grieving Lawrence family has not been inundated with letters of sympathy from Downing Street or Buckingham Palace as have other white families who have lost family members in circumstances just as tragic as this.

What a disgraceful lack of courtesy ... from the leaders of this country. But such official indifference is nothing new.

None of the families who have lost loved ones at the hands of racists have received a word of comfort from Her Majesty's Government.

The British establishment should rest uneasily in their beds after witnessing how ANC leader Nelson Mandela found the time during his busy UK visit to comfort the Lawrence family in their hour of need.

Neither the Prime Minister, the Queen nor any other member of the Royal family or government could spare a few minutes to make a phone call or send an official message of condolence.

Perhaps such gestures are not thought necessary when it comes to the business of winning votes or raising the popularity stakes.

In the wake of Nelson Mandela's visit, *The Voice* offered a £1,000 reward to anyone with genuine information leading to the arrest and conviction of Stephen Lawrence's murderers.

The murder of Stephen Lawrence was to dominate *The Voice* letters pages in the months ahead. Over this time period, readers wrote into the paper to express their horror:

I am now beginning to wonder how much more it will take for us as Black people to get out there and directly confront the neo-Nazis.

We should start by channelling the aggression among ourselves – Black on Black violence – into fighting the real enemy, who are now getting a little too big for their bovver boots.

We cannot keep on relying on sympathetic white people to fight our battles for us. We must begin to take charge of this situation and start doing things for ourselves.

Having been brought up in a predominantly white community in the East End of London in the 1970s, I know that not all white people are racist bigots. But in all societies, there are bad apples and it is these people whom we need to target and stamp out from society.

Britain is a great place to live and work in. The multicultural society that has built up over the years is working quite well and we must not let a minority of racist vermin continue to stir up trouble.

As a Black person, I am a very loyal subject of Britain, but I am now beginning to wonder whether Britain is being loyal and supportive to me.

I urge all political leaders to monitor the situation very carefully so as to avoid a future bloodbath. If this ever arises it will most certainly not be of the Black man's making.

I hope people reading this do not think that I am inciting people to commit acts of violence. This is most certainly not my intention. I merely wish to highlight a growing trend within British society.

Patrick

The most important form of self-defence is for Black people to realise their vulnerability. Whether we are dirt poor or professionals, we are exposed to the whims of sections of the dominant group.

Perry, Bedfordshire

To echo the words of the last letter, it was no longer about being dirt poor or professionals. As much as the decade began with the optimism of upward mobility for Black Brits, the murder of a Black teen had shattered the dream of being seen as equal citizens in Britain. Stephen's death had united buppies, ragamuffins and every other type of Black Briton. For now, the most important consideration was the strategies that Black Britons would formulate to protect their children.

Increasingly, the Black middle classes were waking up to the realisation that they needed to deploy a strategy to maintain and retain before they ended up, like so many of their peer group, being ultimately demoralised. They needed to strengthen their position through alliances. The notion of 'having each other's backs' was one that was becoming a subject for discussion. Some people turned to the church as a source of 'togetherness'. Others turned to the mosque. 'Profit theology' became a thing where the pursuit of material wealth was not frowned upon by, in particular, some African-heritage Christian denominations that were popping up in units on industrial estates. There was no need to feel guilty about wanting to earn money. Such churches became a repository of the Black middle classes with their mantra of 'liberation through wealth and traditional values'. Hard work, for the church-going middle classes, was next to godliness, and even harder work was the road map out of your current situation. Working two jobs was better than working one when it came to making ends meet. Working two jobs was so commonplace among the Black middle classes that it seemed to be the vital requisite for membership of the club.

The New Year of 1995 was greeted with an unholy battle between British and American entertainers. Black British actors were being shunned in favour of their American counterparts. Either because the likes of Forest Whittaker was seen as being much more believable playing the role of a British soldier for *The Crying Game*, or because they were deemed much more bankable. White British actors experienced the same type of snubbing, but there was something much more cynical when it came to the Black American stars replacing their British counterparts. Black British achievers were simply not valued. Not in entertainment, not in sport, nor in writing or business. It was as if Peter Cook and Dudley Moore as their alter egos Derek and Clive had permanently prejudiced Black Brits when they joked: 'In America, they've got their soul singers and here in Britain we've got our soul singers.' Chaka Khan was the American import that got the frustration of the Black British thespians in the neck when she starred in the new West End musical *Mama I Want To Sing*, the more or less real story of Doris Troy, the singer behind the classic 'Just One Look.' The front page of *The Voice* on January 10 1995 read simply: 'Chak Em Out.'

The May 16 issue of that year showed a haunting photograph of a Black man lying unconscious in a hospital bed, the first victim of a new police baton. It was a scenario that we had seen played out over and over again. 33-year-old Brian Douglas was stopped for a minor motoring offence. A scuffle broke out during the arrest resulting in him being rushed to hospital with a fractured skull. The image was accompanied by the headline: 'How many more, Mr Major?'

If anything, the fallout from the Stephen Lawrence murder intensified the existential questions that were being addressed through the letters page of *The Voice*. Who are we NOW? What are we NOW? Where are the fault lines of Britishness and Black Britishness? And how can we, as Black Brits, decolonise our minds and thought?

> I totally agree with reader Roselyne Mawere (*The Voice*, January 6) when she criticises Black British people for their clothing, manners and lack of education.
>
> Black British people are going nowhere fast as long as our minds are only on things like skin shade and quality of hair.
>
> We tend to divide ourselves into fair-skinned, brown-skinned, light-skinned, dark-skinned and so on.
>
> Unless we stop dividing ourselves like this we will be going nowhere fast.
>
> R Clement London, SE17

I was incensed to read Paula Williams's thoughts on the lack of Black male role models in England (*The Voice*, January 13).

It would appear her definition only includes sex symbols with dazzling smiles and good physiques.

A role model to the average person is someone we can respect and set our personal standards by. Basically, someone who has achieved success through sheer hard work, skill and determination.

We are fortunate to have a wealth of talent in music (Jazzie B), sport (Colin Jackson) and broadcasting (Paul Green).

I strongly suggest that your short-sighted reader opens her eyes and ears and starts to appreciate what the UK offers our young males.

I only hope her recognition of female role models is not equally limited.

C Archer London, SW16

Let's hit dead-end dads.

I agree with Pat Younge's views in his article entitled 'Why double standards over single mums?' though he doesn't say much about fathers.

Where are the men, who for the main part do not behave responsibly at all and produce children without thought or the offer of financial support? Why should the taxpayer support such low morals and standards?

It's high time the government stopped single mums from being single mums and dealt firmly with the type of men involved.

Surely it is not a question of colour, race or religion but a question of decent standards and responsible attitudes.

Christopher Beckenham, Kent

I am one of a growing number of Black youths who is sick and tired of being stereotyped by people like Rose-lyne Mawere.

Instead of trying to place the blame she should be encouraging us.

We were brought into the world by someone possibly of her generation and cannot be blamed for being lost.

We only know what we are taught, and if the last generation did not teach us then, that is why we go astray.

It is a vicious circle. What are you doing for Black youths apart from snubbing them?

Remember, knowledge is power and a mind is a terrible thing to waste. Big up all Black youths our future leaders!

Name and address withheld

Young Afro-Caribbeans who were born and schooled in this country cannot be proud of themselves and who we are and where we come from and where we are going, due to the lack of knowledge about our history even though it goes back a million years.

What we, the Black population, do not know can kill us.

Not many (of us) know the story of the Black goddess Isis and the virgin birth which was taken from Africa to Greece and Rome and ended with Mary and Jesus.

Not many (of our) young people know about the Moors, Africans who conquered and ruled many countries in Europe, including Spain where they ruled for over 500 years until the African General Boabdil surrendered to the Spanish in 1492.

Many things we take for granted today were brought to Europe by the Moors, even many names of places. Paris was named after the Goddess Isis, 'Par-Isis' (see Ivan Van Sertimer's book *Golden Age of the Moor*). The list is endless. Each year Afro-Americans celebrate a month of Black history. Why can't such celebrations take place in the UK?

Hugh, Chiswick, London W4

I write after reading the article 'A lighter shade of Pale' (*The Voice*, February 10). I wholeheartedly agree with all that was said. Nonetheless, I must add my tuppence. The fact that an individual chooses to have lighter skin shows a need for education. Intelligence has no skin colour. Each of us should strive to be the best that we can be, within our physical, emotional and intellectual boundaries. Once we have achieved what is for us our highest standard then let that standard be the guide.

This is the message we should be conveying to our young people. Let your entire make-up ooze with confidence, morality, sincerity and honour. Those qualities will carry you wherever you wish to go. Remember, the only person who is better than you is the person who does not turn to dust when he or she dies.

Skin colour is transitory, the qualities I have listed above are eternal.

R D Ransom London, W1

I enjoyed reading Sam Pragg's article (*The Voice*, February 10) on skin lightening.

I blame the parents as well as the media for low self-esteem. As a child my parents favoured my sister because she is light-skinned. I often hear parents praise their children because they are fair-skinned.

As Black people we not only bleach our skins, we change the colour of our eyes and the texture of our hair to conform to the expectations of society. We are constantly being told that white is right and are letting this influence us.

It is up to Black people to change the situation and be proud of what they are – as opposed to what they are not.

Ms J Smith London, SE17

It was with great pain that I read Lynda Kheir's letter on Michael Jackson (*The Voice*, December 16).

Michael Jackson has done more damage to Black people than most people acknowledge. He reconstructed his features along European lines and reconstructed himself as an asexual European man.

Jackson was a role model. But he has emasculated the Black man and in one decade, in my view, has damaged the pride and love Black people had for their culture, their features, their colour, their very Blackness, which men such as Malcolm X, Martin Luther King Jr. and Marcus Garvey fought so ardently for.

When Michael was accused of being an Uncle Tom, he released 'Black or White and 'Liberian Girl'. He also releases politically correct songs whose purpose seems to be, in my view, to boost his sales and popularity by projecting the image of a naive and caring young man.

I regard Michael as an egotistical, selfish man who will do whatever it takes to maintain his popularity, including compromising himself and his people.

I view the media's stories with scepticism, but sadly Michael's actions indicate to me that he does not care one iota for his people.

Adela Surbiton, Surrey

I can fully understand Black and white people detesting Michael Jackson for his lifestyle. However, to blame him for the damage and disintegration of the Black race is grossly misguided.

If one takes a walk into the Black neighbourhoods of inner-city America, they would find that Black pride has been eroding for years – and it has nothing to do with Michael Jackson.

What has Jackson got to do with Black-on-Black crime and fatherless children?

I do not think that Jackson's programme of restructuring his face has had a great impact upon the Black race. To me, he has hurt himself more than anyone else.

Kemi London, E8

As a Black actor living and working in Scotland, I recently set up my own multi racial drama group, The Media Theatre Company.

We are an anti-racist group committed to presenting new writing and directing from a Black perspective, portraying positive images of Black people.

We often joke about how great it would be to have full-time funding or, dream of dreams, money to make a film. So, I cannot tell you how shocked and offended I was after seeing the Damon Wayans big-budget film *Mo Money*.

In the movie, the object of desire is a fair-skinned Black actress with straight hair and green eyes, while the actress who is ridiculed is dark-skinned, brown-eyed with Afro hair. This negative portrayal of Black women is offensive and very depressing, but no more depressing than the fact that Mr Wayans is himself a Black man. Sometimes we are our own worst enemies.

Troy

After reading all the hubbub last week about 'ebonics' I felt motivated to write in. Young Black kids in this country should stop trying to ape their American counterparts and grow up. If children are encouraged to speak badly there can be no future for Black people in this country.

The American experience is very different from our own. We do not have the history of segregation that they have in the States. Working-class white kids and working-class Black kids speak more or less the same.

In Britain, region is more important than race when it comes to language.

Let the Black Americans keep their slang and keep their low-paid jobs and pitiful position in American society. We are on the up and up.

Margareti, Manchester

I write in response to your article 'Ebonics Rules Okay' (*The Voice*, January 20). As a child, I had a strong Jamaican accent and my teacher encouraged me to speak standard English. She did not want me to feel different in any way.

I found that I spoke 'well' at school, but at home I spoke using Jamaican.

As a mother, I spend time with my daughter explaining to her what is acceptable at home and what is expected of her in society.

This is an important issue that should be taken on board by parents and educators.

Listening to some young people, I can understand the need for some form of Ebonics.

Brenda, Northolt, Middlesex

When will music promoters stop taking advantage of the Black public? We enjoy our music and are prepared to spend our hard-earned money on entertainment. We do not mind a little inconvenience, but it seems that more and more these days we are expected to put up with expensive tickets, overcrowding, and the threat of artists not turning up.

To all the promoters out there: remember, what goes around comes around. We will not be fooled forever. And where will that leave you?

Jeanette London, SW12

I am writing to you about an issue of double discrimination: being Black and fat in British society.

In Jamaica, I never experienced the kind of treatment that you get in this country for being above average size.

I have talked with many of my naturally slim Black girlfriends and they do not experience anything like the abuse that I get from white people – much of which is directed specifically at my size. White people seem to have a hatred of abundant flesh. It is no surprise to me that the Duchess of York is reportedly putting her child on a diet.

I recently went to an exhibition publicised in *The Voice* which celebrated fat women from all over the world. I felt I belonged. It is about time that we see big, beautiful Black women in the media.

Ruth Barnet, Hertfordshire

At the start of 1997, the Lawrence family were at their lowest ebb. The campaign to get justice for their son had been running for almost four years and, at this point, it seemed like nobody would be charged and convicted of the murder. *The Voice* had increased its reward for any information leading to an arrest or conviction to £5,000. But it had not unlocked the silence. What it unlocked instead was the overwhelming feeling among people who felt they needed to do something to

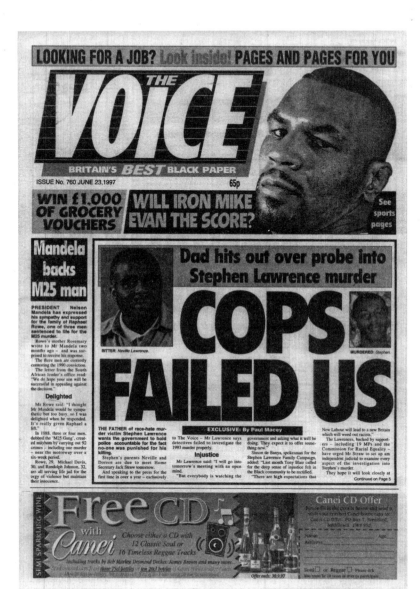

In 1997, Neville Lawrence spoke exclusively to The Voice *ahead of a meeting with then-Home Secretary Jack Straw*

help the Lawrences pursuit of justice. Not for the first time, *The Voice* became the beacon around which the Black community could gather to help the cause, to make their feelings known and to fight the good fight.

In February 1997 the paper stepped in to help:

> *THE VOICE* is offering a £5,000 reward for any information that could lead to the murderers of Stephen Lawrence being brought to justice.
>
> Over the last week, we have been inundated by readers wanting to donate money and offering support to the campaign to catch Stephen's killers. Once more the strength of the Black community has been clear for all to see.
>
> One London pensioner phoned *The Voice* to donate money as a 'protest against injustice.'
>
> We have passed on your kind offers of help. Now with the support of Stephen's mother, Doreen, we have added our own contribution, which we hope will lead to justice for Stephen and his family,
>
> If anyone has any information that could lead to the capture of Stephen's killers, please contact Crimestoppers.

The Lawrences were doing all they could to keep their son's name in the headlines but there seemed little hope. Their private prosecution in September 1994 against three of the accused had collapsed and hopes of the continuing police investigation bringing anyone to book was dwindling. Doreen and Neville could not have imagined that it would take this length of time. They could not have imagined that they would spend their entire lives not giving up in their search for justice. Neville had by now resumed his work as a painter and decorator, albeit with a broken heart. It was his aura of sadness that was noticed by a client whose house Neville was refurbishing. That client coincidentally happened to be the editor of the *Daily Mail*.

It was on Valentine's Day 1997 that the *Mail*, a right-wing national newspaper, took the calculated risk on its front page of identifying five white men suspected of killing Stephen, calling them murderers and challenging them to sue the paper.

This intervention by the paper regarded as the conscience of Middle England was a game changer. The Stephen Lawrence story was now mainstream. It was not a Black story any more. Everybody in the country now knew that a Black teenager had been murdered for no other reason than his colour by thugs who were walking our streets having got away with murder. A year and a half later at Elephant and Castle, the five suspects who had been ordered to attend a public inquiry were met by a huge angry crowd of Black and white protestors and a punch-up ensued.

The Voice newspaper was surprisingly unconvinced by the *Mail*'s 'trial by media'. It had one big question about the national newspaper's intervention: Why would a paper, which normally takes a less than supportive stance of Black people, feature a Black cause celebre on its front page?

'We as Black people feel aggrieved by the injustices heaped upon us and you have to look no further than the Lawrence case to see that even with a fight, justice does not always prevail,' *The Voice* editor wrote.

'What if the next time the *Mail* or any other newspaper decides that a Black person should be pictured on the front

This ad from 2000 shows then-Prime Minister Tony Blair reading the 1999 Stephen Lawrence Inquiry special edition of The Voice

page and called a murderer after he or she had been through the courts and was found innocent.

'There are already a disproportionate number of Black people being charged and jailed.

'There would also be a disproportionate number being held up by the newspapers as criminals.

'While the *Mail* took a welcome stance by saying this is not good enough perhaps it should have found another way to be so bold.'

Instead of featuring the murderers on its front page in the February 17th edition of that year, *The Voice* took the decision to focus on what Stephen's mother, Doreen, was going through. The headline read: 'A mother's grief, Britain's shame.'

The tears shed by Doreen Lawrence for her murdered son Stephen at the end of the inquest into his death hit us all. Her dignity and pain were there for all to see.

Stephen's murder nearly four years ago was a tragic waste of a vibrant young life. His mother's pain runs so deep because his killers still walk free.

Somewhere, someone is harbouring brutal murderers. One can only wonder how they can live with themselves. As a result, there is a strong chance Stephen's killers may never see the inside of a prison cell.

The case is not only an indictment of those who have lost their humanity, but of the British judicial system – a system that has failed Stephen and his family.

Many praise the British legal system for effectively protecting the just and punishing the unjust. Such praise would now seem a mockery.

The Voice will continue to support the Lawrences in their quest for justice. Their bravery is a lesson to us all.

Let us hope their struggle will force those in authority to ensure that not only is justice found for Stephen but that our legal system is as it should be – fair, accessible and just to all.

Relations between the police and the Black community was at an all-time low. This was primarily because of the failure to properly investigate the murder of Stephen Lawrence. Through the Lawrence family's tenacity in trying to get to the bottom of why the police did not even bother to do their due diligence in what should have been a relatively straightforward manhunt of local teenagers, we learned more and more about the racism that allowed Stephen's killers to get away with murder.

It was bad enough that police assumed it was a gang fight and that Stephen somehow was linked to drugs. It was shocking that they then turned their attention to Duwayne Brooks, Stephen's best friend who was with him at the time of the murder and tried to portray him as an unreliable witness to the crime, and it was almost criminal that they did not pursue the leads to the murderers with the names that was passed on to the Lawrence's by a local woman. As if that were not enough to put on the grieving family, it was later revealed that at least one leading officer in the investigation of Stephen's death was linked to a local mobster who happened to be the father of one of the suspects. To say that there was no trust between Black people and the police is an understatement. The mistrust would unite much of the community irrespective of social class, salary and political affiliation. It ignited a suspicion of miscarriages of justice when it came to police evidence. As was highlighted by this letter asking for support for the man who was initially jailed for the murder of PC Keith Blakelock in the 1985 Broadwater Farm riots before that conviction was quashed based on a fabricated confession to the police:

> Thank you and the staff of *The Voice* for your kind and unwavering support for brother Winston Silcott.
>
> As you are aware, Winston is currently being held in Gartree Prison in Leicester on charges of murder.
>
> The Winston Silcott Defence Campaign exists to highlight his case, to link with other campaigns – such as the Orville Blackwood Campaign and to press the Home Secretary to, firstly, refer his case back to the Court of Appeal and, secondly, to release him.
>
> Now that new evidence has come to light which shows clearly that Winston acted in self-defence (corroborating what he said all along) we are asking for his immediate release.
>
> Winston will make legal history by becoming the first person to be cleared by the Court of Appeal twice. In the meantime, we invite you to join us. The struggle continues for real justice.
>
> Julietta Joseph, Winston Silcott Defence Campaign, Selby Site, Selby Rd, London N17

Justice for Black Brits at the time never tasted so sweet as when a boxing champ fought the law and, for once, the law didn't win. Colin 'Sweet C' McMillan won an out-of-court settlement after he accused police of harassment. He was awarded more than £2,000 in compensation after he was stopped by police, who assumed he had stolen a car. After leaving a fast-food

THE VOICE

REMEMBER

BRITAIN'S BEST BLACK PAPER

ISSUE No. 846 MARCH 1, 1999   65p

COME ON, CONDON

PAUL Condon has to go.

In an interview with The Voice last week Sir Paul Condon gave a veiled warning that we, 'the Black media', should be careful not to be 'police-ist' in our reporting of the Lawrence Inquiry. If by that he meant we should not criticise him then, unlike him, we must apologise straight away for our failings.

He is the head of the Metropolitan Police service, which has been so heavily criticised in the Macpherson Report into the 'matters arising from the death of Stephen Lawrence'. This is the same service which last week allowed Stephen's memorial plaque to be desecrated by racist morons for the third time – after cleverly fitting a 'dummy' camera to a nearby tree for security.

It is also this same force that is apparently 'spitting blood' over the criticisms it has faced.

Ultimate responsibility for its failings must surely rest with him. Rank-and-file officers can only do what management directs and allows them to do.

Blood

Condon says he wants to stay to see through the process of change but surely, after seven years it's fair to say he's had his chance and blown it.

His removal would by no means be the most important thing to come out of the Lawrence Inquiry, but surely if Condon is as principled a man as he and Home Secretary Jack Straw tell us he is, he should want to stand down and let a new man have a go. They couldn't do any worse, could they?

If Jack Straw really had any respect for the Black community wouldn't he have got rid of the man who must ultimately be held responsible for the police's actions?

After all, when any family of a Black person who has died 'mysteriously' in police custody goes to the inquest to find out why they died, they are faced by a bank of highly paid Barristers representing the police commissioner.

When a member of the Black community is wrongly arrested or charged or falsely imprisoned by police, isn't it the commissioner who settles out of court 'without liability' or has to pay the compensation?

And if the Macpherson Report really is a fresh start for the police and the Black community, why hasn't anyone lost their job over this staggering display of incompetence?

WE HAVE A DREAM

THE VOICE is adding its weight to calls for the memory of Stephen Lawrence to be preserved by a special day named in his honour.

Following last week's momentous events, Voice editor Annie Stewart said: "The idea of a Stephen Lawrence Day is a good one. It will be a huge symbolic gesture and a lasting testament to Stephen.

"It will also act as a permanent reminder of the need to respect Black communities and, hopefully, British society's determination to bring an end to racism."

The call for a special day to be

By Paul Macey

declared has long been mooted by organisations and individuals close to the Lawrence family and their six-year campaign for justice.

Now we hope it will gather a massive groundswell of support at a time when many are determined that Stephen's death will lead to real changes in race relations in this country.

Steven Jacobs of Covent Garden, central London, believes that the idea is a good one.

"There is a Martin Luther King Day and we should have a similar event here. If nothing else, at least it

will mean it can't be forgotten."

We call on Voice readers to write to the Prime Minister and urge him to consider a special day, to be marked on the day of Stephen's death.

● Lee Jasper, director of Black think-tank the 1990 Trust, has threatened to urge members of the government's influential Race Relations Forum and the Race and Violent Crime Task Force committee to join him in walking out if Paul Condon does not quit.

The walkout would be a great embarrassment to both the government and Home Secretary Jack Straw as they seek to create a dialogue with the Black community.

FOR MORE TURN TO PAGES TWO TO TEN

LOOKING FOR A JOB? Look inside! PAGES AND PAGES FOR YOU

In 1999 The Voice *called for Met chief Sir Paul Condon to step down*

restaurant, the boxer was getting into his sports car when he was approached by two policewomen – one of whom was Black.

They asked for his licence and log book and, although he did not have them, he produced identification and the officers confirmed over the radio that the car was not stolen.

'They asked me how much the car cost,' McMillan told *The Voice*. 'When I said that was irrelevant, the white officer decided to take everything out of the glove compartment.'

She justified her behaviour by telling the boxer that his eyes looked glazed and he was acting irrationally. She said that she was searching for drugs.

Then three male officers arrived in a car. 'When they did not find anything, I asked them to put the stuff back. One of the male officers did put it all back roughly, including a half-eaten hamburger and frenchfries . . .'

'They even opened the bonnet and looked at the chassis number to see if it was a ringer,' added McMillan. 'There are certain police officers who abuse their authority and stereotype individuals.'

The Voice continued to focus on bad police behaviour, highlighting the death of yet another Black man, Wayne Douglas, in police custody at Brixton police station on December 5 1995. But the newspaper's campaigning work was not welcomed by the Met police commissioner Sir Paul Condon. He decided to go on the offensive and publicly accused the newspaper of being 'inflammatory and irresponsible' for continuing to demand the truth about Black deaths in police custody. *The Voice* responded with a counter-attack of its own and a front-page headline in the January 30 1996 issue read, 'If this man were Black,' across a full-page image of a uniformed Sir Paul.

We feel we must rebut his ill-founded charges in the strongest of terms,' read the article.

For his claims are not just a slur on *The Voice* – which after all is your paper. When he accuses us of 'fuelling discontent' he inadvertently attacks the whole Black community.

If he really wants to understand our frustrations, he might stop to consider that had he really been a Black Londoner, he would be:

*Three times more likely than White youths to be mugged. Just 1 per cent of all white people, but 3 per cent of Black and Asian people are victims (British Crime Survey/Home Office)

*Twice as likely to be burgled. Six per cent of white people but 12 per cent of Black people suffer break-ins (British Crime Survey/Home Office)

*Five times more likely to be stopped by the police. One in seven Black Londoners are apprehended – but just one in 32 white people (Scotland Yard)

*Three times more likely than white people to be imprisoned. Black people make up 16 per cent of the jail population – but just 5.5 percent of the general public (1991 census/Home Office).

*Three times more likely to be jobless. Unemployment is 8.3 per cent among white people and 24.7 per cent among Black people (Labour Force Survey)

*Seven and a half times more likely to be poorly paid. Some 12 per cent of white men but 88 per cent of Black men in full time employment earn under £4 an hour (Low Pay Unit)

*Two and a half times more likely to be homeless. Ethnic minorities make up 20 per cent of London's population but 49 per cent of households deemed homeless by the capital's councils. (Shelter).

Black people do not have to be told what to think - despite what Sir Paul would believe.

You do not need *The Voice* to tell you to be incensed that 50 Black men have died in police custody in the last two-and-a half decades – but only once in 25 years have officers been convicted.

When it was put to Sir Paul that many Black Londoners saw his force as heavy-handed, he snapped: 'Talk to people in the real world.'

Yet, he is the one dealing in make-believe if he thinks that distrust of police is limited to a few vocal Black activists.

Sir Paul claims that if he were an inner-city Black teenager, he would still join the police – his ham-fisted attempt, perhaps, to empathise with our disillusioned youth.

For the record, *The Voice* never claimed that police killed Wayne Douglas in Brixton last month.

But his death was met by deafening silence from police and the mainstream media – at a time his grieving family and the rest of the Black community wanted openness and answers.

An eyewitness – who later signed a sworn statement - came forward. We felt it our duty, given the absence of information from elsewhere to make public his statement, and we would do exactly the same again.

And that wasn't the end of it. Inside that issue, the great and the good of the Black community lined up to come to the paper's defence.

Bernie Grant MP said: 'Paul Condon was widely criticised for being too liberal in the early part of his term in office. He is now desperate to rush in the other direction to curry favour with his political masters. He has a great deal to answer for the damage he has caused to race relations with his comments on mugging.

'His political master is the Home Secretary and, weeks away from a general election, they have decided that race is going to be a crucial election battleground. The battle is on for the white middle-class vote.'

Diane Abbott MP added:

I am appalled by Sir Paul's comments about *The Voice* newspaper's coverage of the Brixton riots and the death of Wayne Douglas. He accuses the paper of being 'dangerous, 'wildly irresponsible' and of 'inflammatory' reporting. This is nonsense. The paper is attempting to report the truth. And sometimes for some people the truth is unpalatable. *The Voice* is a community newspaper based in the heart of Brixton. Its journalists are fully aware of the issues which concern people living in the area. The paper is important because it focuses on what is happening in Black communities across Britain, and the mainstream press does not deal with issues which concern Black people living in Britain. In the interview, Mr Condon also remarks that the Black communities have complete faith in the Met. He also believes that the Met is the best police force in the world, and feels that it is unfairly lambasted by the press. He rejects the idea that police officers are becoming increasingly segregated from society and unrepresentative of the communities in which they work. And he thinks that Black teenagers would seriously consider a career in the Metropolitan Police. His remarks show that he has lost touch.

I cannot take Mr Condon's comments seriously. I think that he should retrieve a copy of the statement he made last summer in which he accused young Black males of being responsible for the majority of street crime if he wants to get an idea of what constitutes 'dangerous', 'wildly irresponsible' and 'inflammatory.'

Herman Ouseley, Chairman of the Commission for Racial Equality, said:

The Voice newspaper does an excellent job in serving the Black community with relevant news that other parts of the media fail to cover. It must continue to do so fearlessly and objectively. I have not always agreed with *The Voice's* treatment of some important stories and I hope it will not sensationalise sensitive issues in the same way as the majority of the tabloid media. As Britain's leading Black newspaper, *The Voice* has enemies among those who are envious of its success, those with grudges and others with their own political agendas.

The Voice must set high standards and not be deflected in uncovering and in commenting responsibly and objectively on the many difficulties which the Black communities are facing on a daily basis and which the rest of the media ignores.

It did not end there. *The Voice* then asked young readers if they had faith in the Met and would happily join the force. Speaking on a radio show to commemorate his three years as Metropolitan Police Commissioner, Sir Paul Condon said that if he was a Black young person, he would be happy to join the police force. But did Sir Paul accurately reflect youngsters' hopes and aspirations? *The Voice* asked some young people if they would serve in the police.

Audrey Taaff, a 29-year-old secretary from Brixton, said: 'I wouldn't. The force just doesn't appeal to me now that I've decided my career. I am encouraged by the Black and Asian people who do. It helps the community.'

Sales rep Marlene Martin, 27, also from Brixton, said: 'No way, they might try and corrupt me and make me like them and I know that they're going through a lot of trouble right now.'

28-year-old choreographer Lee Elliot, from Brixton, said: 'I don't respect police, plain and simple. I don't respect the way they treat the community. That's an absolute no-no. How seriously can you take a profession like that?'

Jerry Sereboh, a 17-year-old architecture student from Tulse Hill, added: 'They're too racist in their dealing and the way they carry out their work for me ever to consider joining them. The way they searched and stopped me for no reason. Then they say there's a robbery in the area and I look like a suspect.'

Teacher Linford Dunstan, 32, from Brixton said: 'There are not many Black police officers in the force and the ones that are there get a lot of stick not only from people on the street – but also from their colleagues in the force. You don't need that extra hassle. There's not as much hassle in teaching.'

Photographic assistant Sharon Price, 27, from Carshalton, Surrey said: 'Years ago, I would have, yes. But now the politics are too sensitive for a Black woman to join up. It's far more trouble than it's worth.

On the letters page there was a powerful argument by a reader headed with 'Questions needing answers':

> Regarding ex-police sergeant Mark Newberry's letter (*The Voice*, January 16) in which he criticised your coverage of last month's Brixton riots as 'provocative and lacking restraint', the real questions we need answers to are:
>
> Are suspects beaten to death in police custody?
>
> Are Black suspects particularly singled out for this sort of punishment? Or do all deaths in custody have innocent explanations, with the police being unfairly criticised for natural or accidental deaths?
>
> The way to answer these questions once and for all would be for the government to publish a comprehensive racial breakdown of arrests and deaths in custody.
>
> The Black community – and the police too, I presume – would welcome this. It would end individuals relying on prejudice or misinformation when discussing this emotive issue.
>
> Patrick, London, E5

As demoralised as relations with the police was for the Black middle classes, all they could do was just get on with it. There were people who simply had enough and packed their bags and left these shores. Their stories appeared sporadically through the pages of the papers. But for most Black Brits they had no option but to stay. The 1990s saw the emergence of a third generation of Black Brits who knew nothing else and nowhere else. For them and their parents, 'getting on with it' meant getting a good education.

Long before a British prime minister coined the phrase, 'education, education, education' had long been a mantra for the Black community. The first generation of post war immigrants had drummed into their children that as a Black person, you have to work twice as hard as your white counterparts. The second generation in turn drummed it into their children. So it was no surprise that questions about education were never far from the pages of *The Voice*. In 1994, a report by the Institute of Race Relations found Black children were four times more likely to be excluded and stereotypes about Black children being 'difficult' persisted, even in primary schools. The report suggested that every permanent exclusion should be challenged by parents through the appeal system, but added that the appeal system was a minefield of problems in itself.

There was a lively debate about this in the letters pages. One teacher from Manchester wrote:

As a teacher, I think it is a gross oversimplification to blame teachers for the exclusion of Black children.

It is very difficult to exclude pupils from schools on a permanent basis; more bums on seats means more cash for schools. African-Caribbean girls do much better than boys at school. Are the girls immune to racism? I think not. At the end of the day, we need to look at the way we are rearing our Black boys in the community and at why some of them pose problems when in schools.

Even if our Black boy pupils experience racism from teachers, we need to teach them ways of dealing with this that will not leave them educationally disadvantaged.

Miss E Russell, Manchester

The middle classes, although engaged in the conversation about exclusion were, in the main, less likely to have their children barred from the classroom. For them, in the Black community, the discussion was about intellect in general:

I am writing with regard to Pat Younge's article concerning Black intellectuals in Britain (*The Voice*, March 10).

I have three points to raise:

First, I would like to know how he can make such a generalisation about the lack of Black intellectuals in Britain. On what evidence is Mr Younge basing his claim?

Second, what is his definition of an intellectual? I think what he describes is being a public spokesperson for the Black community.

Third, as far as I can see, given that Mr Younge is the series producer of *Black Britain*, he is in an ideal position to set the Black agenda.

Maybe he is not looking in the right places. I would describe myself as an intellectual - and I know plenty of others.

I Warner, London NW6

Black stars dominated British sport in the 1990s and were cheered on throughout the decade by *The Voice*. Unusually for a sprinter, Linford Christie only started sprinting when he was 19 and at the age of 32 became the oldest man to win Olympic gold in the 100m. Christie, who was born in Jamaica, followed his parents to England at the age of seven. He went on to have an international career spanning 17 years.

He is the only British athlete to have won gold medals in the 100m at all four major competitions and was the first

European to have run a sub ten-second 100m. His career best of 9.87 seconds was recorded at the World Championships in 1983, when he took gold.

After hanging up his spikes he became a successful coach, leading the likes of Darren Campbell, Katherine Merry, Mark Lewis Francis and Laura Turner to glory.

In an interview with *The Voice* Christie said:

> The papers (tabloids, naturally) said I was too old and after a while it got to me. I've been at the top in Britain for nearly six years and for three years people have been telling me to retire. I made that decision to retire because athletics isn't my whole life. It doesn't pay that much and through my other activities I've carved a niche for the future. After Tokyo they were saying 'Wow! He ain't so old!'

Curiously, Linford has not been held in the same regard as other world-class British athletes, and wasn't even included in the London 2012 bid.

Neil Duncanson, author of *The Fastest Men on Earth* interviewing every living Olympic gold medallist in the process, told *The Voice*: 'When he went out there on the track it didn't matter who was against him, he'd eat them anyway. He would spit blood at anybody.

'I think that alienated the standard media pack over here who wanted the nice boy like Seb Coe. Linford was "take me for what I am or not at all" and I think that did him a lot of disservice.

'I think only with time will we come to regard Linford Christie as one of the greatest athletes this country has ever seen.'

When heavyweight Frank Bruno burst onto the boxing scene in the early 1980s it would be fair to say that excitement was at fever pitch. He was a boxing Adonis who had all the skills to succeed in a sport dominated by Americans. The charismatic South Londoner had a dream and had the ability to deliver it while gaining the nation's love and support. Bruno was championed by *The Voice* from the beginning of his career. In an early interview with the paper, a 20-year-old Bruno said: 'I want to be the World Heavyweight champion. I think it will take me four years. I want to be a millionaire as well! I'm not going to waste my time gallivanting and messing around, I know what I want in life.'

His early career culminated with Bruno becoming the youngest ever Amateur British Champion at 18 years of age. He became a professional boxer in 1982, starting with 21 consecutive wins by knockout. The 1980s were a rollercoaster for the popular pugilist and he suffered key defeats to Tim Witherspoon and famously Mike Tyson.

Further angst arrived in October 1993 when he battled Lennox Lewis in a bout that was dubbed the 'Battle of Britain'. Unfortunately Bruno lost to Lewis by technical knockout. The loss would have curtailed the career of a lesser man, but Bruno was to bounce back again. On September 2 1995, Frank finally became world champion when he outpointed Oliver McCall over twelve rounds. In 1996 a 34-year-old Bruno hung up his gloves after losing to Mike Tyson for the second time.

Frank was to suffer mental health issues and the nation was once again to show their support and admiration during his greatest battle. It is his candid approach in talking about his mental health that continues to earn him the respect of his contemporaries and the wider community.

In his autobiography he shared the benefits of talking and sharing his experiences, which has not only enabled him to help

The Voice Interview

JEREMY GUSCOTT

JEREMY GUSCOTT: Helped the England team to its current successes.

Whenever thoughts of his baby daughter enter his mind a magnetic smile appears on Jeremy Guscott's face. It's doubtful that even a third unprecedented Grand Slam with the England rugby team could match his delight of being a father for the first time.

"It's strange that when I come home these days it's not just my wife, Jayne, it's Imogen I greet. It's like, 'Jayne move out of the way I want to see my daughter I haven't seen her for eight or nine hours'," beams the happily married ex-brickie.

Imogen Lily Guscott, born on August 4 last year, has become the apple of her father's eye. It took him a while to grasp the magnitude of his new responsibility, but, once it sunk in, her birth made him more conscious than ever before of the world beyond the rugby field.

"I suppose my initial reaction was 'wow this is my daughter, my wife and I produced her.' You just can't believe she's yours. Later you become more aware of social problems and diseases. Anything that can effect your daughter, even Green issues," he said.

But eventually he turns his thoughts away from his daughter to talk about the sport which he's made his own.

Guscott, 27, has just finished his first serious run - around the lush green playing fields of Bath University - since England's opening win in the 1993 Five Nations Championship against France a few weeks before.

Now fully recovered from his run, he sits in a quite corner on the top floor of the university's sports hall overlooking the gym where students are playing badminton on the courts below.

He speaks eloquently about his squad's chances in the championship. If England can win their remaining games over Ireland, Scotland and Wales, they will make history by becoming the first team ever to win three consecutive Grand Slam titles.

> 'What I've got at the moment I enjoy and I don't really want to change'

"Everybody's talking about it and we as players can't help but think about it," he admits.

"Although we try to put it to the back of our minds, every time it gets closer to a game the back pages of the newspapers are covered with 'are England going to do it, are they going to fall at this hurdle or the next?'.

"As a team we are very confident in our ability. We keep asking ourselves whether we have reached our full potential. I don't think we have. If we really looked closely, there hasn't been an entire 80 minutes of rugby in which we've totally played to the best of our ability. We've had periods, small periods against all the different sides we've played. But we've just never been able to sustain that impeccable performance. We are all looking for perfection and that's what we are aiming to achieve.

"From a personal point of view I think we can

Mr Magic Man

England rugby player Jeremy Guscott's got a reputation for being a wizard on the field because of the way he can turn around a game in a few seconds. Colin Ennis hears how that magic has touched other parts of his life

definitely do it, if you look at the quality of our side compared to the others. But we have been together for such a long time - three to four years - and so we have more confidence in each other to pull it off. "

There's no doubting that the England squad includes some of the most talented rugby players in the world and Guscott is one of them.

The Bath-born man simply oozes class. He has the gift of being simultaneously exciting and deadly. One

moment of his magic can turn a game on its head.

That was something the Australians learned to their cost during the 1989 summer series against the British Lions. As several Aussies advanced towards him, Guscott cheekily chipped the ball over them and then reached out to score.

The try ensured that Britain won the Second Test match in a three- match series and propelled him firmly into the international spotlight.

"I think everything I trained for and worked for were all summed up in those few seconds of scoring," he enthuses.

"My elation, my reaction after scoring" - his eyes lit up as he recalls that glorious moment - "I've never acted that way before or since."

This cavalier style has won him the admiration of rugby enthusiasts throughout the world as well as 25 England caps and two appearances for the British Lions. He has also scored

15 tries and a drop goal at international level.

At club level he has inspired Bath to seven Pilkington Cup titles (two of these titles occurred when the competition was named the John Player Special Cup) and three Courage (English) League Championships.

Guscott's skills have inevitably attracted lucrative offers from rugby league's professional teams. It was rumoured that Leeds once offered him a £300,000 contract but he refused.

"The games are very different and it would have meant learning from scratch again," he explains. "Although the money, over three, four, five years, sounded quite substantial, had I not broken through and gained the same status in rugby league as rugby union, that money would have drifted away.

"I may not be portraying an image of a get up and go person, but what

Continued overleaf

In 1993 The Voice *interviewed Jeremy Guscott, who was one of the first high-profile Black rugby players to compete for England*

others but also the public responses empowered him to accept his own mental health challenges. Frank Bruno will always be a winner in and outside the ring.

While a Black man playing rugby might be the norm now, it was not the case in the 1990s. But Jeremy Guscott was a player of astonishing natural gifts, bucking the trend to forge a notable and successful career. A veteran of three British and Irish Lions tours in 1989, 1993 and 1997; Guscott famously converted a winning drop-goal against South Africa that clinched the series win in 1997.

The ex-Bath centre – who played for England 65 times, scored 30 tries and represented his country in three World Cups helped England to a final appearance in 1991. His outstanding career was forged early in his life. He once said: 'I liked all sports really. I loved rugby but I also enjoyed football, cricket and judo. Sport was my thing and I was quite good at everything I tried.'

The Voice writer Colin Ennis, who interviewed Guscott in 1993, wrote: 'the Bath-born man simply oozes class. He has the gift of being simultaneously exciting and deadly. One moment of his magic can turn a game on its head.' Sir Clive Woodward, who led England to Rugby World Cup victory in 2003, once dubbed Jeremy as the 'Prince of Centres' and when Jeremy left the field at the end of his final England match, the entire packed Twickenham crowd gave him a standing ovation. In 2016, Guscott was inducted into the World Rugby Hall of Fame, an accolade that puts him into the list of the world's greatest rugby players of all time.

In the 1990s no footballer would ever dream of 'taking the knee.' But the issue of racist abuse against Black players was a big issue, one which featured in the letters page of *The Voice*. A fan wrote:

I would like to comment on the story about Black players being abused by fans at Everton Football Club (*The Voice*, February 3). I think that it is a disgrace that we should have to put up with the lunacy of such racial hatred. And it doesn't only occur at Everton: this happens at Millwall, West Ham and some clubs abroad. Paul Ince has suffered racial abuse in Italy.

The Football Association has announced a campaign against racism. Are the clubs doing enough to ensure that racism is kicked out of football by the FA?

S Aboagye, London, E15

The seeds of kicking the racism out of football was beginning to bear fruit in the boardrooms and in the mindsets of football fans. On the terraces, things needed to get better, much better and fast. This reader's letter encapsulates this viewpoint:

Footballer John Fashanu recently got together with other Black footballers and the Commission for Racial Equality to start a campaign called 'Let's Kick Racism Out of Football.' Millwall chairman Reg Burr voiced his support for the campaign, but claimed that there was no racism on the terraces. My experiences suggest otherwise. I have been standing on the terraces watching football since I was seven, I am now 35. Admittedly, most of the football I've watched has been at Watford, but then you can't help where you were brought up can you?

Back in February, one of my best friends, who is a Millwall fan, invited me down to the Den to watch Watford's away fixture there. Now I've been to a lot of away games and I am not easily shocked. I have also been privy to a fair amount of abuse from supporters, and comments directed at Black players are depressingly common. However, nothing could prepare me for what I heard at Millwall last season.

Watford have four regular Black players in the first team and the abuse coming from members of the crowd behind me was astonishing.

I'm sorry to have to print this stuff, but in order to make my point I feel I have to. The comments had a limited range but were frequent. What I heard with nauseating regularity throughout the first half of the game whenever one of Watford's Black players received the ball was 'kill that Black c**t', 'f***ing stab the Black c**t' and 'burn him, ****ing Black bastard'.

As I said, these insults were very frequent and delivered with vicious ferocity. No one within earshot made any comment to stop it. I couldn't stand any more and told my friend I'd prefer to leave. He suggested we move to the other side of the terrace.

Admittedly no one there screamed 'c**t' or 'burn' every few seconds, but the words 'Black bastard' were often heard throughout the second half and greeted with the same degree of complacent amusement that I witnessed in the first half. In some way this was more shocking because these were not young delinquents, but people who are old enough to know better in front of children.

Maybe I am naive or maybe the relatively mild nature of the Watford crowd, who have had successful Black players in their team for some years now, have made me a touch sensitive. Either way, seeing Mr Burr on national television paying lip-service to the anti-racist lobby while dismissing the problem at Millwall was something that I couldn't ignore without comment.

I am not much of a letter writer – in fact this is the first complaint I have ever written. If Mr Burr is serious about the racial issues in the game, he needs to examine the behaviour of his own crowd a little more closely. There are, I understand, laws pertaining to racist comments during matches. It would have been nice to see the police having a word with someone, even if they are not prepared to make an arrest.

Suffice to say, I will not be going to any game at Millwall's new ground at the somewhat ironically named Senegal fields.

As it is an all-seater stadium, one doesn't have the option of moving about the ground in an attempt to find a racist-free zone.

With the police not prepared to intervene at football matches where the laws were being openly disregarded and made a mockery of, one reader feared that the race relations laws in the country were about to fall into 'even more' disarray:

Last week I read about a white man who went to an industrial tribunal because he lost a job to a Black woman. He lost the case – and I am glad. Discrimination of any form is wrong. But no one should forget that the race laws and positive discrimination were to a small extent, an attempt to address the real and terrifying effects of racism against Black people. It would seem that in these days of anti-political correctness there's a tendency to jump on the bandwagon, which means that our struggles gets belittled.

Tony, Luton

Sadly, the decade would ultimately be book-ended by two deaths.

Whereas the coverage of the murder of Stephen Lawrence in 1993 shone a light on the racism – casual and institutional – that Black Britons faced on a routine basis, the killing of ten-year-old Damilola Taylor on the stairwell of a council estate in Peckham, would highlight a plethora of different problems and resonate with so many new Britons who came with their parents to this country as children, with distinguishable accents and customs, and a 'work hard' ethic to take advantages of the opportunities their adopted country had to offer. A classic immigrant story.

Though it would be some time before the police would arrest and subsequently charge anyone for his death, *The Voice* would once again make the right call in its front-page headline of December 4 2020: 'Damilola, we failed you.' Putting the blame for his death on WE – the community.

This was about us, the comment piece read. We needed to ask ourselves the uncomfortable questions. When two brothers, only a couple of years older than the ten-year-old, would later be convicted of Damilola's manslaughter the questions would be even more profound with the realisation that sometimes, in the inner-city neighbourhoods in which we live, other Black boys pose an existential threat to the safety of our children.

The profile headshot of a sweet young boy with the cutest smile endeared Damilola to the nation.

Like the Lawrence family before them, his parents represented their grief in a dignified, if heartbroken, manner in front of the media cameras. Their son had only been in Britain a few months. On the day he was killed he had been attending an after-school computer class. He was caught in what would be the last footage of him by CCTV cameras outside the local library moments before his life would be taken away by the two boys who stabbed him in the leg with a broken beer bottle.

Ultimately it was not the law changes that made the main difference in this decade that began with so much hope and aspiration, but descended very quickly into the same old challenges for Black Brits. While murderous racism demoralised Black Brits, we were not beaten. *The Voice* is witness to that. It was a reminder that no matter how high you reach, no matter how successful you become, there is always a danger that you and your family's lives are at risk while institutional racism influences the thinking of the worst forms of humanity. Institutional racism treats Black people as less. It is what the murderers of Stephen Lawrence treated him as.

2003–2012
Has Anything changed?

By Winsome Cornish

As *The Voice* entered its third decade, escalating reports of youths being gunned down on the street sparked serious concern. Depressingly, discrimination and bias in the workplace continued to be rife, despite the introduction of government-backed initiatives to tackle racial disparities.

The unrelenting climate of discontent that saw uprisings and rioting flare up across North England, chiefly in Bradford, Oldham and Burnley in 2001 resulted in several commissioned government reports recommending initiatives to tackle racial disparities.

Among them, the Ouseley Report called for the introduction of new policies to strengthen partnerships between government and community groups, and foster better relations between the diverse ethnic groups that is multicultural Britain.

These proposals helped pave the way for the implementation of community cohesion policies and the funding of diverse groups working together to improve civic participation and political involvement in the wider society. By 2003, many of these policies were in place, and many new Black and minority ethnic voluntary and community organisations sprang up to tackle issues such as youth disaffection and mental health.

Operation Black Vote, a leading campaign spearheaded by activist Simon Woolley was already firmly established and on a mission to put 'Black faces in high places.' Woolley would tell anyone who would listen that levelling the playing field had to involve better representation of Black politicians and civic leaders within the UK power structure.

But on the ground, the stark reality was gross disaffection and the unrelenting menace of gun crime and gang violence. In tandem with integration initiatives and an equal opportunities agenda, bloodshed and mayhem on the streets was the major threat pounding at the collective Black door.

Many in the community felt uneasy in 2004 when it became clear that moves were afoot to dissolve the Commission for Racial Equality (CRE) – the main body for minorities seeking to pursue cases of discrimination. Those fears were realised when the CRE met its end in 2007.

However, amid these obstacles *The Voice* celebrated a number of successful Black men and women who defied the odds to find success in their chosen fields, from politics and the judiciary to the police and the arts.

The inauguration of Barack Obama in 2008 also brought hope and inspiration across the pond. Obama fever hit *The Voice*, and Barack and Michelle found a second home within its pages throughout 2009.

And after nearly 20 years of relentless campaigning, in 2012 the Lawrence family finally achieving some measure of justice as two men were at last jailed for the 1993 murder of their son Stephen. As we look back on the first decade of the new millennium it is important to consider what, if anything, has changed.

Over the course of 2002 gun crime rose by 35 per cent. There were 9,974 incidents involving firearms in the year up to April 2002, an increase from 7,362 the previous year.

Revenge attacks predictably follow gun attacks, so the expectation was of more violence to come.

True to the word, by the end of the first week of 2003, the disproportionate Black youth death toll had risen.

A violent onslaught had ended the lives of two young women – shot dead by ruthless gunmen in gang-ridden Aston – a multicultural neighbourhood of the Birmingham area.

In its 2003 New Year edition, *The Voice* headline screamed; 'Gunned down!'

Charlene Ellis, 18, and Letisha Shakespeare, 17, were the latest victims of the nation's escalating gang and gun violence. Both were killed when 'evil' gunmen sprayed a hail of 30 bullets from a semi-automatic submachine gun at a group of young Birmingham partygoers. The young girls were out to enjoy themselves and to see in the New Year. But for the revellers, the party at a makeshift venue turned into a nightmare. The criminal gangsters were well known to law enforcement and had developed a fearful reputation in the area. The young women were fired on as they were leaving the party. While Ellis and Shakespeare died at the scene, two others survived after undergoing surgery to remove multiple bullets.

The tragic deaths invariably added to the heart-rending media appeals from inconsolable mothers who beseech the public to help find those responsible for the untimely loss of their children.

The Voice reported that '2002 was the worst year for 'Black-on-Black' shootings and every year sees more gun-related killings' and state that, 'if these deaths are anything to go by, 2003 will be even worse.' 'When will the madness end?' *The Voice* questioned.

In 2004 four men were found guilty of murdering Ellis and Shakespeare, and were also convicted of three counts of attempting to murder Ellis's twin sister, Sophia, and their friend Cheryl Shaw. The prosecution claimed it was a 'botched' revenge attack by one rival gang on another. Ellis's half-brother and three other young men, who were all alleged to be members of the Burger Bar Boys gang, were convicted of the murders. A fifth man and the alleged target of the shooting, was cleared of possessing a firearm on the night of the shooting.

A 24-year-old man who was alleged to be a member of the rival Johnson Crew had taunted the Burger Bar Boys on stage at a nightclub earlier that evening. The prosecution alleged that the taunt was a 'catalyst' for the shooting. One of the convicted was also said to have wanted to avenge the death of his brother, who was shot dead in 2002. The attack was blamed on the Johnson Crew.

Letisha's mother, Marcia Shakespeare, said the court had reached the 'right result.' She said gun crime was a 'terrible thing that has brought misery to my family.' At the sentencing, the three older men were sent to prison for at least 35 years each, and the youngest convicted, was sentenced to 27 years. Three of the convicted launched an appeal but lost their case at the European Court of Human Rights in 2012.

Sadly the deaths of young people at the hands of gun crime did not end there.

Later in 2003 seven-year-old Toni-Ann Byfield became one of Britain's youngest gun crime victims when she was shot dead. The bodies of the child and her father were found in a Harlesden bedsit. Toni-Ann, who was under the care of

VOICE

Can we clean up the police force?

A BBC documentary last week showed that despite attempts to stop racism and discrimination in the police force, some new recruits still hold shockingly racist views. Dominic Bascombe took to the streets to gauge the reaction to the programme and ask: can the problem really be eradicated?

PRISCILLA DANKWA, 25, ARCHITECT, STREATHAM, SOUTH-EAST LONDON: "I was outraged at the programme. There needs to be more black people involved in the police force. I think that would help to combat the perception that the police is governed by white people. The recent appointment of a black chief constable in Kent [Michael Fuller] is a good way to move forward."

ESTHER JEMMOTT, 36, STUDENT, WEST LONDON: "The programme revealed nothing new. I don't think the police can stop racists from getting into the police force because they're always going to be there. It's going to be really hard to do. They are going to have to do a lot of vetting, because it will always be there. Racism is part and parcel of it."

DELROY DWYDR, 38, HOUSING REGENERATION OFFICER, LUTON: "The issues raised by the programme are not things you like to hear. I don't think racism is something that is welcome among the majority of the police force. I think it's a small minority that have that sort of attitude towards minority ethnic groups. It has to be identified and dealt with. A lot of racism is indirect plus you're not going to be able to discover it because it's not out in the open. In order for the police to try and eradicate it, they would have to go undercover, like the BBC did."

MS SCARLETT, 25, SONGWRITER, ISLINGTON, NORTH LONDON: "I think the officers involved should have been sacked. Racism is deep-seated, so I don't know what can be done about it. The police have got a pretty negative attitude towards black people in general. They've tried to curb that in the past couple of years, but people still get stopped. Psychological tests would help, but then you probably wouldn't get a lot of people applying. Black people aren't going to go in to the police when they know they are going to get picked on and get racially abused."

ADE BISI, SALES REPRESENTATIVE, 32, SHEPHERD'S BUSH, WEST LONDON: "On the surface you think England is a tolerant society, but at the end of the day the documentary shows what black people still have to go through. Maybe it's a wake-up call for black people and other minorities to get into the force and make changes rather than running away from it. If they would give me a job I'm sure I could make a change. Bringing in more black people would solve the problem because we understand what our people go through, we know how people feel, we know their reality. It's difficult for black people to step on a brother. The police need to have more minorities in there to make a change."

JAD VITALIS, 21, ACTOR, STONEBRIDGE, NORTH-WEST LONDON: "Black people bring it upon themselves with all the gun crime. If people stop carrying guns it can change communities. The police are there to do their job, but it's how they go about it that is the problem. You can't stop racist police officers in the force, but maybe bringing in more minority officers would help."

yourvoice@the-voice.co.uk

A LIGHT IN THE DARK

Community mourns the tragic loss of seven-year-old Toni-Ann at funeral

By KENNETH TAYLOR

SIDE by side they died, side by side they were finally laid to rest.

As the funeral cortege of Bertram 'Bony' Byfield and his seven-year-old daughter Toni-Ann rolled into George Street, Lozells, Birmingham on Friday, one mourner yelled out: "Oh my God!"

With sorrow and grief etched on their faces, some 250 relatives and friends turned out to pay their final respects to the 41-year-old father and his little girl. She was shot in the back as she tried to flee the scene of her father's brutal murder in a north-west London bedsit on September 14. Many wept openly, others hid their tears behind shades.

"She was like a rose taken from a garden," Bishop Derek Webley told the congregation at the New Testament Church of God. "She offered us a lot of joy and comfort and placed smiles on many people's faces. She was a jolly person, like a light in a dark room.

"On September 14, along with Bertram, Toni-Ann's life was brought tragically to an end by the bullets from the gun of an assassin and executor. A beautiful girl's life was taken away from us, slain in cold blood."

REWARD

In a powerful and moving address, the bishop branded their killer a "coward hiding behind the death of a child".

He said those who used the gun or peddled illegal substances were not concerned about the lives they destroyed as long as they could have a nice home, a nice car, feel big in the community and appear to be untouchable. "I probably can't touch you, but there is a God in heaven who is alive."

He said Toni-Ann used to attend his church with her godmother Audrey Smith.

Toni-Ann had attended Lozells and Slade primary schools in Birmingham since moving to Britain from Jamaica. She was in the care of Birmingham social services department when she was allowed to spend a weekend with her father in London. In the early hours of September 14 they were both shot dead. Despite four arrests, no one has been charged with the killings. A £20,000 reward is being offered to help catch the killer.

Toni-Ann's mother Roselyn Richards, who was flown over from Jamaica for the double funeral, wept uncontrollably inside and outside the church. A wreath on her daughter's tiny white casket read: "To my dear Angel, Toni-Ann Byfield. I love you very, very much, but remember God loves you more."

In a statement later released by the Metropolitan Police's Operation Trident team, Richards said: "The last thing she saw was the face of evil looking down at her. The people in this area are angry about this, but the people who know what happened need to help the police – the people who know whose face my baby was looking at."

Anthony Robinson, who flew in from Jamaica especially for the funeral, described Byfield as his mentor who had helped to fund his schooling and had once paid for him to visit England.

Holding back tears, he said: "My friend, my mentor, Tony shone a light that brightened my darkness. His body is resting before us, but his spirit lives on."

Before the funeral cortege made its way to Handsworth Cemetery, Det Supt. Rick Turner appealed for information in tracing of red Renault Clio, registration RK02 OXC, which was seen in the vicinity of Byfield's flat in Harrow Road between September 8 and 15. He said: "Anyone who knows who is responsible for the murder of a seven-year-old girl must contact us."

If you have information that could help, contact 020 8733 4704, or Crimestoppers on: 0800 555111

Grief: (clockwise from top) mourning family, mother, sister and Toni-Ann (inset)

Seven-year-old Toni-Ann Byfield became the youngest victim of gun violence in 2003

Birmingham Social Services, was hit in the back after she witnessed the shooting of her father by a rival drug dealer. The drug dealer, Joel Smith, was convicted of her murder in 2006 and jailed for life.

In 2008, *The Voice* revealed that knife and gun murders involving youths rose dramatically in the UK since the start of 2007. By June of that year, 29 people under 25 had been killed, more than the total for the same period in 2006. Most of the victims were male and the youngest was a boy aged 14.

As part of its report into the 29 murders, *The Voice* approached community leaders for their thoughts on how the crisis can be solved.

Youth mentor Phillip Morris, told *The Voice*: 'There are no bad kids just lost kids. The youth of today are killing each because they lack a sense of identity, which comes from low self-esteem.'

'Violent crimes are committed by youth because they have lost their sense of belonging. They are like lost sheep roaming in the wilderness. They have no reason to care for their fellow "brother" because no one cares for them.'

Bishop Wayne Malcolm of Christian Life City said: 'Ultimately, all human beings have the same fundamental needs, which is to feel secure, significant and have a sense of self-worth.'

'If a young person fails the educational system or the system fails them, they will create their own system and their own way of how to make money and survive. They create their own entrepreneurship.'

'Early intervention is a big must in preventing young people joining gangs, which must be done at an educational level. One of the solutions to help save young people from joining gangs is to influence their thoughts. Behaviour is driven by belief.

Young people carry knives because they feel a knife will protect them and bump up their street cred. If you are able to influence young people's thought you can challenge their belief system and stop their negative behaviour.'

In 2011 Richard Taylor was also honoured with an OBE for the years he dedicated to raising awareness about knife crime. The father of Damilola Taylor, who was killed on his way home from Peckham Library in 2000. Taylor attributed his award to his late wife, Gloria, who died of a suspected heart attack in April 2008, eight years after ten-year-old Damilola was stabbed in his leg with a broken bottle. Taylor told *The Voice*: 'Receiving the OBE from the Home Secretary in the House of Commons was an honour, but the recognition was largely for the strength and courage my late wife Gloria showed after we lost our son. I wanted to make this clear to the Home Secretary, that I was receiving it in Gloria's honour as well.' Taylor had set up the Damilola Taylor Trust along with his wife.

Despite a worrying rise in knife and gun crime at the start of the decade, *The Voice* also celebrated leading members of the Black community who were finding success and influence in politics and public life. It was their aim to enfranchise and empower their community to engage in civic life and stand up for what mattered to them.

In 2003, *The Voice* celebrated Valerie Amos becoming the first Black parliamentarian to join the cabinet. Amos, who was appointed International Development Secretary by then-Prime Minister Tony Blair, was hailed 'Blair's First Lady' on the cover of the newspaper.

The announcement was hailed as a watershed moment in British history, and fellow upper house member Lord Herman Ouseley said: 'it's a great day for British politics and for our

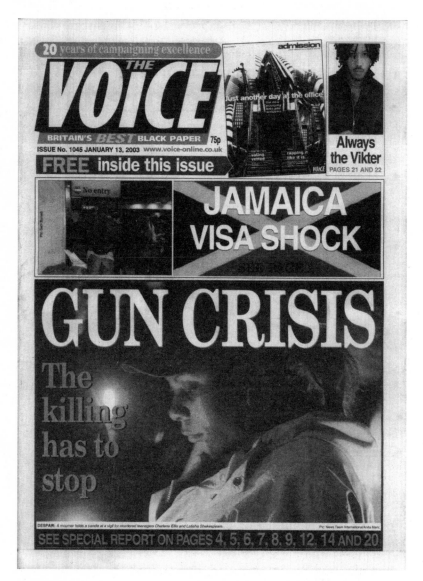

The Voice *campaigned for an end to gun violence with a special edition in January 2003*

position in society to see a Black woman succeed at this level. She has built up a base of respect through all she has done. She's a role model for Black women and for all women.'

Tottenham MP David Lammy added: 'She has been one of the strongest *voices* for Africa and the Caribbean in government. She has a significant track record in the Black community both in Lambeth, Camden and the Equal Opportunities Commission. Her work advising the South African government and Nelson Mandela as the Foreign Office spokeswoman for international development was outstanding.'

Commission for Racial Equality boss Trevor Phillips said the appointment should help address apathy among Black voters. He hoped it would inspire those who may feel disengaged from British politics.

Politics was not the only area in which many Black Brits felt disenfranchised. As the vast majority of criminal cases in England and Wales begin and end in the magistrates' courts, a new initiative was set up to demystify the justice system.

In 2003, Operation Black Vote (OBV) head Simon Woolley lobbied the then-Lord Chancellor Derry Irvine for his approval to begin a programme to raise awareness of the urgent need for Black magistrates. Magistrates were typically white and many in ethnic minority communities felt that bias and prejudice could influence the outcome in cases where they sought justice. Despite this, many didn't know they could simply apply to become a magistrate. So, in order to begin to address the under representation of Black officials within the court system, it was imperative that the wider public was informed about the process of application and the role of a magistrate.

That was the start of the on going yearly OBV Magistrates Shadowing Scheme. A programme that gives access to ethnic minority communities and encourages them that they too can apply and, if appointed, sit among judges dispensing justice. The nationwide scheme, in partnership with the Department of Justice, paired participants with mentor magistrates. They sit in court sessions observing cases, learning about the work of the courts and how judgements are made.

The Lord Chancellor backed the initiative saying it would send a clear statement that the magistracy must be a microcosm of the whole of the community it serves, and improve confidence in the criminal justice system. He said: 'It is excellent community service that we have together been able to put in place.'

I headed the initiative for OBV back in the early 2000s and saw first-hand how imperative the scheme was in inspiring new magistrates and ambassadors – those who will inform others about how the system works. The scheme demystified the court process and is aimed to significantly increase the number of Black magistrates in courts around the country.

Five years later, *The Voice* reported how the Magistrates Shadowing Scheme had seen nearly 40 graduates appointed magistrates across the country, while a further 200 participants were expected to apply in 2008. What's more, the average age of appointees from the scheme had lowered from 57 to 35.

Its successes came after a report by the Department for Communities and Local Government revealed that the lack of Black judges was one of the main reasons Black people expected to be discriminated against by the courts.

Then-justice secretary Jack Straw said: 'My concern is that such an expectation, however false it maybe, exists at all. That is where this scheme adds incredible value.'

⊗BV
Operation Black Vote
Celebrating 25 years

"Power is never given"

HISTORY IN
THE MAKING:
OBV House of
Commons launch,
1996. From left,
Lee Jasper, Yvette
Williams, Rita
Patel, Simon
Woolley and
Kumar Murshid.

OPERATION BLACK Vote was launched in July 1996.

In just 10 months we held over 100 meetings at schools, colleges, community centres, local party offices and town halls up and down the country.

We distributed over 250,000 voter registration cards, 500,000 leaflets in six different languages and 50,000 posters. Over 200 articles appeared in the national and international press, the black press, and a host of other journals and publications.

Ninety-seven radio interviews and 37 television broadcasts spanned every region in the country and eight countries worldwide.

An Early Day Motion tabled on OBV's behalf received support from all sides of the House of Commons.

IMPACT
An OBV collaboration with Rock the Vote and MTV saw Linford Christie make time to

Trevor Robinson (of Tango fame) and Jon Daniel spearheaded a controversial poster and cinema ad campaign.

do an ad specifically for the music channel.

But we knew from the outset that it would be OBV's impact in two specific areas which would determine success or failure: the response of the political parties to black concerns and of the black

community to Operation Black Vote.

In comparison to any election before 1997, the positive attention the black electorate received from the major parties was unprecedented.

And the party leaders led from the front.

OBV special: A word from the editor

"This Operation Black Vote 25th Anniversary supplement to The Voice newspaper is a deliberate and unapologetic nod to

Black History Month. In the next few pages, we wind you through the last 25 years of political activism and our tough, but

well fought, proud journey to the success OBV is today. Power is never given."

Mayowa Ayodele

Contributors and special thanks

Editor: Mayowa Ayodele
Sub-editor: Meesha Cru-Hall
Contributors: Thanks to the founders of OBV,

the board and staff, alumni and associates who helped in the formulation of this publication.

F: facebook.com/ OperationBlackVote/
T: @OpBlackVote
I: @opblackvote
W: obv.org.uk

Supported by VOICE and JN Bank UK

Founded in 1996, Operation Black Vote played a large role during the 2000s in empowering Black people to make a difference in their local community

Participant Derrick Hogg also told *The Voice*: 'We need an equal playing field and OBV have begun the process of making this a reality. I intend to make my application to the magistracy and make a positive contribution to society.'

The following year 2004 also saw progress higher up in the judiciary as barrister Linda Dobb QC became the first Black person to be appointed as a High Court judge. Taking up her role, Dobbs commented that she will be 'the first of many'. At the time in England and Wales, there were just nine Black circuit judges out of 623, or 1.4 per cent.

Dobbs said: 'It is a great honour to have been invited by the Lord Chancellor to become a High Court judge. Whilst this appointment might be seen as casting me into the role of standard bearer, I am simply a practitioner following a career path. I am confident, nevertheless, that I am the first of many to come.'

Dobbs's appointment came in the same year a government report showed that the percentage of women and ethnic minorities being appointed to the judiciary was increasing. People from ethnic minorities made up 14.8 per cent of all appointments between 2002–03 compared to 8.9 the previous year, the Judicial Appointments Annual Report announced. Caroline Herbert, chair of the Law Society's diversity committee commented that while the increase was a step in the right direction the reality was somewhat different.

She said: 'Any increase must be welcomed, but there is a lot more they can do. We can't tackle diversity on the bench if we're not tackling it at the entry level and progression. How can there be a diverse judiciary if we are not given the opportunity in the beginning to get into the profession?'

THE VOICE  INTERVIEW
By CLARE GORHAM

SIMON SAYS

Political activist explains why he is so determined to get

Woolley's thinking: OBV head believes passionately in getting involved in the electoral process

Picture: KEN PASSLEY

THE EPN (Executive and Professionals Network) Awards is an event where the corporate black world comes together to network, fly the flag and fight the good fight together. The nominees scoop up their award in all its perspex splendour and we all bask in their glory, encouraged by the notion that it's possible. The food ain't bad either.

Simon Woolley is a co-founder of Operation Black Vote (OBV), which got just such an award – for being an "Outstanding Voluntary Grass Roots" organisation. It's his third award in as many years.

As a non-party political organisation, OBV wants black people to vote and become part of the democratic process so they can demonstrate their collective community potential.

They also offer such pioneering initiatives as the MP and magistrate shadowing scheme with a view to getting greater black representation in the judiciary and in Parliament. It's the first national initiative to focus on the black democratic deficit in the UK.

Woolley speaks in seamless soundbites, every answer perfectly formed. He's a real visionary when asked what his political fantasy would be for the future:

"For Britain to have a black

'You ignore the black vote at your peril'

Prime Minister. Someone – unlike Colin Powell – to make the black community proud."

He attributes his determination and tenacity to his first job in London, a door-to-door shower salesman. "Knocking on people's doors and getting them slammed in your face gives you resilience. Since doing that, I'm afraid of nothing!"

He was born and raised in Leicester by white adoptive parents, who he describes as

"wonderful people". Sadly, both parents had died by the time he was 20. "Their love gave me the confidence that I believe has made me. They said, 'Go and be who you want to be, do the best you can with the skills you have,' which is what I've done."

When asked his views on trans-racial adoption, an issue that's become incredibly contentious over the years and hijacked by political correctness, he replies: "Ideally, a black child should

be placed in a black adoptive home, but the love I had was something that override the fact that I didn't know what Caribbean food was or that I sometimes had difficulty with my hair.

"But not everybody in my position comes to a point where they can regain their lost blackness."

He had a very positive and multicultural experience on the estate where he grew up, and remains friends with his mates 30 years on.

He left school at 16, having been told he could become either a bricklayer or a plumber. He also trained as a car mechanic and sold advertising space for Pearl & Dean, which enabled him to buy a flat in a relatively

salubrious part of London.

While living there, he was stopped outside his home by the police one morning and asked for ID. Unable to produce it, he took them back to his flat where they followed him inside uninvited.

When he questioned their advance, he was promptly arrested and handcuffed to his own gate while they knocked on his neighbour's door, asking them for a positive ID. No apology was ever made.

"I didn't complain because I knew I would have been consumed with anger, so I decided to let it go, but vowed to get even. What I'm doing now is getting even ten-fold.

"Having graduated from Middlesex University as a

Co-founder of Operation Black Vote, Simon Woolley, told The Voice *in 2003 his political dream would be for Britain to have a Black Prime Minister*

'For barristers, there is still racism in how their cases are allocated in chambers. If they don't get good quality cases to shine in court, the judges don't see them and can't give them a reference on their advocacy skills.'

'And if we look in the lucrative areas, such as the Chancery (financial law) there is nobody there at all.'

She said Black lawyers are in lower paid areas and moving on from a deputy to a district judge is nigh on impossible.

At the same time, ethnic minorities had become the majority in three London boroughs. A Labour Force Survey revealed that Black and Asian people outnumber the white population in Brent, Newham and Tower Hamlets.

But Simon Woolley told *The Voice* the figures masked alarming realities. Concerned that the three boroughs were among the poorest, not just in London but in Britain as a whole, he responded: 'Although we are the majority in these boroughs, we are the minority when it comes to who's controlling the borough. The lack of Black councillors and people in positions of power in these boroughs is lamentable. We must take responsibility for changing these boroughs. We have the numbers to demand it and we should use that power to give our communities the opportunities we deserve.'

Woolley's sights were set on empowering the Black community to make sure their *voice*s were heard at polling stations across the country. In the run-up to the 2005 General Election, *The Voice* reported OBV's findings that only three in four of those entitled to vote in minority communities are registered.

OBV calculated that in 70 seats there were significantly more Black voters than the margin between the sitting MP and their nearest challenger in the 2001 election. They knew that strategic voting in those seats could determine the winner on the day. The organisation's nationwide pre-election campaigning resulted in increased voter turnout and saw a record five new minority MPs elected to Parliament.

There were now 15 Black and Asian MPs sitting in the House of Commons. The new parliamentarians included Labour's Dawn Butler and Adam Afriyie, who became the Conservative Party's first Black MP. Paul Boateng resigned his seat is to take up the post of the UK's ambassador to South Africa. And Oona King lost to anti-war campaigner George Galloway and his Respect Party.

While OBV welcomed the arrival of five new minority MPs, but the loss of two others was 'bitterly disappointing'. Woolley said: 'It shows Black people now refuse to vote just on the colour of skin, policies such as the war and education also have a big impact.'

In 2004, Michael Fuller made history when he became the first Black Chief Constable in the British police. Fuller, who had joined the Metropolitan Police at 16, was Deputy Assistant Commissioner and head of Intelligence at Scotland Yard before he was promoted to Chief Constable of Kent Police. In *The Voice's* report of his appointment, headlined 'Hail to the Chief', Fuller said: 'I've always felt that the police should reflect the community they serve. When I joined, there were only five other Black officers on the force and we worked really hard to bring others in.'

But despite this historic moment, a leaked memo from the Morris Inquiry into racism in the Metropolitan Police found that around half the race cases taken before employment tribunals were brought by white officers. In one case, reported by the Black Police Association (BPA), the promotion of one Asian sergeant led to discrimination suits from six white officers.

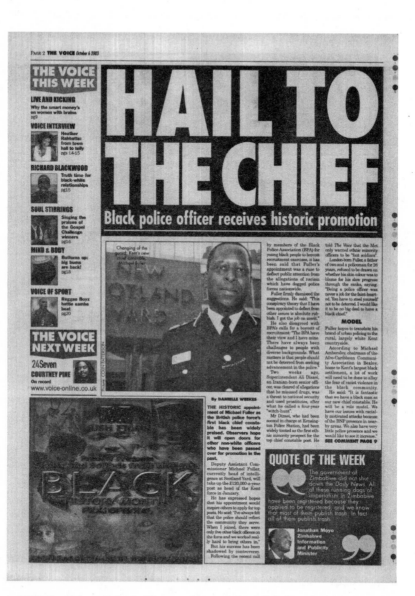

THE VOICE THIS WEEK

LIVE AND KICKING
Why the smart money's on women with brains
pg9

VOICE INTERVIEW
Heather Rabbatts: from town hall to telly
pgs 14-15

RICHARD BLACKWOOD
Truth time for black-white relationships
pg15

SOUL STIRRINGS
Singing the praises of the Gospel Challenge winners
pg16

MIND & BODY
Bottoms up: big bums are back!
pg18

VOICE OF SPORT
Reggae Boyz battle samba beat
pg20

THE VOICE NEXT WEEK

24Seven
COURTNEY PINE
On record
www.voice-online.co.uk

HAIL TO THE CHIEF

Black police officer receives historic promotion

Changing of the guard: Kent's new chief constable Michael Fuller

By DANIELLE WEEKES

THE HISTORIC appointment of Michael Fuller as the British police force's first black chief constable has been widely praised. Observers hope it will open doors for other non-white officers who have been passed over for promotion in the past.

Deputy Assistant Commissioner Michael Fuller, currently head of intelligence at Scotland Yard, will take up the £120,000-a-year post as head of the Kent force in January.

He has expressed hopes that his appointment would inspire others to apply for top posts. He said: "I've always felt that the police should reflect the community they serve. When I joined, there were only five other black officers on the force and we worked really hard to bring others in."

But his success has been shadowed by controversy. Following the recent call by members of the Black Police Association (BPA) for young black people to boycott recruitment exercises, it has been said that Fuller's appointment was a ruse to deflect public attention from the allegations of racism which have dogged police forces nationwide.

Fuller firmly dismissed the suggestions. He said: "This conspiracy theory that I have been appointed to deflect from other issues is absolute rubbish. I got the job on merit."

He also disagreed with BPA's calls for a boycott of recruitment: "The BPA have their view and I have mine. There have always been challenges to people with diverse backgrounds. What matters is that people should not be deterred from seeking advancement in the police."

Two weeks ago, Superintendent Ali Dizaei, an Iranian-born senior officer, was cleared of allegations that he misused drugs, was a threat to national security and used prostitutes, after what he called a four-year "witch-hunt".

Mr Dizaei, who had been second in charge at Kensington Police Station, had been widely touted as the first ethnic minority prospect for the top chief constable post. He told *The Voice* that the Met only wanted ethnic minority officers to be "foot soldiers".

London-born Fuller, a father of two and a policeman for 28 years, refused to be drawn on whether his skin colour was to blame for his slow progress through the ranks, saying: "Being a police officer was never a job for the faint-hearted. You have to steel yourself not to be deterred. I would like it to be no big deal to have a black chief."

MODEL

Fuller hopes to translate his brand of urban policing to the rural, largely white Kent countryside.

According to Michael Ambersley, chairman of the Afro-Caribbean Community Association in Bexley, home to Kent's largest black settlement, a lot of work will need to be done to allay the fear of racist violence in the black community.

He said: "It is fantastic that we have a black man as our new chief constable. He will be a role model. We have our issues with racially motivated attacks because of the BNP presence in nearby areas. We also have very little police presence and we would like to see it increase."
SEE COMMENT PAGE 9

QUOTE OF THE WEEK

The government of Zimbabwe did not shut down the *Daily News*. All of these running dogs of imperialism in Zimbabwe have been registered because they applied to be registered, and we know that most of them publish trash. In fact all of them publish trash.

Jonathan Moyo
Zimbabwe Information and Publicity Minister

In 2003 London Assembly chairman, Trevor Phillips faced criticism as he took up a new appointment as Head of the Commission for Racial Equality (CRE). It was well known that the government were planning to transform the CRE into an equal opportunities commission was in the pipeline. Many feared the CRE would be abolished and merged with groups representing disabilities and women's rights, and that race would fall to the bottom of the equality agenda. Trevor Phillips stated: 'I am delighted to be given the opportunity to lead the CRE in its twin tasks of helping to bring all our diverse communities together and in rooting out racism and discrimination in all its forms.'

However, former CRE chairman Lord Herman Ouseley told *The Voice*: 'We have to wait and see how Trevor does. It is a challenging job.'

Conversely, Dr Raj Chandram, a former CRE commissioner, told the paper that the head of the CRE should be white. 'It's the only way discrimination can be fought,' he said. 'There are too many racists in the ethnic community. If a Black person is chosen, Asians feel they get a raw deal and vice versa. A white chairman would have been more impartial. I hope Trevor will overcome this. He has a great task ahead of him.'

Four years later equalities campaigners continued to criticise Phillips when he was announced as the head of the new Commission on Equalities and Human Rights (CEHR). Phillips was accused of reducing the effectiveness of the CRE and many said his appointment would seriously deter progress in race relations in the UK.

Lee Jasper, senior advisor to the mayor of London said his concern about Phillips was largely because of what he perceived to be a lack of progress at the Commission for Racial Equality (CRE).

Trevor Phillips gets death threat

EXCLUSIVE

By Andrew Clunis
yourviews@gvmedia.co.uk

Trevor Phillips

A VIOLENT, racist thug has threatened to kill former Commission for Racial Equality (CRE) head Trevor Phillips and dump his body into the River Thames.

The threat was made on a forum hosted by the fascist website Blood and Honour, which is operated by the Nazi Fundamental group Combat 18.

Phillips, who is the new head of the Commission for Equality and Human Rights (CEHR) has reported the matter to the police, who are conducting an investigation.

The threat was made last Tuesday by a forum participant who goes by the name 'Adolph the Geordie'.

The poster ranted: "I've just been reading in the paper about the CRE being wound up, and some f****king new human rights creation taking its place. "Does anyone know where its new offices are going to be? I suggest we burn the f****ker to the ground, and that worthless piece of c**n filth, Trevor Phillips along with it. Kill the c**nt and throw him into the f***king Thames."

CONDEMNED

The threat against Phillips' life has been condemned by race campaigners. Joint Secretary of Unite Against Fascism, Denis Fernando said: "These comments show the true function of fascist websites – they allow violent racist thugs to organise and proliferate unchecked. Thousands of people have supported our campaign to remove fascists from Facebook. Ultimately, the Government must act now to close the legal loopholes and shut down fascist sites. It is grotesque that fascism is being allowed to organise itself openly in a modern society."

The development has once again brought into focus the need for more stringent regulation of the Internet in the UK. Organisations like Searchlight have been demanding tougher action by the government against persons who operate such websites. A spokesman said: "Searchlight does not accept that nothing can be done against these websites because they are hosted outside the UK. Most of the people who run the hate websites and provide information to them live in the UK."

He continued: "The authorities have been repeatedly informed about certain individuals but no action has been taken." It is believed the sites are run by neo-Nazi groups operating across the country. Among other things, they offer advice on how to make bombs similar to those used in the July 7, 2005 terror attacks.

A spokeswoman for Phillips said he was not prepared to comment beyond saying that the matter was in the hands of the police.

Soul protest at the MOBOs

By Janelle Oswald
yourviews@gvmedia.co.uk

Soul artists protesting for a soul category.
Photo: Colin Patterson

A NUMBER of UK soul artists gate crashed last week's MOBO Awards, registering their protest at the organisers' refusal to include a soul music category among its slate of awards.

As other stars from the world of black music arrived to pose for the assembled media, soul singers Omar, Bluey Maunick of Incognito, Ola Onabule and American soul artist Rahsaan Patterson brandished posters asking: 'MOBOs Where's Your Soul?'

"We are at the MOBOs to ask: Where is the soul category?" Omar told The Voice. "I wasn't invited so I invited myself. If there is no soul award that means you are narrowing the music down to two categories – R'n'B and hip-hop. That is not what music is about. I am a soul artist and my music cannot be categorised or compared to someone like Ne-Yo who is R'n'B," he said.

The MOBO organisation is no stranger to controversy. It has been blasted over the years for "diluting its concept to embrace white performers". This, the 12th year was no different. The soul protest was orchestrated and organised by Chris Wells, the editor of Echoes magazine who has been campaigning for several years to get Kanya King, the founder of the MOBOs to recognise the need for a soul grouping.

Wells told The Voice: "Soul artists sell millions of albums and perform to 'sold-out' signs all over the world – frequently eclipsing other cornerstone black music styles such as Gospel, Jazz and Reggae, all of which are recognised at the MOBOs.

"I organised the protest because I wanted well known artists like Omar and Rahsaan Patterson to be at the forefront because they are the ones that are being ignored by the MOBOs."

He continued: "Unlike the Royal Albert Hall, the O2 is private property so we were unable to be as vocal as we would have liked without getting the police involved so Omar and the boys conned themselves inside the Arena so they could voice their opinions.

"Soul music needs to be recognized because it one of the core elements of black music. The MOBO organization keeps arguing that soul music is not successful enough to have its own category but that's rubbish."

MOBO founder Kanya King remained defiant. She argued: "What is soul music but R'n'B, and gospel? And we already have those categories. We can't have all the categories, it is just not possible. However, we have had many soul artists in the past that have been honoured and are continuing to be honoured."

HONOURED

English signer and songwriter Corinne Bailey Rae who picked up two MOBO prizes last year told The Voice: "I'm very honoured to have been awarded, however, I truly believe that the MOBOs should preach for all Music Of Black Origin and as such it seems very strange not to have a category for soul music.

"When you have artists such as Jill Scott, Joss Stone, Beverley Knight, Raphael Saadiq and Angie Stone all successfully creating modern soul music I'd suggest that soul is very much alive and well, and continues to be a massive influence. Without soul music I know I wouldn't be making the music I make."

* See GSWORLD (pages 24-25) to find out who won hot and who was not at this year's MOBOs.

In 2007 former Commission for Racial Equality head Trevor Phillips received a death threat, where a racist thug threatened to dump his body in the Thames

But Phillips did not just receive criticism from the Black community. In 2007 police investigated when a racist thug threatened to kill him and dump his body in the Thames. The threat was made on a forum hosted by the fascist website Blood and Honour, operated by the Nazi fundamental group Combat 18.

The end of 2008 saw euphoric celebrations across the world when Barack Obama was elected President of United States of America. The historic election reached fever pitch on the momentous event of his 2009 inauguration. As Obama readied himself for the Oval Office, a *The Voice* Inauguration special captured the wonder, joy and expectations of Black Britain. In London especially, grassroots organisations and the political community became uplifted by Obama's accomplishments and excited about the changes his presidency could bring.

According to Simon Woolley, Obama's election renewed a sense of Black pride and gave more Black people the confidence to be involved in the political system, where currently there are only 15 Black and Asian members of Parliament.

'What Obama has taught us is to have the audacity to believe again. I think that people will now see that they can go for the top jobs and lead communities', he said. Woolley says he has been inundated with offers of help towards the work of OBV.

'We are direct beneficiaries of the phenomena that is Barack Obama. People are excited by our campaign and they want to be involved. They want to be part of a movement for change', he said.

Speaking to *The Voice*, Britain's first Black female Attorney General Baroness Scotland said: 'I think it's the most exciting thing that has happened in our generation. I think it confirms so many things that I believe in so fervently, mainly that if you have passion and ability and dedication, you will succeed.'

'Obama has demonstrated to all of us, to all our children, of whatever colour, or race, or orientation, that you can achieve great things. I think he's an inspiration not only for us but for the world.'

David Lammy, then-Labour Minister for Higher Education said:

> I have tremendous respect for Barack Obama. I draw huge inspiration from the way he ran his campaign, the way it has drawn people together. There will be young people who truly believe they can realise their dreams and have an image of what is possible, something other than the hip hop image that has been an issue for many years …We draw inspiration but there is a lot of work for us to do in Europe.

Meanwhile Sam King, a Windrush pioneer and Southwark's first Black mayor said:

> I feel good. God is good. We should give thanks to Dr. Martin Luther King Jr. People have been through great tribulation. Sixty years ago, Blacks were chased with dogs when they went to vote, but these young ones here, playing around with guns and knives, don't realise that people have gone through great difficulty just for them to live with a little dignity.

Just a year later, American civil rights icon Reverend Jesse Jackson paid a visit to Britain to help launch a campaign to encourage people to register to vote in time for the 2010 general elections. The campaign, featuring a 100-foot billboard poster with the slogan was unveiled by OBV: 'Expect the best from yourself and society. Register to vote.'

Jackson said he believed that voting would help Black people set right the inequalities they faced in health provision, employment and society. He said: 'If we expect much, we receive much. If we don't expect much and we don't vote much then we should not expect much. Therefore, we must raise expectations for our nation by voting. Every vote matters.'

The election result was later hailed as a 'historic victory for the ethnic diversity of British politics.' The number of minority MPs in the Commons rose to nine – Labour's Diane Abbott, David Lammy and Mark Hendrick were joined by Chi Onwurah and Chuka Umunna. Onwurah became the first African woman to win a parliamentary seat in Newcastle Central while Umunna won with an Obama-style campaign in Streatham, supported by a multitude of well-organised young graduates. The Conservatives also added three new Black faces to their benches. Adam Afriyie kept the seat he won in 2005 as MP for Windsor. However, the mixed-heritage millionaire businessman told the *Evening Standard* in 2012 that he considers himself 'post racial', not Black. Conservative strategy had placed Black candidates in strong winnable constituencies, which resulted in Oxford graduate and businessman Sam Gyimah taking Surrey East. Fellow Ghanaian, Kwasi Kwarteng won for Spelthorne. The writer and entrepreneur, who was educated at Eton, Cambridge and Harvard, was the first Black MP to be elected in the Surrey constituency. Solicitor Helen Grant took Maidstone and Weald, Ann Widdecombe's old seat, to become the first Black female MP for the Conservatives. Grant, of mixed heritage, had already established her own family law practice before she decided to run for political office. New Brent voting boundaries merged two constituencies, which meant two candidates were contesting one seat. Sadly, Dawn Butler was temporarily unseated in the new North London seat of Brent Central by Liberal Democrat Sarah Teather. This was also the election that saw future Home Secretary Priti Patel win her seat in Witham, Essex to become the Conservative's first Asian female MP.

Swiftly following the 2010 election was the Labour Party leadership contest, when Diane Abbott became not only the first woman to enter the battle but the first Black woman to run for leadership of a major political party. After Prime Minister Gordon Brown stepped down as leader, the Miliband brothers, Ed Balls, John McDonnell and Andy Burnham were the first to declare their intentions to run for leadership. But concern over the lack of a female challenger saw the long-standing Hackney MP step forward to take her chance.

Abbott told the media that she wanted to see a more diverse range of candidates, and that so many people had asked her to put her hat in the ring that she finally agreed to do so, adding that her nomination would 'broaden the debate'.

She said: 'I want to provide a platform for debate about who should be the next leader, and that debate would not be complete without a candidate, like me, who represents a more diverse choice.'

The media can be brutal but no one could have imagined the unprecedented assault of aggressive and negative media coverage that Abbott faced. Abbott's decision to run was hailed as 'historically significant' by many. When the dust had settled and the votes counted, Ed Miliband emerged as Party Leader. Battered but not broken, Diane Abbott took up the position of Shadow Minister of State for Public Health in Miliband's cabinet.

A few good men

No BME candidates run for Labour's deputy leader job

By Dominic
Bascombe

yourviews
@gvmedia.co.uk

AS Labour gears up for the election of a new leader and deputy leader, the absence of a black or Asian candidate has become plain.

While chancellor Gordon Brown is widely expected to take over the leadership from Tony Blair this summer, a host of candidates have come forward for the deputy position. Party chair Hazel Blears, backbencher Jon Cruddas, constitutional affairs minister Harriet Harman, education secretary Alan Johnson, Northern Ireland secretary Peter Hain, and the international development secretary Hilary Benn, have also declared their intention to stand.

Jack Straw, the leader of the Commons, is also tipped to stand. Diane Abbott and Keith Vaz, who both entered parliament in 1987, have chosen not to declare themselves as candidates.

However, the small number of black and Asian MPs could largely explain their reluctance to put their names forward. Candidates have to get the support of 44 MPs to stand.

Ashok Viswanathan, of Operation Black Vote, said: "It's a shame that they are not coming forward or feel that they won't have the support within the parliamentary Labour party.

"It is also revealing that no black MPs have come forward in the sense that if there were 50 or 60 MPs, not only would there have been more black MPs coming forward but also more black MPs to support them," said Viswanathan.

Abbott, who has never held a Cabinet post, was amongst the first batch of black women to enter the House of Commons 20 years ago.

Diane Abbott

A well-known left winger, she certainly has the experience comparable to backbencher Cruddas, who will contest the deputy PM position.

CABINET

A spokesperson for Abbott told The Voice: "Most deputy leadership contenders are at the cabinet level and because there are no black or Asian MPs in the cabinet, that could be a reason. Diane is looking forward to a time when a black or Asian MP would stand for the deputy leadership."

Dewsbury MP Shahid Malik explained that the absence of a BME candidate could be down to lack of experience.

"Most people believe to do that job you need to have higher level experience. Had Paul Boateng still been about he would have made a brilliant deputy PM.

"I don't think there's anybody else that could have fulfilled the cabinet criteria. Most people would rather support somebody else because they believe that cabinet-level experience is pretty important for that kind of job. If you look at the MPs we've

Keith Vaz

got, some of us are far too fresh and just trying to get to grips with being an MP let alone anything else. Others don't fancy it, and others are supporting other contenders," he said.

Tooting MP Sadiq Khan also added: "We have to look at the pool of candidates from which the deputy candidates are being chosen. When you bear in mind that the most senior Labour member was elected in 1987 and the rest of us elected recently, it's hardly surprising that there isn't that depth of experience."

Brent South MP Dawn Butler said that more time was needed to see changes.

She said: "Obviously there is not enough diversity so we haven't got enough black or black Britons were not as advanced as their American cousins in terms of black participation in politics.

Shahid Malik

'Know your Commonwealth'

AS Commonwealth Day is celebrated today (March 12), Ransford Smith (pictured right), deputy secretary-general of the British Commonwealth, believes that the organisation could do more to help average people understand what it does.

Smith, a former Jamaican diplomat, told The Voice that the Commonwealth remained a relevant institution.

"It is very difficult to conceive of an organisation like this not being relevant or exerting some influence," he said.

"It's a diverse group."

The Commonwealth currently consists of 53 member states, 47 of whom are developing states and six are developed states, and makes up one-third of the world's population, one-quarter of the world's government, and one-fifth of global trade."

Although diverse, the member states share a common historical tradition as former British colonies.

But do the historical ties account for much in today's politicised world?

"Why do countries seek to help each other? That is a simple but important question. It can have many answers and one cannot really delve into the motive behind each and every act amongst individuals or in the context of states," he said.

"Countries do have a sense of common aspirations and do seek to achieve those goals with members that can impinge on their collective and individual wellbeing. Certainly there is today, more than ever before, the recognition that no country can exist in an isolated habitat or cocoon."

Smith also dismissed the idea that the colonial legacy was maintained with the queen remaining as head of the

Ransford Smith

Commonwealth.

He said: "The queen is head of the Commonwealth but it comprises of member states that are constitutional monarchies; states with their own national monarchies; and states that are republican in status."

He continued: "As an organisation it has evolved. That evolution has allowed it to accommodate new states with various forms – that has allowed it to provide a service that connects with the everyday man."

He told The Voice that even if the organisation remained somewhat less well known, it would be measured by it's good works in assisting member states.

"In the final analysis, the measure of the Commonwealth as an organisation will be to see what it does to change life for the man on the ground. The two pillars of the Commonwealth are democracy and development.

"The pursuit of those two pillars will affect and change life on the ground. It has to do with the quality of the institutions, the delivery of services, the right of citizens, and social transformation," he said.

> ## "Had Paul Boateng still been about he would have made a brilliant deputy PM"

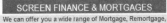
In 2010, Diane Abbott stepped forward as candidate for leader of the Labour Party after no other minority politician did so

Abbott's bruising experience of the 2010 leadership election was indicative of an Equal Opportunities Commission
(EOC) survey from three years earlier, which suggested it might
take up to 200 years to achieve gender equality in the top levels
of professions in Britain.

Sex and Power: Who Runs Britain? said it would take 40 years to
achieve an equal number of senior women in the judiciary and up
to 60 years to achieve an equal number of female directors at FTSE
100 companies. But the commission forecasted it could take up to
200 years to achieve an equal number of women in Parliament.
The EOC lamented that 6,000 women are 'missing' at the top of
professions in Britain. Back in 2007 women made up just 10 per
cent of directors of FTSE 100 companies and barely 20 per cent of
Parliament. At the very top, ethnic minority women were especially under-represented, accounting for just 0.4 per cent of FTSE
100 directors and 0.3 per cent of parliamentarians.

But while the EOC focused on the absence of 6,000 women,
especially from ethnic minorities, at the top *The Voice* writer
Trudy Simpson highlighted many successful high-achieving
Black women who were bucking the trend and leading the way
in their chosen professions.

One, Angela Sarkis, was the only Black female head of a
major charity, the Young Men's Christian Association (YMCA).
Sarkis also contributed to the development of government
initiatives on young offenders, urban regeneration, faith communities, diversity and education and was a founding member
of the Social Exclusion Unit.

She told *The Voice*:

Black women must not give in to negative talk and to racist
and sexist attitudes. Often we are told that we are not worth

much – sometimes by our families, our communities and white society – because we are women or Black. But people such as Maya Angelou and Martin Luther King Jr. demonstrated that even when you are brought low, if you hold onto ambition, things would change for the better.

As executive deputy chairman of Millwall Football Club, Heather Rabbatts showed that Black women could break into even the most traditionally male spaces. Rabbatts, who was given a CBE in 2000, was a barrister and television executive before moving to Millwall. She also worked in local government until 1989 when she became Deputy Chief Executive of Hammersmith and Fulham. She was also Chief Executive of Merton and Lambeth councils. After leaving local Government, she founded and headed iMPOWER, a public sector consultancy, and later moved on to be Managing Director of Channel 4's education programmes and business, 4Learning.

PR expert Yvonne Thompson CBE was also celebrated by *The Voice*. When she was featured, Thompson was at the helm of her own company ASAP Communications, as well as being a board member of Britain in Europe, an observer on the Board of Business Link for London and a member of the DTI's Small Business Council.

When asked her advice for other Black women, she said: 'Stay Focused and be passionate about what you do as without the passion there's no determination, and in the end its determination and strong will that will get you through. Know what you do and be known for it. Free yourself of mental slavery and keep your eyes on the prize.'

Having experienced discrimination and prejudice throughout her career, Thompson's formula for success included having focus, determination, discipline, willpower and being single-minded. A founding member of Black-owned radio station Choice FM and a director for 15 years, Thompson said: 'The challenges are not as many as they used to be, as I mature and grow in confidence, I stand my ground. The biggest barriers are within the institutions which are still male, pale and stale. But they are fading in numbers.'

Gloria Mills CBE won acclaim for her work in trade unions. She had worked as a senior national official and manager in the trade union movement for more than 20 years, using her voice to promote equal rights and race issues. In 2005, she became the first Black woman to be elected president of the Trade Union Congress (TUC). No stranger to making history, Mills, was also the first Black woman to reach the TUC's ruling general council. She also worked as a Unison equalities champion and as a commissioner at Commission for Racial Equality. She was awarded a MBE for services to trade unions and the former Black Socialist Society chairperson, was later became a CBE.

Kanya King MBE had to re-mortgage her house to help finance the MOBO awards, which she founded. She told *The Voice*:

I have overcome a multitude of barriers throughout my career ranging from ignorance, lack of support and of course barriers can take the form of a glass ceiling. I refuse to let any prejudices prevent me from achieving my vision. Times are changing and it's never been a better time for a woman to be in business, as they have an important role to play and different skills to bring. You have to have the ability to overcome adversity, to bounce back from disappointment and face failure squarely and know how to recover from it. It's important to enjoy

NEWS

BLAIR'S FIRST LADY!

Baroness Amos takes over as head of government department

By Shirin Aguiar

THE APPOINTMENT of Valerie Amos to the British cabinet last week has been described as a watershed moment in British history.

Prime Minister Tony Blair made her head of the Department of International Development, taking over from Clare Short, who resigned over his handling of the Iraq crisis.

Leaders in the black community say the appointment will inspire young people to engage in the political process. Amos's appointment was warmly welcomed by senior race equality figures, including former CRE boss Lord Ouseley and current leader Trevor Phillips.

Lord Ouseley, who knew Amos when she served as chief executive of the Equal Opportunities Commission in the 1990s, said: "It's a great day for British politics and for our position in society to see a black woman succeed at this level. She's built up a base of respect through all she has done. She's a role model for black women, and for all women. She's a highly competent person, a doer and very practical."

Lord Ouseley – who, like Amos, is from Guyana – added that there would inevitably be expectations that she might not be able to fulfil.

Amos served in the Foreign Office, where she had responsibility for Africa, before her promotion. She is the first peer to be made head of a full-scale Whitehall department by a modern Labour leader.

She expressed delight at her promotion, performing an impromptu jig outside the Foreign Office.

'I hope her appointment will be an inspiration to black voters'

Amos's rise comes almost a year after Paul Boateng became Britain's first black cabinet minister and Tottenham MP David Lammy became a junior minister at the Department of Health.

Tony Blair trusts the single 49-year-old deeply. She was marked out for elevation after he made her his personal envoy to Africa after the last election. The PM will be hoping she can take some of the political heat out of the sensitive issue of the reconstruction of Iraq.

Trevor Phillips said the appointment was a step in the right direction and should help address apathy among black and Asian voters. He said: "I am delighted that Baroness Amos has been appointed international development secretary and wish her the best of luck in this new role. Ethnic minorities continue to be under-represented in many aspects of British politics. I hope her appointment as the first black female Cabinet minister will be an inspiration to young black and Asian voters, many of whom currently feel disengaged from British politics."

Julie Mellor, chairman of the Equal Opportunities Commission, said it was an historic day, declaring: "I hope we will see many more black and ethnic minority women following Valerie Amos into every level of politics."

However, while the plaudits flowed, some pointed out that she was not an elected representative. Linda Bellos, ex-leader of Lambeth Council, who worked with Amos at Hackney Council, was delighted but had reservations. She said: "It's really good to see a black woman in the cabinet, but she's not elected and I look forward to the time when more black women are elected. We should temper our enthusiasm with a commitment to democracy."

Amos found herself in the spotlight during the recent Zimbabwe crisis. She demonstrated courage when she attacked President Robert Mugabe in a speech in South Africa at the end of March.

She catalogued his "outrages" against human rights and dismissed his accusations that Britain was acting as a colonial power.

Her appointment also raises hopes that the African aid budget will be increased.

AMOS: Highly respected by Tony Blair.

Lady Valerie Amos

BIRTHPLACE	Guyana, 1954
EDUCATION	Townley Grammar School for Girls, Bexleyheath, Kent. Studied at the universities of Warwick, Birmingham and East Anglia and was awarded an honorary professorship at Thames Valley University in 1995 in recognition of her work on equality and social justice.
POLITICAL CAREER	Went into local government, rising to prominence as a top official for Labour-run London councils, including Lambeth, Hackney and Camden, during the '80s.
	Appointed head of the Equal Opportunities Commission in 1989. Masterminded a series of campaigns with PM Tony Blair to promote fairness at work.
	Appointed to the House of Lords after Labour's 1997 general election victory, becoming, briefly, Clare Short's spokeswoman in the Lords.
	Made a government whip in July 1998. As a Foreign Office minister her portfolio included Africa, the Caribbean and consular issues.
	Chosen by the PM to accompany him on trips last year.

'I'm so pleased for Valerie'

HEALTH minister David Lammy said: "I'm delighted, very happy and very pleased for Valerie. It's tremendous that we now have the first black woman appointed to the cabinet. Valerie is extremely capable. She has been one of the strongest voices for Africa and the Caribbean in government.

"She has a significant track record in the black community, both in her work in Lambeth and Camden and at the Equal Opportunities Commission.

"Her work in South Africa, advising the South African government and Nelson Mandela, and within government in the Foreign Office as spokeswoman for international development was outstanding.

"She has formidable talent. She's someone I respect. I was so pleased for her. I spoke to her on the day and she was surprised and very happy."

Baroness Valerie Amos was regularly celebrated by *The Voice* *as being one of a number of successful Black women breaking the glass ceiling*

what you do as success is always the by-product and not the catalyst.

In 2005 Grace Ononiwu became the first Black Chief Crown prosecutor of African Caribbean heritage. She told *The Voice* that she had always known she would end up in law. When she was eight years old, she remembered being inspired by the television programme, *Crown Court*. But she was discouraged from pursuing her dream job by a careers officer, who told her she should consider becoming a legal secretary instead.

'There is nothing wrong with that,' Ononiwu said. 'But being told I couldn't achieve my goal created a barrier in my own mind. But ambition continued burning. I had to recognise that (what was said) didn't mean that I couldn't do it. It was my responsibility to overcome these barriers.'

Ambition and determination saw her become District Crown Prosecutor and Head of the Blackfriars Trial Unit, later taking the position of Chief Crown Prosecutor for Northamptonshire.

Ononiwu advised young aspirants to recognise they have something valuable to contribute and be determined and enthusiastic to succeed. 'Everyone who spends the time to try to improve and develop themselves could be where I am today,' she said.

A legend in public service circles, Valerie Amos, Baroness of Brondesbury, started, she said, by her commitment to social justice and fairness. In addition to her 2003 appointment to the cabinet, she also became the first Black woman to become Leader of the House of Lords.

This made her only the third woman in history to lead the upper house of Parliament. 'I have never been afraid of being first. There has been the argument that if you are the first person to be selected for a role, you got there because you are

Black ... but I believe you get where you get because you are capable,' said the Guyana-born Baroness.

'Never be afraid to be first. Someone has to be.'

She credited her supportive family, who believe in the importance of education and using focus to achieve goals.

The 2000s also saw a worrying number of reports about Black people who had died in police custody. In 2003 an exclusive feature in *The Voice* revealed that campaign group Inquest reported that 655 people had died in police custody in the past 13 years, 70 of whom were Black. But so far, no police officer had been convicted of any offence in relation to any of the deaths of Black people.

In January 2007 a mother told *The Voice* how she heard her son's desperate pleas for help over the phone, minutes before he died after being arrested by police. Jason McPherson, who had asthma, phoned his mother from his mobile and left the line open as he was being arrested by police in West London on suspicion of drugs possession.

Sandra Richardson said she heard her son cry over the open line: 'Get off me, get off me – I can't breathe.' He was later pronounced dead at St Mary's Hospital in Paddington.

This was yet another death in custody and another mother's desperate plea for answers and justice.

In 2012 the Families and Friends Campaign (UFFC), called for a judicial inquiry into all suspicious deaths that occur in state care. They sought a government debate and action over almost 6,000 deaths in custody. They said the inquiry must include the deaths of people in police stations, immigration detention centres, youth and adult prisons as well as those detained under the Mental Health Act. The call followed a statistical analysis of recorded deaths in custody conducted by the Independent Advisory Panel, published in 2011.

THE VOICE

85p

Jade fades

SHILPA STAYS
P6

WorldNews Letters **Opinion**
Health **SoulStirrings** Sport
BlackHistory Features

BEYONCE TURNS ON THE STYLE
Golden Globe winners
P24

Issue No. 1253   www.voice-online.co.uk   January 22 - 28, 2007   www.jamaica-gleaner.com

WHO KILLED MY SON?

Distraught mum in desperate plea for justice after son dies in police custody

By Andrew Clunis

A MOTHER heard her son's desperate pleas for help over her mobile phone, minutes before he died in hospital, after being arrested by police. Asthma sufferer Jason McPherson telephoned his mother from his mobile and left the line open as he was being arrested by police in west London on Thursday night, on suspicion of drugs possession. Sandra Richardson said she heard her son cry over the open line: "Get off me, get off me – I can't breathe". He was later pronounced dead at St Mary's Hospital in Paddington. Now his distraught mother is desperate for answers and is demanding justice over her son's death.

See Page 3 for details

In 2007 The Voice *revealed a mother listened to her son's pleas for help over the phone minutes before he died in police custody*

The report showed there were 5,998 deaths from January 2000 to December 2010. Despite the fact there have been 11 unlawful killing verdicts since 1990, there has never been a successful prosecution.

This issue of police brutality came to a head eight years later when reports circulated that police had shot dead a Black man, Mark Duggan. Police had been tailing Duggan, who was in a mini cab. When they stopped him, police said they believe Duggan had intended to draw a weapon and shot him twice. Social media ran wild with the claims that armed officers had shot Duggan in the face in cold blood, at close range. A peaceful protest, including the Duggan family, marched from Broadwater Farm to Tottenham Police Station and demanded an explanation for the shooting.

But according to reports the unrest took hold when a 16-year-old girl demanding answers from the police was allegedly attacked by them. A number of youths then left the demonstration and set fire to police cars, a double-decker bus and buildings nearby. This was the spark that triggered the biggest riots in UK history.

In the week that followed in August 2011, youths across Britain ran rampant. Fire, rioting and looting broke out across London and other cities across the country. Unlike previous unrest, which was largely supported by Black communities, the onset this time left campaigners and the community asking; 'Have race relations gone up in flames?'

Simon Woolley told *The Voice*:

The initial protest in Tottenham was a peaceful one and asked legitimate questions. They were faced with another death at the hands of the police, with another set of shockingly conflicting reports of what happened. The

hijacking of the initial protest in Tottenham will undoubt-
edly set race relations back possibly a decade.
He added:

Politicians are not talking about racial injustice and
deprivation. Because of the looting, the focus is on thug-
gery and theft. The fallout from the looting will hand
the police stronger powers not just to deal with the looting but for a long time afterwards. Sadly, this focus I fear
will target Black communities and individuals.

Young people of colour were already seven times more likely to
be stopped and searched by police. In fact, some campaigners
told *The Voice* they knew of youngsters who had lashed out at
police because of their anger over stop and search, deaths in
custody and cuts to youth services.

Speaking to *The Voice* reporter Marc Wadsworth, Broadwater Farm campaigner Stafford Scott said:

The situation is just as bad in terms of the stopping and
searching of Black youth by the police, Black students
being thrown out of schools and unemployment.

Add to that volcanic mix the unexplained fatal
shooting of Mark Duggan and it is not difficult to see
why the Tottenham riot spawned a series of disturbances
across the UK.

People in Tottenham felt that local MP David Lammy was late
with a response as the crisis unfolded. Local youth worker
Symeon Brown pointed out that civil rights leader Martin
Luther King Jr. said riots are the voice of the unheard.

IT'S BEEN A GREAT QUARTER OF A CENTURY   THE VOICE 1982 - 2007

THE VOICE
25th YEAR OF PUBLISHING

85p

VOICE Tilda
Baby Beautiful competition is back
[see details on page 18]

Black Britain speaks
FIRST MAJOR SURVEY OF BLACK OPINION IN NEARLY TWO DECADES...
ON POLITICS, RACE, CRIME, THE STATE OF BRITAIN — AND MORE

Issue No. 1274   www.voice-online.co.uk   JUNE 18 - 24, 2007   www.jamaica-gleaner.com

WorldNewsLettersSportOpinionHealthSoulStirringsLifestyleBlackHistoryFeatures

A youth being questioned by police officers.

CRIME TRAP
BLACK BRITONS SNARED BY JUSTICE SYSTEM

RACISM WITHIN the British criminal justice system has created a crisis among black communities by criminalising young black men, a new report has revealed.

A Home Affairs Select Committee, chaired by Labour MP John Denham, looked into the overrepresentation of young black men within the criminal justice system and found that Black people of all ages are three times more likely to be arrested than white people and six times more likely to be stopped and searched by the police. This is despite no evidence that black people are more likely to commit crimes.

Three-quarters of the young black population will soon be on the DNA database. The committee cited social deprivation, educational exclusion and racial discrimination as the main reasons why a disproportionate number of black youths end up in British jails.

essentially confirming a view held by black Britons, according to a poll commissioned by The Voice. In The Voice's poll, findings from which are being published in this issue, nearly half of country's black population say

Turn to Page 9

A 2007 report also revealed Black people are three times more likely to be arrested than white people

He said: 'That doesn't mean that I expected local MP David Lammy to be a Malcolm X and spout "no justice, no peace". But I would have expected Lammy to say that, while he did not condone violence and looting, he demanded swift answers about Duggan's slaying.

'He should have voiced what many of his constituents on the streets said, "the police killing of a young man was more violent than the burning of vehicles and buildings".'

While sections of the community believed social and political injustice underlined the unrest, others condemned the looting and arson as 'wanton criminality'.

Richard Taylor of the Damilola Taylor Trust said: 'They should not forget that we are a community. They should not take matters into their own hands and destroy their communities ... We all need to work together to address concerns and we give local authorities and the mayor a chance to deal with the situation.'

Ex-footballer Ian Wright said: 'I don't want young people to ruin their lives by getting involved in the opportunist violence ... Whatever frustrations you feel, destroying our communities is not the answer.'

A Black professional told *The Voice*: 'A colleague looked at my genuine Gucci Loafers and joked, 'Where did you get those Gucci loafers? Were you out looting? I found it humiliating.'

Meanwhile a *Voice Online* reader wrote: 'In the aftermath, the decent law-abiding Black citizens have to pick up the pieces of their shattered communities, which took years to build and nurture, but only a night to destroy by gangs of marauding youths.'

The independent Riots, Communities and Victims Panel inquiry conducted shortly after the riots concluded that the factors responsible for the riots were complicated. It found that most of those arrested were not gang members. The majority were under 24, with poor academic records and at the bottom of society. 'Poor parenting' and the inability to change their lives for the better were noted as contributing factors. The inquiry also found that some crimes committed were carried out by opportunists taking advantage of the disorder.

The Voice also emboldened members of the community to hold power to account and speak out against wrongdoing. In 2003 *The Voice*'s 'Soul Stirring' columnist Marcia Dixon demanded that errant ministers should get their house in order. Marcia brought church leaders to book by setting out ten commandments intended to halt their sinful ways and have them set top-down examples of good behaviour.

She wrote: 'Last year was an *annus horribilis* for the Black church. Although much good occurred, too often headlines were for the wrong reason.'

Some of her column was aimed at a clutch of leaders who had strayed from the narrow way and found themselves in the dock. The leader of one of Britain's largest Black churches, who was accused of abusing a number of his congregation, was among the targets, and three separate allegations for financial mismanagement were made against other members of his church.

Another mega church was mentioned, which was also under scrutiny from the Charity Commission, who had sent in temporary managers to oversee the church's financial accounting. Dixon also advised Ministers to curtail their weekly prosperity gospel sermons as the lessons encourage a climate of financial greed among the congregation. Marcia admonished: 'This constant coaching on how to get wealthy is unworthy and some of it is anti-Christian.' She called for 'honesty, transparency, accountability and impartiality.' Asked for: 'less pride and more humility and diversity.'

She also criticised the custom of pastors asking their congregation to pay for prayers and blessings, citing Jesus's principle of freely giving and receiving.

She ended with advice for the backward-looking leaders to 'humble themselves, seek forgiveness and return to the true message of Christian living.'

'Amen!' resounded throughout Black Britain.

In 2007, then-London Mayor Ken Livingstone broke down in tears as he issued a formal apology for London's role in the slave trade. Livingstone marked the 200th anniversary of the abolition of the slave trade with an emotional ceremonial apology on behalf of London and its institutions. US civil rights leader, Reverend Jesse Jackson, who happened to be in Britain at the time walked over and placed his arm around the Mayor, as Livingstone dabbed tears from his eyes as he spoke. Livingstone spoke of the cruelties inflicted on the millions transported from Africa and the fact that London still benefits from the fortunes made through slavery.

He apologised, saying:

As mayor, I offer an apology on behalf of London and its institutions for their role in the transatlantic slave trade. It was the racial murder of not just those who were transported but generations of enslaved African men, women and children. To justify this murder and torture, Black people had to be declared inferior or not human. We live with the consequences today.

The Mayor issued the apology on behalf of London, and said Prime Minister Tony Blair should 'follow suit immediately.' Some months earlier, the prime minister had released a statement which said that Britain's role in the slave trade was a 'crime

20 years of campaigning excellence

THE VOICE

BRITAIN'S **BEST** BLACK PAPER 75p

ISSUE No. 1058 APRIL 14, 2003   www.voice-online.co.uk

Choose your baby/toddler of the year   See pgs 16-17

STEPHEN LAWRENCE: 10 YEARS ON ...

NO JUSTICE JUST PAIN

"I have this feeling that I should have been driving past when they attacked him. If I had been there, I might be in prison now - but I would have stopped it"
Neville Lawrence

"I am sad and disappointed that we have not been able to uphold Stephen's rights. His killers remain free and this should not be forgotten"
Doreen Lawrence

See Stephen Lawrence 10th anniversary special, pages 4, 5 and 6

20 years of campaigning excellence

THE VOICE

BRITAIN'S BEST BLACK PAPER 75p

ISSUE No. 1063 MAY 19, 2003 www.voice-online.co.uk

INSIDE
247

Fash: out of the jungle into the hotseat
PAGE 31

GINUWINE and fine

BLAIR'S FIRST LADY!

Historic move as Amos joins the cabinet

SEE PAGE 2

THE VOICE
85p

BRITAIN'S BEST BLACK NEWSPAPER

December 1-7, 2003 Issue No. 1091   www.voice-online.co.uk

24Seven

Action Jackson

Fox wants to star in biopic

ZEPH OFF MA'AM!

Rasta poet slams OBE as an insult, not an honour

EXCLUSIVE BY ANDREW CLUNIIS

CONTROVERSIAL POET Benjamin Zephaniah is calling on the Queen to apologise to African Caribbean people for the atrocities committed by the British Empire during slavery.

After refusing an OBE last week, the firebrand wordsmith challenged PM Tony Blair to discuss issues affecting the black community with him.

And he called on the monarchy to accept responsibility for slavery, declaring: "I get angry when I hear the word 'empire'. It reminds me of slavery. OBE? No way, Mrs Queen. I am profoundly anti-empire."

SEE PAGE 10

Zephaniah believes the Queen should say sorry for slavery

Picture: COLIN PATTERSON

Vivica ready for Whitney

KILL BILL star Vivica A Fox wants to play Whitney Houston in a biopic of the singer's life – because she thinks it's time the troubled songbird was painted in a positive light.

The 39-year-old actress believes she could play the R'n'B diva, who has had a drugs problem, in the way Angela Bassett portrayed Tina Turner in *What's Love Got To Do With It?*. She said: "She has been very overlooked both in terms of music and acting. She was fabulous in *The Bodyguard*. People forget how great she was."

Pick Miss
Jamaica UK
2006
See page 8

THE
VOICE
85p

COMING IN
The Voice
The Londoner
September 25

Issue No. 1235   www.voice-online.co.uk   September 11 – 17, 2006   www.jamaica-gleaner.com

EQUAL WRONGS

Community upset as Phillips is named equalities chief

By Dominic Bascombe

EQUALITIES campaigners have slammed the appointment of Trevor Phillips as head of the new Commission on Equalities and Human Rights. Phillips, who is current head of the Commission for Racial Equality (CRE) has been accused of undermining the credibility of the CRE and reducing its effectiveness. He has fallen out of favour with BME groups over his stance on integration and multi-culturalism and he was broadsided by London Mayor Ken Livingstone for 'pandering to right-wing views'. His detractors say his appointment will seriously deter progress in race relations in the UK.

❝ Commission for Racial Equality used as a career stepping stone – Lee Jasper

❝ It's absolutely disgraceful – Mayor Ken Livingstone

❝ It's a terrible decision – Milena Buyum of the National Assembly Against Racism

❝ We're very unhappy that the new CEHR is being set up against the background of uneven and unequal equality laws – Peter Tatchell, of gay rights group Outrage ❞

THE VOICE

FREE

25th

YEAR OF PUBLISHING

RACIST MANCHESTER TEEN SLAPPED WITH 2 YEAR ASBO

SEE PAGE 13

Issue No. 1,285(B)   www.voice-online.co.uk   SEPTEMBER 3 - 9, 2007   www.jamaica-gleaner.com

WorldNewsLettersSportOpinionHealthSoulStirringsLifestyleBlackHistoryFeatures

MANDELA FOREVER

'MADIBA' GETS PERMANENT PLACE ON ONE OF THE MOST POWERFUL SQUARES IN THE WORLD

WORLD STATESMAN Nelson Mandela was last week immortalised in statue at Westminster Square, just outside the British Houses of Parliament. His bronze memorial joins those of other world figures including Britain's Second World War leader Winston Churchill and the 19th anti-slavery president of the United States Abraham Lincoln. The statue of former South African Prime Minister General Jan Smuts also stands in the Square. Mr Mandela, whose life is defined by his triumphant fight against apartheid which included a 27-year-prison term, is the only person honoured with having a statue placed in such a prominent space while still alive.

Supermodel Naomi Campbell reaches out to Nelson Mandela's statue while proud members of the black community, (l-r) Jeanette Arnold AM, Diane Abbott MP, David Lammy MP, Dawn Butler MP, Baroness Valerie Amos and Lee Jasper, Senior Advisor to London Mayor Ken Livingstone look on.

20 years of campaigning excellence

THE VOICE

BRITAIN'S *BEST* BLACK PAPER 75p

ISSUE No. 1052 MARCH 3, 2003 www.voice-online.co.uk

STEVIE WONDER:
Legendary singer is one of many big names expected to appear at anti-gun bash.

SONGS ARE THE KEY TO LIFE

Anti-gun concert gets backing from Stevie

A MASSIVE anti-gun concert to kick off a month-long weapons amnesty is to receive a huge boost with the likes of Sean 'P.Diddy' Combs and the legendary Stevie Wonder being lined up to appear.

The Voice can exclusively reveal that the concert, earmarked for the London Arena in Docklands, is to be the high-profile centrepiece of the guns amnesty in May.

Other stars who have been approached include Ms Dynamite, So Solid Crew, Mica Paris,

EXCLUSIVE
by Shirin Aguiar

Mis-Teeq and Run DMC from the USA.

Last week So Solid's Megaman told *The Voice*: "This gun violence thing has to stop. The glamorous path isn't always the best path. We have to think of ourselves as a unit."

● See full story on pages 4 and 5.

Issue No. 1422A   May 10 - 16, 2010

THE **VOICE** 85p

www.voice-online.co.uk

HEART 2 HEART

THE PLACE TO FIND YOUR SOULMATE

Page 42

IN THE HOUSE!

General Election creates NINE black MPs - Double the previous number

Pages 8 - 9

MUST READ FEATURES!

What's on this weekend *Steppin' out*
Pages 32-33

Dear Prime Ministers, Page 14

Reggae Icon: Jimmy Cliff Page 25

Issue No. 1506 JANUARY 5 - 11, 2012

See special reports pages 2-6

Britain's top black weekly

THE VOICE

90p

www.voice-online.co.uk

Stephen Lawrence:
The fight for justice

JUSTICE AT LAST!

...but shock *Voice* poll says nothing has changed since murder

STRUGGLE: The Lawrence family

973

EDUCATION PULL-OUT
See pages 27 to 30

WEST MIDLANDS SUPPLEMENT
See inside

THE VOICE 25th
YEAR OF PUBLISHING

85p

WIN 4 FREE AIR TICKETS TO NIGERIA
See page 36

WIN BUMPER CD COLLECTION & TICKETS FOR GREENSLEEVES 30TH BIRTHDAY!
See page 26

Issue No. 1,284(A)   www.voice-online.co.uk   AUGUST 27 - SEPTEMBER 2, 2007   www.jamaica-gleaner.com

WorldNewsLettersSportOpinionHealthSoulStirringsLifestyleBlackHistoryFeatures

WEEPING KEN

Mayor sheds tears as he apologises for slavery and launches London Memorial Day

Ken Livingstone

MAYOR KEN Livingstone broke down in tears last week as he issued a formal apology for London's role in the slave trade and backed calls for the Government to declare August 23 as Slavery Memorial Day in Britain.

The Voice had exclusively reported last week that Livingstone would issue the apology at a civic function at City Hall, to mark the International Day for the Remembrance of the Slave Trade and its Abolition, whose commemoration is promoted by UNESCO.

Among Livingstone's guests at last Thursday's event was the Rev. Jesse Jackson, the black US civil rights leader who was in Britain supporting the 1990 Trust's new initiative – Equanomics-UK – a vehicle, which its fashioners hope to use for economic research and analysis and to encourage the BME community to flex its economic muscle to shape the national agenda.

SEE STORIES ON PAGES 2-3

Rev. Jesse Jackson addresses audience in Bristol

Black power through economics

A NEW initiative, aimed at bringing black economic power to the centre of the discourse on race and the empowerment of Britain's black and ethnic minority communities, is being launched here with the support of the US civil rights leader, Jesse Jackson, who traipsed across the UK last week helping to promote the idea.

SEE FULL STORY ON PAGES 2-3

London Mayor Ken Livingstone shed tears and apologised for London's role in the slave trade in 2007

against humanity' and expressed 'deep sorrow' that it happened. But he had stopped short of making a full apology.

A week later, after seven years of struggle and argument about permission, positioning, funding and location, Nelson Mandela's memorial bronze statue finally found a home at Parliament Square, Westminster. A packed square welcomed the former South African President for the unveiling. Prime Minister Gordon Brown led the tributes alongside Ken Livingstone. Mandela's second wife Graca Machel was among those on the podium. Among the other VIPs were David Cameron, writer Ben Okri, supermodel Naomi Campbell and Queen's guitarist Brian May. Reverend Jesse Jackson was also there to support his friend.

Crowds packed the square to welcome the statesman who they had grown to know as 'Madiba'. The ceremony was a success, but an undercurrent of quiet discontent had run through the crowd when they arrived and caught sight of the casually clad statue. Perplexingly to many, the monument stood near ground level within reach of a pat on the head. Many felt that 'the man of the people' monument was not as impressive as other memorials hoisted on towering plinths, and out of the reach of ordinary people.

Nelson Mandela said the statue and its sitting would have pleased his friend and former Leader Oliver Tambo. 'Oliver would have been proud to have been here,' he said.

Over the course of the decade *The Voice* highlighted a variety of healthcare issues, from uncovering care scandals to celebrating heroic campaigners.

The tragic death of eight-year-old Victoria Climbie, who was fostered by her aunt for a better life, must have sent lightning bolts through many first-generation parents who relied on the help of extended family as they pursued work or study as young parents. Born in 1991 on the Ivory Coast, Victoria was taken to France, then England, by her abusive great-aunt, who later murdered the child with her boyfriend. The Laming report into Victoria's death, published in 2003, blamed 'poor practice within and between social services, the police and the health agencies'. It said the tragedy was a consequence of ineffective and inept management among a catalogue of other errors.

Chilling stories are told by Caribbean children left behind and raised by extended family, a role reversal in the case of Victoria Climbie. The evil perpetrated against babies and toddlers, whose cases have reached the courts in recent years is truly shocking. And the cases are even more disturbing when we learn that the abuse had consistently gone unchallenged by care teams and law enforcement officers who are paid and trusted to take action when a child's life is at risk.

In the same year, another report was published into the death of two-year-old Ainlee Labonte, who died in 2002. Ainlee's mother Leanne Labonte, 20, and her boyfriend Dennis Henry, 39, were both found guilty of the child's death and were sentenced to ten and 12 years in prison respectively.

'Newham Council gets off "Scot-Free" reported *The Voice* after the independent report into Ainlee's death, which under its protection, was branded a whitewash.

A catalogue of failings between healthcare and social services staff was listed as contributing to the child's death, but the council said that none of its staff would be disciplined for the 'shortcomings'.

Ainlee's tragic death was blamed on 'collective' rather than 'individual' failure.

But the December 2003 report investigating Newham's child protection role after the abuse came to light was woefully lacking, and stopped short of holding the local authority social services team responsible.

The Council was accused of failing to protect the child after several referrals were made to Social Services. Frequent police visits to the violent household were on record, but it came to light that Social Services had closed the casefile as far back as May 2000 when the child was only 11 months old.

The report blasted the local authority for repeatedly failing to protect the two-year old from her parents but concluded that 'Ainlee got lost in the system.'

It was therefore understandable that both reports caused fury and distraught when the news hit the community.

Sadly, lessons were not learned and we have seen the same neglectful local authority scenarios played out again and again within social services departments, resulting in the death of many more children.

The Voice was inundated with letters and emails condemning the results of the report. One Londoner said: 'We have heard this kind of thing before, children are suffering and there's no guarantee that it's not going to happen again.'

In 2008 tributes poured in following the loss of one of the most inspirational young men within the Black community. Daniel De-Gale, whose childhood battle against leukaemia inspired a surge in bone marrow donors from Black communities, died surrounded by his family.

The 21-year-old London Metropolitan University undergraduate aspired to be a physiotherapist and completed a year of his BSc Honours degree course in sports therapy. In an interview with *The Voice*, he described himself as a 'thrill seeker.' 'I love experiencing adrenaline rushes and living life on the edge. Life is too short not to have fun,' he said.

'Everybody should learn to live life to the max and be grateful for each day that God gives us.' Despite his youth, Daniel lived up to his own words and experienced a rich life, meeting personal heroes as he campaigned for more people to register as donors.

In 2012 Orin Lewis, co-founder of the African Caribbean Leukemia Trust (ACLT), was honoured with an OBE. He said he felt 'deeply touched' after collecting his award.

Lewis was awarded for his contribution to healthcare and accepted the OBE on behalf of his children, family and everyone associated with the life-saving work of the ACLT.

The ACLT was set up with partner Beverley De-Gale to raise awareness of the need for Black and mixed-race donors, while trying to find a matching bone marrow donor for his stepson Daniel De-Gale.

Daniel later found a donor and overcame childhood leukemia. But he sadly died at age 21, in 2008 from an unrelated health condition.

The arrival of *SS Empire Windrush* in Britain in 1948 carrying 492 passengers from the Caribbean is considered a key moment in the development of multi ethnic Britain. The newcomers had travelled to the UK on the invitation of the government. Faced with a serious labour shortage following the devastation of World War II, an appeal went out to commonwealth citizens to start a new life in Britain helping to rebuild the war-torn country.

But as Britain celebrated the sixtieth anniversary of the arrival of the Windrush Generation in 2008, another side of the story was also told by *The Voice*. While most of the public consider the Windrush Scandal to have been uncovered in 2018, *The Voice* uncovered a different scandal a decade earlier.

The paper told of how the Windrush Generation's hope and aspiration had turned to isolation and hardship over the years. One of the stories the article highlighted was George's. The Hammersmith pensioner, who arrived in Britain from Jamaica in the late 1960s, had lived in the same council-owned bedsit since he moved to London, but the council had failed to maintain living standards for George. The pensioner's plight was discovered by workers at a day centre for African Caribbean elders, which George attended.

'He was a regular at our group but after a while we noticed that his whole demeanour had changed and that he was becoming depressed and uncommunicative' centre manager Jazz Lewis Brown told *The Voice*:

> It was then that he told us about the situation he was in. And it was then that we got involved. When we visited him at his bedsit, we were shocked at what we saw and we asked if we could take pictures. You could clearly see from the pictures that there had been no repairs done to this property in a very long time. It was shabby and run down, the paint had no colour, and in some cases was peeling off the walls. It was really horrible to see.

Immediately Brown and her team got on the phone to the council. Within six months, George was rehoused in a one-bedroom flat with new furniture.

But George's case was not an isolated one. Many members of the Windrush Generation faced homelessness, mental health problems and disconnection from utility services because often they were too afraid or too confused to question contentious decisions made by utility services, local councils and care agencies.

Brown told the paper that many members of the Windrush Generation had negative experiences of dealing with bureaucracy when they arrived in Britain in the 1950s and 1960s, experiences that were rooted in racism. As a result, elders developed a fear that they would lose what care or support they received if they complained about an expensive bill or healthcare they were not happy with. It's a situation that amounts to what Brown calls 'institutional abuse'.

She said:

> We have to recognise that a number of these elders, when they first came to this country, had minimal contact with local authority and social service agencies and so now that they are old, they are reluctant to engage with them. These people have made the ultimate sacrifice. They moved from a place which they knew and which they loved. They came over to an inhospitable environment to start families and now in their hour of need they are being left to fend for themselves. People of younger generations need to recognise that they have to step forward to improve the quality of life for our elders in their later stages. A lot of us are in good positions in life because of the journey that they've made, so we need to honour that journey by contributing back.

As we entered the new millennium, the Black community's contribution to the arts was more widely celebrated than ever. But in 2003 dancehall music became mired in controversy when reggae artists including Beenie Man, Elephant Man and Bounty Killer were threatened with legal action from lesbian and gay rights campaign OutRage!

The dancehall stars were due to visit the UK for the MOBO Awards, but as a consequence of the trio's homophobic lyrics OutRage! spokesman Peter Tatchell presented a ten-page dossier to the Metropolitan Police hate crimes unit demanding for the artists to be jailed if they set foot in the country. The artists's management claimed that much of their lyrics were metaphorical, but Tatchell was not deterred.

He said: 'We object to the inciting of violence against people, which is clearly put in a song as the beating, shooting and burning of lesbians and gay men. We would adopt the same attitude if a white singer advocated violence against Black people.' The artists eventually decided against the UK visit. The campaign signaled a revision of attitudes by raga and dancehall artists whose charted hits came to be labeled 'murder music.'

The 2000s saw an increased visibility for Black artists and writers, and in 2003 the news that acclaimed poet Benjamin Zephaniah had rejected an OBE was met with surprise, pride and humour. Speaking to *The Voice*, Zephaniah said:

> It's remarkable. I've had people coming up to me in the streets saying: Thank you. You dared to do what many others never would. It tells me that there are Black people here who are ready to work on the new British project, which is to bring our community up to a level where we see equal rights and justice manifested.

Zephaniah felt that leaders were failing the community and were drunk with power.

He said: 'There are too many coconuts in office playing to the establishment.' In his 2001 book *Too Black. Too Strong*, he says many people in high office are not serving their community.

Zephaniah refused the award because he did not want to give legitimacy to the monarchy. 'I have to be critical in my work. If I had accepted it, would I have been able to criticise them?'

After refusing the award, Zephaniah invited PM Tony Blair for a sit down to discuss Black community issues.

> He said: 'I have been trying for months to talk to Tony Blair about my cousin Mikey Powell, who died in police custody in Birmingham. He hasn't responded. And clearly they have not read my work because if they had, they wouldn't even have considered me. I consider it an insult. I don't take tokens. I don't do my work so that I can belong to an empire that was built off the sweat, blood and tears of my forefathers. I don't write to win awards. I get my respect in the street. When I saw the letter, my first reaction was "Up yours".

He added: 'Come on, Tony Blair, I'll meet you any time. I'll talk about your Home Office being tough on crime and about the disgusting way we are being policed. Let's talk about why there are so many guns in the Black community.'

A year later, the BBC came under fire for perpetuating harmful stereotypes rather than investing in positive programming for the Black community. Black media professionals raised their concerns over the BBC's constant negative portrayal of Black people. The complaints centred on a three-part documentary – *The Trouble with Black Men: A Polemic* – that commentators said described Black men as lazy, promiscuous and family wreckers.

In a move to redress the balance, *The Voice* launched its own campaign to highlight positive male role models.

Film magazine publisher Menelik Shabazz said; 'The Black community does not have a problem with controversial programmes that stimulate debate. But we do have a problem when negative programmes are all we see.'

But in 2008, Lenny Henry blasted the BBC and ITV for not employing enough Black actors and staff. Henry heavily criticised the television industry, accusing them of discriminating against ethnic minorities. He said TV had not moved on from the 'Alf Garnett' generation of programmes and said racism was rife in the industry.

He told *The Voice*: 'When I first started watching TV, there were no Black people on it at all. That was in the days of black and white television. They should have called it white and white television.'

Calling for 'affirmative' action in order to increase the number of Black and Asian people, Henry told *The Voice* that 'urgent steps were needed to give people who did not benefit from an Oxbridge education the chance to get a job in the industry.'

That year the National Film and Television Awards Survey also reported that 84 per cent of the Black community thought there wasn't a strong enough Black presence on television or at the movies.

The underrepresentation of Black people on British TV revealed that those surveyed could name their favourites among Americans in film and TV, but were unfamiliar with the work of new British stars such as Thandiwe Newton, Chiwetel Ejiofor, Colin Salmon and Naomie Harris.

The Voice reader Sharon Fearon said: 'We need to see Black actors in magazines and TV adverts.'

In 2006 The Voice *questioned whether Leona Lewis would become the first Black winner of the X Factor*

Monica Clarke added: 'If they are not exposed to us and we are not given information about them, we will never know who they are.'

In the 2000s television had been taken over by reality and competition formats. Among these programmes, talent shows such as *The X Factor* produced water cooler television as well as providing a platform for talented Black stars of the future.

In 2002 the soul singer Lemar finished third on the BBC's *Fame Academy*, while future West End star and television presenter Brenda Edwards came fourth on *The X Factor* in 2005. But by the middle of the decade, no Black person had won a reality TV contest in the UK.

So when a 21-year-old Leona Lewis started to progress in the 2006 series of *The X Factor*, *The Voice* echoed concerns she might not win because of her race.

'She's young, a smashing beauty and a super talent. But do all these attributes add up to *The X Factor*? Sighting a long list of previous talent show competitors who were strong contenders and tipped for the top but lost out before the final' *Voice* reporter Janelle Oswald wrote: 'The reality is, none of them ever won. Some have gone on to have successful careers, often outshining those who beat them in the finals. But the fact is, when it comes to the crunch, females and non-white males simply do not get the public endorsement on the night – when it matters most.'

Leona's mother Maria said: 'It is hard to think that my daughter could never win *The X-Factor* because she is Black. There's never been a Black reality talent show winner in Britain. Racism does play a part.'

Thankfully Leona did win the £1 million recording contract with more than 8 million votes, 60 per cent of the total.

Just two years later, 20-year-old Alexandra Burke became the second person of colour to win *The X Factor*. The final show attracted a whopping 15 million to see her duet with Beyoncé. Boyband JLS we also thrilled to finish in second place.

In 2009, the BBC aired an all-Black episode of *EastEnders*, which drew in an audience of 8.4million viewers. A BBC first, the popular soap included references to civil rights leader Martin Luther King Jr. and racism. The episode showed a viewer increase of more than one in comparison to episodes that aired around the same time.

The show centered on the Trueman and Fox families, and no white characters were featured for the first time in the soap's 23-year history. The BBC has previously featured episodes with an all-female and all-Asian cast, but this is the first time all the performers were Black. However, the BBC received more than 200 complaints over the ground breaking episode.

In 2011, Black Britain was shocked by the sudden death of cheeky chappie and reggae icon Smiley Culture. Smiley, whose real name was David Emmanuel, was charged with conspiracy to supply drugs but a few days before the trial it was reported he had died while a police search took place at his house.

Emmanuel's family was told that Smiley had taken his own life. That he had stabbed himself while making a cup of tea, despite the presence of four police officers. The family was not convinced by the police explanation and sought community help to investigate the incident that led to their relative's death. Protesters and sympathisers organised a march past Parliament, ending in a rally outside New Scotland Yard, calling for a public inquiry into the sudden death of the reggae star.

The protesters chanted 'No Justice, No Peace', played reggae music and carried placards reading 'No more deaths in police custody' and 'Who killed Smiley Culture?'

A post-mortem examination revealed that Smiley had died from a single stab wound to the heart.

The death was investigated by the Independent Police Complaints Commission, which returned a verdict of suicide. It stated there was no evidence of misconduct that justified pressing criminal charges against any of the four officers who carried out the raid. The final report was not made public nor was it available to Smiley's family.

However, the report said the raid was 'significantly flawed' and called for the Metropolitan Police to improve the planning and execution of drug raids.

Smiley's family said they felt let down and that there were many unanswered questions surrounding the death. The Black and wider community remained unconvinced that the verdict and investigations told the whole truth.

The beginning of the 2010s, however, saw an explosion of Black talent in film and music. In 2011 Daniel Kaluuya and Labrinth were named in a list compiled by *The Voice* of budding talent, aged 25 and under, from the worlds of TV, music, business and fashion. 22-year-old artist Labrinth released the UK number one hit, *Pass Out* – a collaboration with rapper Tinie Tempah.

21-year-old Daniel Kaluuya became one of the youngest people to pen an hour-long episode of drama for prime-time television when, at 18, he was asked to write a full episode of the BAFTA Award-winning E4 programme, *Skins*. He later starred in the acclaimed Jordan Peele horror film *Get Out*, as well as in Marvel's *Black Panther*.

But despite the plethora of Black talent, the 2012 BRIT Awards attracted criticism for ignoring too many Black musical acts. Just two of the 48 2012 BRIT Award nominees were Black – JLS, and newcomer Emeli Sandé. In an online poll from *The Voice*, readers were asked 'Do you think that the BRIT Awards represent Black talent?' An overwhelming 85 per cent of readers responded 'No.'

Over the course of the 2-00s Black British sport blossomed into an international powerhouse, culminating in a triumphant summer Olympics and the birth of a motorsport superhero.

At the Sydney Olympics in 2000, Audley Harrison became the first British super heavyweight to win gold. By that time, he was already a Commonwealth champion and well placed to step out of the amateur ranks and make his name as a professional. From 2001–05, the Londoner won his first 19 professional bouts, including 14 knockouts. During that run, in 2004, he claimed the WBF heavyweight title, when he stopped Dutch fighter Richel Hersisia in the fourth round at Wembley Arena.

Injuries were to curtail Harrison's progress over the next few years and even though there were moments when his boxing career seemed to be over, Harrison returned to winning ways in 2009 at the one-night Prizefighter tournament in London.

While he received adulations from fans across the community, Harrison could not always win over the press. In an interview with *The Voice*, he said: 'The British public have been magnificent to me. I can honestly say that there has not been a single negative letter, no matter what the press might have written about me. I've got the skills to pay the bills.'

Harrison's true legacy, however, is as an Olympian who played a fundamental role in securing funding for the GB Boxing World Class Programme. Harrison marched to Parliament with a petition of 2,000 names and handed it to then-minister for sport Tony Banks. The subsequent funding of the programme bene-fited the likes of Amir Khan, Anthony Joshua and Joshua Buatsi.

When she was interviewed for *The Voice*'s Olympic special issue ahead of the 2004 Athens games, Kelly Holmes knew exactly what she wanted to achieve.

'I am very focused at the moment because I realise that this is my last chance at the Olympics and I personally want to do as best as I can in my last few years as a competitor,' she said. And sure enough, just a few weeks later, Holmes won gold in both the 800m and 1500m. With two Commonwealth golds already under her belt, she was able to retire with her reputation as Brit-ain's greatest female long-distance runner secure.

Holmes, who was born in Kent to an English mother and Jamaican-born father, joined the British Army at the age of 18 and eventually reached the rank of sergeant. Holmes was later crowned the service's judo champion and, at one athletics event she won the 800m, 3000m, a relay race and the heptathlon on the same day. She was set on the path to elite athletics during the 1992 Barcelona Olympics where she watched British run-ner Lisa York competing in the televised heats.

Holmes had previously taken on and beaten York so knew that she could reach the required level. She combined her ath-letics career with her work as an army PT and eventually went full-time in 1997.

By then, she was already a Commonwealth cham-pion, claiming 1500m gold in Victoria in 1994, and later stood on the podium at the European Championships, World Cham-pionships and World Indoor Championships. Her second 1500m Commonwealth gold came in Manchester in 2002. Hol-mes was made an MBE in 1998 for services to the British Army and, upon her retirement from the track, was elevated to Dame for services to athletics.

It was thanks to the tireless work of Holmes and fellow athletes such as Denise Lewis that London won its bid to host the 2012 Olympics in 2005. As the city geared up to host the ultimate international sporting event, *The Voice* was delighted to hear that the stadium was to be built in East London, a historically diverse area of the capital.

But, as the Olympics drew closer, the paper discovered with horror that they had been denied accreditation to report from the Games itself. Sports editor Rodney Hinds told the *Guardian* the decision was 'outrageous', while managing director George Ruddock told the paper: 'We are truly disappointed that *The Voice* which has covered the glorious achievements of British, African and Caribbean athletes for many years will not be inside the Olympic stadium.'

However, following petitions and high-profile figures such as Boris Johnson and Nick Ferrari lending their support, *The Voice* gained accreditation days later.

One sportsman in particular defined *The Voice*'s sports coverage in the 2000s. He first appeared on the paper's sports pages in 2000 when he was a talented kart racer with a drive to succeed. The news report read: 'He has only just turned 15, yet his skills are such that one of the most powerful men in motor racing – Ron Dennis of Formula 1 World Championship winning team McClaren Mercedes – has now become his personal racing manager. This young man happens to be Black, and his name is Lewis Hamilton.'

In the years to come, Hamilton would establish himself as one of the greatest drivers of all time, winning seven World Drivers' Championship titles, equalling Michael Schumacher's

SPORT SPORT SPORT SPORT SPORT SPORT SPORT SPORT SPORT SPORT SPORT SPORT SPORT SPORT SPORT SPORT SPORT SPORT SPORT SPORT

HINDSIGHT

with
RODNEY HINDS

ZIMBABWE and Pakistan's cricketers must be rubbing their hands in glee. In just a few days' time Zimbabwe's inexperienced cricketers take on the West Indies while the team from the sub-continent engage in battle later in the month. Both sets of tourists are no doubt fired up by the fact that Caribbean cricket is at its lowest ebb for ages.

The Windies are being led by a trio of newcomers in the management team – so you can see why the home side could be in for a torrid time.

New captain Jimmy Adams, coach Roger Harper and assistant Jeff Dujon should not underestimate the task they have been assigned. Make no mistake, the resurgence of cricket in the region is firmly in their hands.

After years of woeful displays at home and abroad, they now have to lead players and supporters towards the light at the end of what has been a very, very dark tunnel.

Supporters will still come out in droves wanting above all to see their team play with pride. Defeat faced with class pulled out isn't acceptable but can be tolerated. Defeat faced with apathy is totally unacceptable to those of us who hold the team dear.

Sadly, former skipper Brian Lara seems to have an air of just such apathy around him and has decided to take a rest. While many resent his decision, I think it gives the rest of the team the chance to show exactly what they can do without the player who is still the best batsman that we possess.

Now Sherwin Campbell, Shivnarine Chanderpaul and other senior figures must step up to the plate and deliver the goods. Jimmy Adams would appear to be more of a 'team' man than Lara but that point is negated by the fact that he is never going to destroy a bowling attack like the little left-hander from Trinidad.

I don't expect to see too much improvement from the Windies over the next month. It will take time to pull back from the abyss.

For all their naivety Zimbabwe are making progressive strides in the international arena, with the likes of all-rounder Henry Olonga leading the way. And we all know what the Pakistanis are capable of. They won't be lenient with our boys simply because we are in disarray. In fact they will probably go for the proverbial jugular.

All we can hope is that the Windies pull together so that by the time they come to England in May they are ready to do battle. How the mighty have fallen!

GOT A STORY? WE'D LIKE TO HEAR IT!

Email:
sportsdesk@the-voice.co.uk

RACE TO

TOP level motor racing is one of the hardest sports in the world to get into. More than any other major sport it requires enormous amounts of money to become a champion.

But that doesn't mean you can buy talent. It has to be nurtured, developed, moulded, and for world class motor racing, it has to be as finely tuned as the powerful engine beneath the hood. Those with money but no talent have short careers. No other sport in the world is tougher at the top than Formula 1.

Every once in a while a star is born.

In Formula 1 at the present time it's Michael Schumacher. Before him it was Ayrton Senna. Now there is a new star in the making, and he races karts, the breeding ground for tomorrow's Formula 1 stars. With the help of his father, he's been nurturing his racing talents since he was only eight years old.

He has only just turned 15, yet his skills are such that one of the most powerful men in motor racing – Ron Dennis of Formula 1 World Championship winning team McLaren Mercedes has now become his personal racing manager. This young man happens to be black, and his name is Lewis Hamilton.

Champion

At 15 years old, Lewis is probably the most talked about, written about and photographed kart racing drivers in the United Kingdom, if not the world. By the age of 10 he was the youngest driver ever to win the British Junior Kart Championship, and the only kart driver ever to hold the British Junior Kart Championship, the McLaren Mercedes Champions of the Future Title, the SKY Kart Masters, UK Five Nations, and the Northern Ireland

Championships at the same time.

In 1997 Lewis again established himself as a true champion by winning both the 1997 McLaren Mercedes Champions of the Future series and the 1997 Junior Yamaha British Kart Championship.

In 1998, in the Junior Intercontinental 'A' Class, Lewis won both opening rounds of the RAC British Championship and the McLaren Mercedes Champions of the Future Series, finishing second in the Championship overall.

Lewis was subsequently invited to test for the Italian Top Kart Comer Team based in Parma Italy. The test proved successful and Lewis was then offered a contract to race in Italy for the end of 1998 and all of 1999.

That contract entailed racing in the junior intercontinental 'A' class, in the Italian championships, and the European championships.

Money

Lewis finished third in the championship and won the first final of the Junior European championships. He started on pole for the main final and finished second in the race – all this at only 14 years old!

In a word, Lewis Hamilton has talent. In fact, he is regarded by many as a teenage prodigy who may eventually achieve the heights of some of the greatest racing drivers the world has ever seen. He has already achieved more in karting than either Senna or Schumacher had achieved by his age. That's going some.

Lewis's talent has already helped him to take care of the other side of the motor racing equation that often sees many rising stars become short-lived entities: it's called money. Motor racing isn't cheap. Racing mag F1 Racing

EXPENSIVE RIDE: Karting can cost up to £150,000 a year per team.

CHASING THE BIG WIN AT CHELTENHAM

THIS year's Cheltenham Festival (March 14-16) will see some of the sport's finest hurdlers and chasers try to land the big prizes at the most eagerly-awaited meeting of the season, with much of the Irish turf industry – horses, trainers, jockeys and punters – descending on the West Country in search of a long-priced winner.

Day One will have as its highlight the Smurfit Champion Hurdle over two-and-a-half miles.

For a winner you do not have to look further than trainer Martin Pipe's Nicolashayne stable in nearby Devon. Pipe looks likely to have four runners in the big race: Far Cry, Make A Stand, Rodock and Watihba Sands.

Other horses that represent good value are the Venetia Williams-trained Lady Rebecca and French hope Hors

La Loi fil, both of whom are course and distance winners.

The feature on the second day at Cheltenham is the Queen Mother Champion Chase over two miles. Champion trainer Pipe will be represented by six-year-old Majadou. But it will be difficult to oppose the Paul Nicholls-trained Flagship Uber Alles.

Comfortable

Scheduled to be ridden by the improving Joe Tizzard, Flagship was a comfortable distance winner the last time out at Newbury.

Good each way bets for the Queen Mother chase would be Decoupage and Nordance Prince, who, despite having fallen on the last two occasions, is a quality animal.

Thursday's Tote Cheltenham Gold Cup is second only to the Grand National when it comes to prestige and

the pleasure of having a flutter. Even though it's hard to look beyond last year's winner See More Business (13-8), there are one or two experienced chasers in the race who may give good value.

Pipe could land the big race with the highly impressive Gloria Victis (20-1), who dominated the opposition last time out at Kempton. His other entry is the exotic-sounding Tresor De Mai.

Looks Like Trouble (5-1), to be ridden by the talented Norman Williamson, and the Mark Pitman-trained Ever Blessed (12-1) are other horses worth noting for the three mile, two furlong slog. Pitman, who has taken over the reins from his popular mother Jenny, will be hoping that some of her big race magic rubs off on him and the residents of his Upper Lambourn yard.

Last time out Brother of Iris (14-1)

was a major disappointment, destroyed by Gloria Victis.

If jockey Lorcan Wyer can keep the seven-year-old focused he must be that a good run in the season's biggest race so far. Experience is a great thing around the demanding course and last year's runner-up Go Ballistic (16-1) will have the relevant know-how to get round the undulating track. For me Flagship Uber Alles and Gloria Victis are the two horses that might just represent some consolation for not winning the lottery.

Good news is you can bet on all of Cheltenham's races without leaving the comfort of your home. All of the main bookmakers accept bets by Switch and Delta cards, and can be called on freephone numbers. The above odds for the Gold Cup are only estimates. Prices are subject to fluctuation.

Garrison Savannah

The Voice *championed the career of Lewis Hamilton from an early age, first reporting on his successes back in 2000*

record. Despite this, long-standing sports editor Rodney Hinds noted that the superstar always had time to speak to *The Voice* at his press conferences.

Born in Stevenage, racing for Hamilton was a family affair. His father Anthony, who is of Grenadian descent, encouraged his participation in the sport and bought him his first go-kart when he was just six years old. After introducing himself to McLaren boss Ron Dennis in 1994, he was signed to the team's driver development scheme in 1998.

Nine years later he burst on to the F1 scene, coming second in the driver's championship in his rookie season. Since then he has gone on to dominate the sport, consistently performing at the top of his game. When he won his seventh world championship in 2020, *The Voice* ran a special eight-page tribute edition which hailed the star as 'Simply The Best'.

While Hamilton's achievements on the track have been a key focus for *The Voice*, the paper has also tracked how his rising star has inspired other young people in the Black community to aspire to racing success. When the driver equalled Schumacher's seven world titles in 2020, *The Voice* spoke to three young men hoping to follow in Hamilton's footsteps.

The trio were all supported by BAME Motorsports Foundation. The charity, launched by their respective fathers, aims to help, guide and support young people keen to get behind the wheel and emulate Hamilton's success.

13-year-old Aaron Mensah said: 'I got into racing because I saw Lewis Hamilton win his second world championship on television and realised it was something I wanted to do when I was older. I started watching videos of him and I was even more inspired.'

Corey Alleyne, 18, who started competing in the sport in his teens, said: 'I first started by watching F1 and loving the sport but never knew how to get into it. But my Dad found out that there was a karting championship doing a race in Cork and we went and looked at everything and talked to some teams. We spoke to as many people who knew about what they were doing, and we met a mechanic who actually bought our first car for us.

'He found it on the internet, we paid him back and he tested me three times – at the end of that we realised I was ready to start a championship, so we did.'

Joshua Bugembe – the youngest of the trio at ten years old – was already lauded as a driver of the future by Motorsport UK.

Joshua said: 'He [Hamilton] makes me feel really excited because it's a lot of world records that he's beaten and he's carrying on to beat them. I just want him to have the most world records in F1 until I go up there and then I want to beat him!'

As *The Voice* entered its thirtieth year, and almost two decades after teenager Stephen Lawrence was murdered by racist thugs, parents Neville and Doreen finally saw two men jailed for the crime. David Norris and Gary Dobson were found guilty of the 1993 racist murder in] London and were imprisoned for life. Norris received a sentence of 14 years and three months while Dobson was given a minimum of 15 years and two months.

The pair were the first and only two convicted over the murder carried out by a group of racist thugs. Doreen Lawrence told the media the minimum terms imposed 'may be quite low' but she recognised that 'the judge's hands were tied'. She said 'It's the beginning of starting a new life.'

Neville Lawrence said: 'This is only one step in a long, long journey.' He thanked the police, the judge and the jury, but said they must 'give up' the other people involved in his son's murder.

FAMILY AFFAIR

By Rodney Hinds
yourview@xymedia.co.uk

NO WONDER Formula One sensation Lewis Hamilton is as quick as he is! The rookie that is taking the sport by storm has the middle name of Carl in honour of the legendary United States Olympic gold athlete, Carl Lewis.

Hamilton, the talk of the Grand Prix world and beyond, looked to extend his lead in the world drivers championship last week in Indianapolis, after claiming his maiden Formula One victory in Montreal in only his sixth Grand Prix. Apart from his obvious ability on the track, Hamilton is proving to be a media darling.

His press conferences are assured and articulate for one so young; he is proving to be a a credit to his family. At just 22 years old he looks - with a modicum of luck - set not only to win the world championship but for many more years to come.

However, Hamilton's story has been years in the making.

Awards

Hamilton introduced himself to McLaren team boss Ron Dennis at the 1994 Autosport Awards, asking if he could drive for the team in the future.

In 1998, he was signed to the McLaren driver development support programme, the contract including a future option of an F1 seat, making 13-year-old Hamilton the youngest ever driver to secure an F1 contract.

Behind the scenes of the glitz and glamour of motor sport, Hamilton has been supported by a strong family unit every bit as important as the mechanics and engineers that serve him so well in the pits. Hamilton dedicated his historic win in Canada to his father Anthony.

His mother Carmen and father separated when Lewis was just two. Lewis grew up with his father, stepmother and half-brother Nicholas who suffers from cerebral palsy. Hamilton's paternal grandparents emigrated to the United Kingdom from Grenada in the 1950s.

His grandfather worked on the London Underground. While Hamilton quite rightly grabs the headlines, he has never forgotten the sacrifices made by his family. The motor-racing fraternity had better get used to seeing young Hamilton on the podium.

You know the opposition is worried about his talent when teammate Fernando Alonso, twice a world champion, made a jibe suggesting that McLaren favour Hamilton.

Grenada is noted for its spices. It would appear to have unearthed a man to provide some extra flavour to the exciting world of Formula One.

Life in the Fast Lane: The View on Lewis Hamilton

By Tiffany Maria Joseph

THE VOICE of Sport asked members of the proud black community three question to get their view on the sensational Lewis Hamilton.

■ How impressed are you with Hamilton in his debut season?
■ Do you think he can win the world title this year?
■ Is Hamilton set to make the same positive impact as Tiger Woods and the Williams sisters?

LUTHER BLISSETT, former Watford & England footballer:

■ I am highly impressed; think that everyone is, his achievements so far have been phenomenal.
■ He is leading at the moment and has a long way to go. There has

to be a possibility when you are in the lead. If things go his way and he does not get too many mechanical failures, then he has a good chance.
■ Be definitely will because when somebody has the profile that he has achieved already, its got to inspire others, no doubt about it.

AL HAMILTON, founder of the Commonwealth Sports Awards:

■ I have watched his races including the win in Canada, you don't get that kind of talent often, it only comes about once in a lifetime. He is a remarkable talent, personality, and a lovely human being.
■ I have no doubt. That this is his destiny. Some people are destined like a Bob Marley or Nelson

Mandela; they are put on this earth for a specific reason. Hamilton is a winner. He does not like to finish second. Winning comes naturally to him.
■ He is making that right now! This is the new roost to the block community, well, the whole community. At a time when we are celebrating our history, here is a son of one of our descendants. There was a time when motor racing was only for the elite. I am glad to be alive.

LES FEVRIER, football agent:

■ I think he has done fantastically well-he has worked really hard to achieve.
■ I am very confident that he could win the world championship

at some stage but I hope it is this year.
■ Yes, if he is managed correctly. I am sure he will be up there with them. He is a very young man with a lot of drive and determination, he has got quality.

JENNY DAINTON, customer relations manager at the Football Association:

■ Very impressed and surprised. It is so nice to see a young black face doing so well.
■ Yes definitely!
■ I think so. There are several similarities with him and the Williams sisters and Tiger Woods. Each of their fathers have positive impacts on their lives and very influential on guiding their sporting careers too.

The Voice *regularly celebrated Lewis's wins and highlighted his close bond with his father, who nurtured his interest in motorsport*

TURKISH DELIGHT

■ TURKISH champions Fenerbahce are set to offer Ghana midfielder Stephen Appiah a contract extension. The 26-year-old, who played a key part in Fenerbahce's title win last month, has attracted interest from several top European sides.

TAKE TIME

■ MARLON DEVONISH says Britain should avoid rushing its next batch of promising sprinters into the senior international arena. The Coventry-based Olympic relay gold medallist, 31, said: "There are some good lads coming through, but I think it would be wrong to rush them. "It might result in irreparable damage, and in the long term, it will not be the best policy."

NEW MAN AT ICC

■ RAY MALI has become acting president of the International Cricket Council following the death of Percy Sonn. The 70-year-old president of Cricket South Africa since 2003 will assume the role for approximately 15 months until the ICC's 2008 annual conference.

SIR VIV'S FEARS

■ SIR VIVIAN Richards fears cricket in the Caribbean is near to "breaking point" and is anxious of a total collapse through petty, internal politics that continue to blight the West Indies. "When I was representing my country, I was prepared to battle," Richards told BBC Radio Five Live. "That is how serious we took our sporting profession and that is missing now. When I was involved before, I was criticised for being too hard."

Vivian Richards

In his summary, the judge stated, 'the crime was committed for no other reason than racial hatred,' describing the crime as 'a murder which scarred the conscience of the nation.'

Shortly after Norris and Dobson were convicted, it was revealed that 21 people under 20 had died as a result of racist attacks since Stephen's murder, according to the Institute of Race Relations (IRR).

The IRR, which records all deaths with a known or suspected racial element, showed that five of the 21 deaths took place in 'unprovoked attacks similar to that on Stephen.'

The deaths included those of 18-year-old Anthony Walker, who was killed with an axe in Liverpool after a group of white men attacked him in 2005, and Christopher Alaneme, who was fatally stabbed after being racially abused by a group of white men while on a night out in Sheerness, Kent, in 2006.

Since Stephen Lawrence was killed in 1993, 96 people of all ages had died in racist attacks, with 40 people dying 'as a result of random acts of violence.'

The charity's data also showed victims were overwhelmingly men under 30 years old.

The research pointed out that at least ten of those who died were refugees or asylum seekers. In addition, five migrant workers were also killed between 2005 and 2012.

In the same week as the long-awaited trial of the Stephen Lawrence killers, *The Voice* readers' poll found the case had not changed race relations in the UK. Writer and campaigner Marc Wadsworth reported: 'The 1999 Macpherson report into the police handling of Stephen Lawrence's murder was supposed to have brought changes, but more than a decade later, Black Britons have mixed feelings about whether anything has changed.'

The poll showed a majority of Black people do not believe race relations in Britain have changed since the murder of Stephen Lawrence. 17 per cent said race relations had improved, but 83 per cent of participants thought things had not got any better.

It was a surprising result considering the groundbreaking inquiry was hailed as a milestone when it was published.

The report should have brought about big changes in the way the police handle racist crimes and deal with the Black community. But critics said the disproportionate number of Black people – mainly young men – are still stopped and searched by police, and deaths in custody, are stark examples of how things have not changed.

The Voice's editor George Ruddock said: 'The results of our poll reflect a deep dissatisfaction about the way race relations in Britain have failed to progress. Stephen's brutal murder by racist thugs was a wake-up call for the whole of the nation – Black and white – and for a time the authorities took its lessons to heart. But it is clear the momentum of change needs to be stepped up if we are not to see more inner-city disturbances of the type that happened this year.'

He added: 'Our newspaper, which is proud to be '*The Voice* of Black Britain', will continue to champion the cause of Black people, fight injustice, highlight success stories and promote race equality.'

So we ask ourselves again, what has changed?

In the 2000s community crusades had led to set quotas and initiatives by government and business. These were intended to increase minority employment and status in the sectors. The incentives brought a visible increase of minorities, with a handful in executive positions and in decision-making roles.

But a few years later, many of the same executives moved on, not just because some felt their hands were tied, but also because their options improved and they took higher paid roles on the open market. Once again, *The Voice* and the Black community were on a campaign to remind businesses to fill gaps and maintain their remit for fairer representation.

Relentless campaigning also brought better political representation, but the judgements of some of the Black faces in high places jar with expectations on a plethora of issues, and some gains may well be perceived as set backs. Deaths in custody, general policing, community relations and other areas of conflict and disparity will probably be ongoing battles. Reports may still include platitudes such as: 'We are doing our best, but there is a long way to go.'

Relations between coexisting cultures invariably breeds bias. Racial, religious and cultural politics underlie the fabric of certain societies, and inequalities seem to be a constant in underprivileged lives.

Despite our best efforts inequality still lingers – it is only the continued vigilance of our communities that brings progress.

2013–2022
The Voice in the Social Media Age

By Vic Motune

In the ten years between 2013 and 2022 we have seen unprecedented national discussions about how to achieve race equality, giving many Black Britons hope that their concerns would be taken seriously. Celebrities, from actors and singers to writers and athletes, joined protestors in taking a stand against the police killings of Black people after the Black Lives Matter movement launched in the UK in 2015 and social media became a key campaigning tool for activists demanding racial justice. Following the death of George Floyd in 2020 and the widespread protests that followed, it was clear to everyone on *The Voice*'s editorial team that these events marked an important chapter in history.

Their impact shone an unforgiving light on race inequality in all areas of life, from health and education to entertainment and employment. This became a key editorial theme for the newspaper which, through its network of reporters, grassroots campaigners and high-profile Black Britons, was able to showcase the day-to-day realities of racism. The coverage only further demonstrated why the Black Lives Matter movement had gained so much traction in the UK.

But there was also disappointment. Despite progressive policy statements from former Conservative prime ministers such as

David Cameron and Theresa May, concerns over the police's use of stop and search and the high number of Black deaths in custody saw many campaigners claim that institutional racism was nowhere near to being effectively tackled. As *The Voice* documented, the years following 2013 saw a political shift to the right which, some say, dealt a serious blow to the race equality agenda.

In 2013, mainstream political support for ending racial profiling by police officers came from the unlikeliest of sources. In July that year, Conservative Home Secretary Theresa May announced a major package of measures to reform the way police used stop and search powers. The policy was announced after a Home Office review found Black people were seven times more likely to be approached by police officers. Speaking about the measures in the House of Commons May said that 'no one should be stopped on the basis of skin colour.'

It was a rare acknowledgement by a major politician of what Black people had been saying for many years – the disproportionate use of stop and search represents a deep racial injustice rooted in the false narrative that drug use and crime is more prevalent in the Black community than in others.

It came as a surprise to many that the party long associated with the most racist election in British political history – Smethwick in 1964 – and Enoch Powell's 'Rivers of Blood' speech was now clearly courting Black voters. News of May's plans prompted *The Voice* to ask, 'Is Labour losing the Black vote?' on the front page of its July 25 edition. The article said that the move 'shows how far the Tories have come from the "sus" laws that were rife in the 1980s under Margaret Thatcher, which fuelled riots in Brixton, Toxteth and Handsworth.'

It went on: 'It's also a complete U-turn on Prime Minister David Cameron's 2008 pledge that his party would make it

THE VOICE
CELEBRATING 35 YEARS
OF CHAMPIONING A DIVERSE BRITAIN

www.voice-online.co.uk   £1.00

Jamaican celebrates a century in Birmingham

THE HISTORY MAKERS
Meet the black Nobel Prize winners

'I'LL TAKE ACTION ON RACE INEQUALITY'

TIME FOR CHANGE:
Prime Minister Theresa May

PM Theresa May says the time for merely talking about discrimination is over and asks for your support to help her challenge it

EXCLUSIVE

IN AN interview with *The Voice* Prime Minister Theresa May has promised to end race inequality in Britain.

Her recent Race Equality Audit highlighted widespread discrimination faced by black Britons.

The Prime Minister acknowledged the perception of many *Voice* readers that it was just another report about discrimination but said: "What makes this different is that you will see action coming out if it."

And she asked *Voice* readers for their support in tackling inequality.

In an exclusive interview in 2017, Theresa May promised she would end race inequality in Britain

easier for officers to stop and search the public without having to give a reason.'

'As May launched her public consultation on stop and search, she wrote an exclusive piece for *The Voice*, knowing the audience she needed to speak to would be listening. The Tories have woken up to the possibilities of winning the Black vote and are actively in open discussion with Black communities. They have a natural advantage, too: studies show their conservative values are more ideologically aligned with that of African Caribbeans. As they up the ante, many Black voters might soon start wondering: 'What has Labour done for us lately?'

Lord Simon Woolley, Director and founder of campaign group OBV, shared his thoughts about that question in the article. 'I'm afraid the Labour Party must do better,' he said. 'There's an election to be won and there's no doubt the Black vote will make a big intervention in Britain's political history. What's very clear is that the Conservatives acutely understand they cannot win elections without the Black vote. It's no surprise that Theresa May has almost offered a public inquiry over the Stephen Lawrence smear allegations and stop and search is under review – these are clear policy areas that appeal to Black communities. In response, we don't see the Labour Party being proactive and if they don't, they will lose. It's as simple as that. They need to catch back up.'

While observers like Woolley lauded May's understanding of the need to take seriously the demands of Black voters it was former prime minister David Cameron who championed a drive to detoxify the Conservative brand in an attempt to move it away from its image as the 'nasty' party and back towards the one-nation conservatism of former prime ministers such as Harold Macmillan. In 2001, the Conservative Party had no Black or minority ethnic MPs. But Cameron saw the importance of harnessing the talents of prospective MPs from these communities. In 2005, he launched the 'A-List' of 100 preferred prospective parliamentary candidates aimed at widening the party's appeal to a diverse electorate. Conservative associations were encouraged to choose from this list. Half of the list were women and a significant minority were non-white.

At the 2010 General Election 64 per cent of the Black vote went to Labour, while the Tories achieved a meagre 18 per cent. It was also in this election that the party elected a record number of Black Conservative MPs. The number of Black, Asian and minority ethnic MPs increased from two to 11, including its first Black woman, Helen Grant, who went on to become a minister and later became the party's vice chair for communities. It was this breakthrough that led to Cameron to make a bold pitch for Black votes.

Cameron continued in his efforts to woo Black voters through the pages of *The Voice*. 'I Want To Turn Black Britain Blue' was the headline that dominated the front page in April 2015. In an exclusive interview with news editor Elizabeth Pears, Cameron said that the Black community's concerns would be best tackled by a Tory government. When asked about Black voters who were thinking of voting Conservative, but couldn't bring themselves to do it, he replied:

> I would say, I know why you have been holding back. I think lots of Black Britons look at the values of the Conservative Party and think we agree with you about family and community. We are passionate about enterprise. We want opportunities. The holdback has been people asking themselves if they can get up and get on with the Conservative Party and you can see now that you can. You can see that

with the talent we have got on the backbenches. Black and minority ethnic Britons are not only joining the Conservative Party, they have a seat at the cabinet table. And it's not just the Conservative Party in parliament; you see it in local government. So I say, hold off the hold back.

In subsequent general elections the Conservatives increased the number of minority ethnic candidates it fielded. In the 2019 general election the party ran 76 Black and minority ethnic candidates, a 72 per cent increase on 2017. Sadly, the voices of these MPs have been largely absent from parliamentary debates on the impact of race inequality. Their silence was particularly noted following the widespread criticisms of a 2021 report from the Commission on Race and Ethnic Disparities, which denied the existence of structural and institutional racism in the UK.

Founder of Operation Black Vote and crossbench peer Lord Woolley initially welcomed the emergence of a new generation of Black Tory MPs after years of meeting with party leaders to convince them to diversify their lists of parliamentary candidates. But he later told *The Voice*: 'The only tragedy of that story is that because they put them in predominantly white seats the vast majority of these Black and brown candidates cared not one jot for the broader Black race equality project. On a photo opportunity, it looked good, but hardly any of them would speak out about racism unless they didn't get promoted.'

When Theresa May became Prime Minister in July 2016, following Cameron's departure after the political earthquake that was the EU referendum, one could be forgiven for being optimistic that race equality was now a firm part of the Conservative political agenda. On taking office May promised to fight 'burning injustice' in British society and create a union 'between all of

NEWS

BLACK OFFICERS: POLICE FORCE IS STILL RACIST

By Mary Isokariari

PAYING THEIR RESPECTS: (right to left) Sir Bernard Hogan-Howe, Superintendent Leroy Logan and Met BPA chairman Bevan Powell

LOVING MOTHER: Doreen Lawrence at her son's memorial

DISCRIMINATION IS still prevalent within the Met Police despite the Macpherson Inquiry findings of institutional racism more than a decade ago, an organisation for black officers has said.

The Met's Black Police Association said: "We still believe that the police service is institutionally racist."

Its chairman, Bevan Powell, said: "Institutional racism is not about labelling individuals racists but rather police practice and procedures that bring about disproportionate outcomes for black and minority ethnic communities and police personnel."

The sounding of the alarm by the BPA coincides with the 20th anniversary of Stephen Lawrence's murder on April 22.

A memorial, attended by senior police and politicians, was held in central London to reflect on the teenager's legacy which includes changes to legislation following the investigation into his death in 1999.

The National Association for Black Police Officers also voiced its concern. Its president, Charles Crichlow, said: "It is unacceptable that in the 21st Century less than five per cent of police officers in England and Wales are from black and ethnic minority backgrounds (BME)."

THREAT

They said the underrepresentation of BME officers presents a serious threat to modern day policing and the democratic nature of the service.

One suggestion was for the launch of a 'direct entry' route into the profession, which would give individuals a chance to join the force at the rank of superintendent or inspector to encourage diversity.

Crichlow added: "We support the concept of direct entry, but, with one caveat. It must bring about greater ethnic diversity and new thinking at the senior ranks within the police.

"British policing must adopt radical approaches across the service, if issues of race and diversity are to be successfully addressed."

The NPBA said that stop and search continued to be a concern and the disproportionate numbers of black people being stopped and searched was damaging trust and confidence in the police.

StopWatch, a coalition of legal experts, community activists and civil society groups, expressed similar worries over the abuse of the powers.

INCREASE

Recent statistics shows there has been a significant increase in the use of stop and search over last decade, which peaked at 150,000 in 2008/09 – an increase of 2000 per cent over the preceding decade.

It was also discovered that black people are 37 times more likely to be stopped and searched under this provision than white people, the highest level of disparity ever recorded.

Commenting on the Stephen Lawrence murder, Prime Minister David Cameron said: "The senseless killing of Stephen Lawrence in 1993 was a tragedy. It was also a moment that sparked monumental change in our society - change that has been brought about by the tireless efforts of Stephen's family in challenging the police, Government and society to examine themselves and ask difficult questions.

"I believe that many of those questions have been answered: from improved community relations to more accountability in policing. Much has been achieved, but we know that more still needs to be done. We owe this to the memory of Stephen."

Tell us what you think. **Email: yourviews@gvmedia.co.uk**

STAMP OF APPROVAL FOR LONDON'S FIRST BLACK MAYOR

HONOURED: Great black Briton John Archer

THE FIRST black mayor of London will feature as one of the faces of Royal Mail's Great Britons stamp collection.

John Archer will be part of the stamp issue celebrating individuals across sport, journalism, music, politics and the arts, whose anniversaries of birth fall in 2013.

Archer was the first person of African descent to hold civic office in London and to represent his country at an international conference overseas.

Born in Liverpool in 1863, Archer was a prize-winning photographer before turning to local politics and working as a councillor for three years.

Ranked 72nd in a public vote of 100 Great Black Britons, Archer was elected the Mayor of Battersea in 1913 and upon this achievement, told the council: "You have made history tonight...Battersea has done many things in the past, but the greatest thing it has done is to show that it has no racial prejudice, and recognises a man for the work he has done."

Other personalities included on the commemorative stamps are football manager Bill Shankly, actor Peter Cushing, journalist and broadcaster Richard Dimbleby and fashion photographer Norman Parkinson.

Royal Mail stamps spokesman Andrew Hammond said: "We are delighted to be honouring some of the UK's most distinguished figures in history through our latest Special Stamp collection.

"We hope the stamps will serve as a lasting tribute to their memory and once again encourage people to remember their significant contribution to our Great British way of life."

As Britain marked the twentieth anniversary of Stephen Lawrence's death, a report revealed discrimination was still rife in the Metropolitan Police

our citizens'. 'I'll take action on race inequality' was the bold front-page headline of *The Voice*'s October 26 edition.

In an exclusive interview the Prime Minister outlined her plans to launch a Race Disparities Audit to examine how ethnic minorities and white working-class people were treated by public services such as the NHS, schools, police and the courts. She told the newspaper she acknowledged the perception of *The Voice* readerership that this was just another report about discrimination but said: 'What makes this different is that you will see action coming out if it.' She also asked readers for their support in tackling inequality.

However, the hopes of race equality campaigners were to prove short-lived. The aftermath of Brexit saw Britain's political and social climate move increasingly to the right. Several sources reported an increase in physical and verbal hate crimes amid growing anti-immigrant and nationalist sentiment.

Politicians and commentators called for the concerns of the 'left behind' – white, socially conservative voters who were behind the surge in support for UKIP – to be both heard and acted upon. One direct consequence of the shift to the right was that Black politicians and public figures, especially Black women, increasingly became targets of relentless racist and sexist online abuse.

Following research published in September 2017, Amnesty International revealed that Shadow Home Secretary Diane Abbott had alone received almost half of all the abusive tweets sent to female MPs in the run-up to that year's general election. The abuse directed at her amounted to ten times as much as was received by any other female MP, the study found. In a September 2020, a *Voice Online* report on Abbott highlighted the impact of this continuing abuse on those around her. The Hackney North and Stoke Newington MP said the most upsetting abuse she receives was toward her 28-year-old son. She said: 'It's incredibly hurtful – it's much more hurtful than anything is written about me.' She also discussed the impact it had upon her staff, saying: 'I've had interns who came to work for me, Black women, and they've been really shocked at the abuse. We very regularly have to send stuff to the police because of threats of violence and other threats.'

Another person to feel the full impact of online abuse, both in the run up to and the aftermath of the Brexit referendum, was Gina Miller. The businesswoman became a public figure when, in 2016, she led the successful legal challenge that forced Theresa May to get Parliament's approval before triggering Article 50 and leaving the European Union. Her victory was hailed as the greatest legal upset of modern times. But the businesswoman's success in taking on the government saw her become a hate figure for many hard-line Brexit supporters. In Miller they not only saw a passionate remainer but a feisty Black female who made no apologies about her willingness to fight for what she believed in. These characteristics seemed to trigger an extraordinary range of vitriolic messages, racial abuse and death threats directed towards her. Many of them referred to her as a traitor and mentioned her perceived 'foreign-ness'. The level of abuse on social media reached such a level that Miller was forced to spend up to £60,000 on personal security after a £5,000 reward was offered on social media to anyone who ran her over.

In a 2019 interview with *The Voice* Miller acknowledged that her determination to take on the government over Brexit had come at a huge personal cost. She said: 'The most scary [threats] are ... a message or an email or a letter, which says, we know where your children are, we know where their school is, we're going to take them today. 'The threats against my family and my

Exclusive Voice Interview

'FEARLESS? I'M NOT'

When businesswoman Gina Miller was first thrust into the media spotlight in 2016, she had no idea about the impact it would have on her life

By Vic Motune

IT'S PROBABLY fair to say that Brexit is the most important political event to happen in Britain this century so far.

And businesswoman Gina Miller's role in the increasingly divisive national debate about it has seen her hailed as a remarkable woman of courage and principle, someone who took on the government – and won.

Miller, 52, became a public figure when, in 2016, she led the successful legal challenge which forced Theresa May to get Parliament's approval before triggering Article 50 and leaving the European Union.

VICTORY

Her victory was hailed as the greatest legal upset of modern times. It came as no surprise to many in the black community when she was named as the most influential black person in Britain by the 2018 Powerlist, beating the likes of British Vogue editor Edward Enninful, grime star Stormzy and boxer Anthony Joshua.

The list recognises people in the UK of African and African Caribbean heritage who are rated on their "ability to change lives and alter events".

Praise has also come from other arenas. Journalist and broadcaster Rachel Johnson, sister of Prime Minister Boris Johnson, has described as Miller as a "remarkable woman, whose courage one can only admire, whatever your politics".

And Baroness Helena Kennedy QC said that Miller was "strong, resourceful, principled and brilliant – a heroine for our times".

But her national profile has come at a huge cost.

Her success in taking on the government has seen her become a hate figure for many hardline Brexit supporters.

In Miller they not only saw a passionate Remainer but also a feisty black female who made no apologies about her willingness to fight for what she believed in.

These characteristics seemed to trigger an extraordinary range of vitriolic messages, racial abuse and death threats directed towards her.

In the same month that the Supreme Court delivered its historic judgment, Metropolitan police officers revealed they had issued eight "cease and desist" notices to people

> ❝ The threats against my family and children are terrifying ❞

who had sent Miller threatening messages.

Many referred to her as a traitor and mentioned her perceived "foreign-ness".

Miller's solicitor, Mishcon de Reya, was subjected to abuse as a result of its involvement in the case, and Brexit supporters mounted a protest outside the firm's offices.

The level of abuse on social media reached such a level that Miller was forced to spend up to £60,000 on personal security. In July 2017 Rhodri Philipps, 4th Viscount St Davids, was jailed for 12 weeks for making the offer.

Philipps had offered the sum on Facebook to "the first person to 'accidentally' run over this bloody troublesome first generation immigrant".

Before deciding to legally challenge the government, friends and members of her legal team had told her it was likely to be tough and some close friends even advised her to walk away from the case.

Three years on from her first legal challenge, is she still having to spend a lot of money on personal security?

"It's never stopped," she says. It's worse than it was in the first case because people are at a different place now. Three years on there's a lot more anger, people are actually a bit more extreme on both sides.

ABUSE

"The online stuff I don't worry about so much, because a lot of that is armchair abuse.

"But it's when I get the packages or letters – if I get stuff with white powder and I'm not sure what that is – so have to hand it in to the police.

"Or the most scary ones are if I get something, a message or an email or a letter, which says, 'We know where your children are, we know where their school is – we're going to take them today'.

"The threats against my family and my children especially, that's terrifying. And I still get those all the time. And, in an odd way, it has made me even more determined to carry on. It's had the opposite effect of frightening me."

She continues: "In the beginning my children were very frightened because they were little. Now they're 12 and 14 they understand much more. They understand that I'm fighting for them and their friends and their future. So they do understand. I look in the mirror and the question I ask myself is, Why am I doing this? And I believe that going forward this will have a massive impact on our democracy."

Most people would not have the courage and fearlessness that she has to fight for a cause they believe in.

When put this to her, she says it's not a description of herself that she recognises.

"There's this idea out there that I'm fearless. I'm not fearless. I tend to think of myself as being fearful. I'm fearful of silence and letting people get away with things.

"I'm fearful of what that will happen if we don't stand up for what is right."

It would be no surprise if the fierce criticism and scrutiny that inevitably comes with Miller's public profile would wreak havoc with confidence.

But according to Miller, the inner resolve and sense of purpose it took to face the barrage of racist and threats to physically harm her was shaped by growing up in British Guiana, [now Guyana] where she was born and spent her early childhood.

In particular, she pays tribute to the influence of her father, Doodnauth Singh, who served as Attorney General of Guyana.

"He was a civic rights and human rights lawyer. In a country which has a death penalty that takes on a huge significance, because literally, every case has the possibility of somebody's life ending.

COMMUNITY

"My father's view was very much that the law was there to protect people. But even if you didn't use the law, everybody has a right to protect each other. I think a lot of who I am today is based on actually not just my father, but my mother as well in that I was brought up to believe that the way we live our lives is not just about ourselves, it's about a community and everybody matters."

She continues: "Apart from giving me these values, they also gave me confidence in myself. If you're confident, you don't worry about what other people put onto you. When you lack confidence, it's easier to worry about what other people think about you. But if you are grounded and know who you are and what you believe in, then it's very difficult for people to shake you. You're like a tree that's got good roots in a wind. When you're battered, you still stand. They gave me a belief in myself as well and in my own abilities and my strength and my own goodness."

It was this confidence and willingness to stand up for what she believed was right that underpinned her earliest experience as a campaigner after the birth of her first daughter, Luci-Ann, in 1988.

It was she says, the first real awakening to her own strength.

"In the 1980s the NHS was on its knees just like it is now. There were shortages of midwives, medicines and everything else. I was about to have my beautiful baby girl, but

📷 @thevoicenewspaper   🐦 @thevoicenews   f voicenews   🌐 www.voice-online.co.uk

Businesswoman Gina Miller was became a target for racist abuse and death threats when she led a successful legal challenge on the government's approach to Brexit

children especially, that's terrifying. And I still get those all the time. And, in an odd way, it has made me even more determined to carry on. It's had the opposite effect of frightening me.'

When asked about how courageous she needed to be to fight for what she believed in, she replied: 'I tend to think of myself as being fearful. I'm fearful of silence and letting people get away with things. I'm fearful of what that will happen if we don't stand up for what is right. You know, you wake up one day and the world will be a different place, where the vulnerable or the bullies are winning and the vulnerable people are losing and hurting.'

If Brexit seemed to slow down Theresa May's plan to place race equality at the heart of national life, another event would completely overshadow it. It saw thousands of Black Britons denied their basic rights as citizens and revealed some uncomfortable truths about racial inequality. And the irony was that what came to be described as a 'stain on the conscience of the country' had its roots in policies that May herself had introduced while she was Home Secretary.

On a mid- November afternoon in 2013, *The Voice* news reporter Natricia Duncan was getting ready to file copy when a call came through from a young woman from South London asking if the newspaper could help her. Phone calls invariably come through to the news desk at the same time as journalists hit their deadlines, but Duncan, whose reporting had a focus on community issues, immediately recognised that it was worth taking the time to listen to the person on the other end of the line.

'This young woman was hysterical. You could hear the emotion in her voice,' Duncan recalled. 'She told me that the government was sending her mother back to Jamaica unless she could prove she had the right to stay in this country. From what I understood, this decision had come out of the blue. The family was desperate and had no idea who to turn to.' The young woman's mother was 52-year-old Beverley Boothe, a mother of five from London who had been ordered to leave or 'be removed' after living in Britain for 34 years.

Boothe first came to this country as a teenager to join her parents in 1979 and claimed she was granted Indefinite Leave to Remain (ILR) in 1980 after her mother, who arrived in 1962 as part of the Windrush Generation, made an application on her behalf. Since then, she had achieved a degree in criminology and started a family.

However, when she applied to the Home Office for a new ILR stamp after losing her passport she was told they had no record of her status. When the call came through to *The Voice*'s news desk, Boothe had recently received a letter from Capita Business Services, a company contracted by the Home Office to help it tackle illegal immigration, instructing her to either provide proof of her status or 'make immediate arrangements to leave the United Kingdom.'

Duncan said: 'When I eventually did speak with Beverley, I could sense how overwhelmed she was by what was happening. I remember her saying repeatedly "I didn't bring myself here, I was brought here as a teenager." She had lived in this country for 34 years and had little connection with Jamaica so she was worried about how she would cope being separated from her family if she was forced to leave. And, you know, being a migrant myself, I could imagine how distressing that situation was.'

While she was Home Secretary, Theresa May won plaudits for her pledge to tackle racial bias in police use of stop and search. But this went hand in hand with her tough stance on immigration. She presided over the widely condemned 'Go Home' vans that patrolled areas with sizeable minority

Britain's top black weekly

ISSUE NO. 1830 | MAY 3 - 9, 2018

THE
VOICE
www.voice-online.co.uk £1.00

THE VOICE
CELEBRATING
35 YEARS
OF CHAMPIONING
A DIVERSE BRITAIN

Coming soon
Voice Traveller magazine

AS WINDRUSH DEBACLE CONTINUES
Sajid Javid vows: "I'll do whatever it takes to put it right"

‹‹ OUT   IN ‹‹

DEPORTATION THREAT STILL LOOMS FOR MANY

Windrush family's fears despite Theresa May's promise to halt removals

MAIN CARER: Yvonne Williams with her elderly mother

1948: Windrush nurses helped to build the NHS

2018: They're still sorting out the NHS crisis

SEVENTY YEARS after Windrush, Caribbean nurses continue to support the National Health Service (NHS). Meanwhile, Jamaica is still losing some of its best healthcare professionals to Britain.

The UK government has announced a new partnership with Jamaica that will see nurses from the Caribbean island work in the NHS for three years.

Under the new scheme, nurses from Jamaica will undertake work placements in the UK facilitated by Health Education England in areas such as emergency medicine and intensive care.

EXPERIENCE

Following the completion of their placements, the nurses are expected to return to Jamaica so that they can share their new skills, knowledge and experience in their home country.

But critics claim that the recruitment of Jamaican nurses by foreign countries, such as the UK, has adversely affected the country's ability to provide adequate healthcare for its citizens.

By Vic Motune

THE DAUGHTER of a woman who came to Britain in 1963 as part of the Windrush Generation has said she is fearful of what will happen to her family if she is deported to Jamaica.

Yvonne Williams, 59, who is the main carer for her 82-year-old mother as well as her own seven grandchildren, had been detained in Yarl's Wood detention centre for eight months awaiting to be deported.

FAMILY TIES

Home Office officials told her that she had to leave the country because she didn't have enough family ties to remain in the UK despite the fact that her mother is a British citizen, her daughter has leave to remain and her siblings and grandchildren are also British citizens.

Williams had been booked onto a charter flight to Jamaica scheduled to leave this week.

But following a social media campaign in support of her, she was released from Yarl's Wood in Bedford on Friday (April 27) and told she would not be on the plane. However, her right to remain in the UK is still uncertain. She told *The Voice*, "I'm very worried about my mum. My grandchildren are also very worried. I don't have anywhere to go to in Jamaica. All my family are here."

The Voice helped to tell the stories of the real people whose lives had been turned upside down by the Windrush Scandal

communities in 2013. Critics told *The Voice* their message echoed the 'No dogs, No Blacks. No Irish' signs that greeted arrivals to Britain from the Caribbean and Africa in the 1960s.

The move was part of the 'hostile environment', a set of policies introduced in 2012 with the aim of making life unbearably difficult for those who could not show they had the right to remain in Britain. The government set about trying to cut undocumented migrants off from using fundamental services including the NHS and the police, and make it illegal to work, or for a landlord to rent them a property. Doctors, landlords, police officers and teachers were tasked with checking immigration status and often people who looked or sounded 'foreign' were asked to show their papers so they could rent a home or get medical treatment. The setting of immigration removal targets, a toxic culture at the Home Office that aimed to catch people out and the passing of the Immigration Acts 2014 and 2016 laid the foundation for what became known as the Windrush Scandal.

Many members of the Windrush Generation – people who arrived here from Caribbean countries between 1948 and 1973 – came on their parents' passports and considered themselves British subjects. These people, now in their sixties and seventies, were unable to show their right to stay in the UK after the hostile environment policy was implemented. The situation was made worse by the fact that the Home Office destroyed thousands of landing cards and other records their parents would have had in spite of the complications that this could cause.

According to Home Office officials, these members of the Windrush Generation were now required to submit an official document for every year they had been resident in Britain. People who had done nothing wrong were burdened and, in many cases, had the impossible task of trying to locate old records. Their rights to housing, healthcare, banking and driving were all curtailed as a result of them being classed as 'illegal' or 'undocumented'. Those who had been arrested and held in immigration custody found themselves at risk of deportation to places they hadn't seen since they were children.

This was the unfortunate situation that Boothe found herself in when her daughter contacted *The Voice* in November 2013. Duncan's story about her plight was splashed across the front page of the December 5 edition under the headline 'Mum told to "Go Home": Devastated Beverley Boothe ordered to return to Jamaica after 34 years in Britain.' The story on the inside pages captured Boothe's anguish and frustration about what was happening: 'I can't believe this is happening. Where am I supposed to go? Do they expect me to leave my children here? I was 17 when my parents sent for me and I haven't been back since. My grandparents, who I used to live with, have passed away and all of my close family have moved on.' Trying to get answers from Home Office officials had added to her health concerns – she was suffering from high blood pressure and a heart condition.

She explained: 'I have given them my mom's date of birth; my dad's date of birth, where they were born, (and) information about my two sisters that were born here. I also gave them my fingerprints and proof of my degree – I don't know what else to do, they should be keeping records.' Boothe revealed that the situation had a devastating impact on her children. Despite them all being born in the UK they had been unable to get British passports.

Her two youngest daughters, Reneisha, 18 and Rakiela Drummond, 17, had never been able to travel outside of the UK. Reneisha was unable to fulfil her dream of going to university because she couldn't apply without a passport.

Britain's top black weekly

ISSUE NO. 1846 | SEPTEMBER 6 - 12, 2018

THE VOICE
www.voice-online.co.uk £1.00

National Diversity Awards 2018
Celebrating community champions

'A powerful black woman'
Miss La La, the 19th Century circus star

AN URGENT CALL TO WINDRUSH FAMILIES...

PLEASE COME FORWARD

Met police praise a 'safe' Carnival

Your input can influence a new compensation scheme

► LIFE-CHANGING: A young family leaves the Empire Windrush back in 1948

A N URGENT appeal has been made to families and individuals affected by the recent Windrush scandal to come forward to help shape a new compensation scheme.

A formal public consultation for the scheme was launched in July this year with hundreds of people coming forward.

But with the public consultation due to end on October 11 Home Office officials say they want many more Windrush families to share their experiences and ideas in a bid to redress the difficulties they have faced proving their British citizenship following the introduction of tighter immigration laws.

As a result of recent 'hostile environment' immigration policies, Windrush Generation members faced being denied services, losing their jobs and even facing deportation despite living in Britain for many decades and paying taxes and insurance.

DETERMINATION

Arthur Torrington, director of the Windrush Foundation, *pictured left*, told *The Voice*: "I urge everyone of Caribbean heritage to participate and add your own voice to the consultation. It's important that the Home Office hears from you. This will reflect the community's interest and our determination to assist those who need our support."

Story continues inside

COMMENTS FROM senior Met Police officers thanking revellers for this year's 'safe and spectacular' Notting Hill Carnival have met with an enthusiastic response from the black community.

Last week Met Commander Dave Musker, who led the policing operation, described it as "one of the smoothest and most efficient carnivals I have seen."

He added: "We would like to thank all those who took to the streets to celebrate everything that the carnival stands for, in a kind and considerate manner. Unfortunately there is still a minority that seek to tarnish this celebration and we will continue to review our security measures."

Responding to Musker's comments, readers of *The Voice* welcomed the fact that senior Met officers had positive things to say about Europe's biggest street party.

Mainstream media reports have often painted a picture of the event as one marred by crime. They have also called for the carnival to be moved to a central London park.

Writing on *The Voice's* Twitter page, carnival-goer Eterna C said: "This is the type of Carnival news I want to promote."

Story continues on page 2

The paper was instrumental in encouraging Windrush families to come forward to help shape a new compensation scheme

'I cannot stress how this makes me feel,' Reneisha told *The Voice*:

> How could somebody who was born in this country have to go through this? I have loads of friends who weren't born here and they have British passports. All my life I have been a prisoner and it's not fair because I haven't done anything wrong. My mother and my grandmother have worked and contributed to this country and yet this is happening.

Recalling the interview with Boothe, Duncan said:

> Looking back, I found it interesting that the family decided to call *The Voice*. It wasn't a story that was part of something we were looking into specifically. They decided to pick the phone up and call us. And that really stuck with me because it highlighted how people view *The Voice*. Beverley's family didn't just ring us to say, we've got a story we'd like you to cover. They rang us because they were really looking for help. And that's something that is central to the history of this newspaper and why it was founded. It gives a *Voice* to people who are being side lined or marginalised.

As well as following up on the story, Duncan helped Boothe to find a specialist immigration lawyer. In the years that followed, more stories were emerging of people like Beverley who had been denied their legal rights, wrongly detained or threatened with deportation were emerging. By 2018, the Windrush

Scandal had become a national conversation, prompted by a series of articles by Guardian reporter Amelia Gentleman.

'I was happy to see the Windrush Scandal get the coverage it did but I was disappointed at the same time,' Duncan said. 'If Beverley's story had received the attention it deserved back in 2013, I think there could have been a lot of pain and distress avoided for other people affected and for families. Imagine how many lives could have been changed. By the time the Windrush Scandal became the national story it did things were already reaching crisis point.'

Others affected by the Windrush Scandal followed Boothe and contacted *The Voice* with their stories. Among them was Yvonne Williams, whose mother came to Britain in 1962 from Jamaica. Williams, the main carer for her 82-year-old mother as well as her own seven grandchildren, had been detained in Yarl's Wood removal centre for several months awaiting deportation, and had been scheduled to leave the UK on a charter flight in the week that the family got in touch with the newspaper.

Home Office officials told her that she had to leave the country because she didn't have enough family ties to remain in the UK, despite her mother being a British citizen, her daughter being granted to remain and her siblings and grand-children having British citizenship. However, following a social media campaign in support of her right to remain in the UK and the efforts of her lawyer, she was released from Yarl's Wood and told she would not be on the plane. However, her right to remain in the UK was still uncertain.

'I'm very worried about my mum,' she told *The Voice*. 'My grandchildren are also very worried. I don't have anywhere to go to in Jamaica. All my family are here. I'm the only one look-ing after my mum and my grandchildren. When I was in Yarl's

Wood my granddaughter kept asking: 'Who's going to pick me up from school?'

Describing life in Yarl's Wood, she said: 'We didn't know when they were going to pick us up to be deported. When they give you the plane ticket, they don't give you any warning. When they come for you, they bring handcuffs, belts and strap and they carry you and put a belt around your waist and pull you outside to take you to the airport. It's very traumatising.' *The Voice* carried a series of reports and eyewitness accounts of rallies and marches held all over the country aimed at expressing solidarity with those threatened with deportation. Shadow home secretary Diane Abbott called the revelations a 'complete disgrace' and demanded justice for those affected by the hostile environment policy, while London mayor Sadiq Khan said the Windrush Scandal had 'become a stain on our nation's conscience', shining a light on 'an immigration system which is simply not fit for purpose'.

Prime Minister Theresa May held a meeting with the leaders of 12 Caribbean nations to discuss the issue. She apologised for the Windrush Scandal, assuring them that she was not clamping down on immigrants from Commonwealth countries, including theirs.

A week later, following growing anger at stories that were continuing to emerge of Windrush Generation members whose lives had been ruined by a discriminatory immigration system, May wrote an open letter exclusively for *The Voice* in which she apologised to the Black community for the Windrush Scandal. She wrote: 'We have let you down and I am deeply sorry.' The Prime Minister also acknowledged the role that Windrush Generation immigrants had played in helping to shape Britain and said she wanted to apologise to the families of those affected. She wrote: 'This should never have

Britain's top black weekly

ISSUE NO. 1859 | NOVEMBER 22 - 28, 2018

THE VOICE

www.voice-online.co.uk   £1.00

Thanks for the support!
Windies women big up St Lucia fans

Putting colour on camera
Clare Anyiam-Osigwe on life as a black female director

Taking control of diabetes
How one Birmingham man is helping others fight the disease

'MANY FAMILIES ARE STILL HURTING'

Legal and community groups join forces to hold UK-wide Windrush Day of Action

SHOW OF SUPPORT: A coalition of organisations will hold a National Windrush Day of Action on February 23 next year

DEBATE: Serena Williams has stoked row over black women are treated

Serena: 'Black women are bottom of the totem pole'

TENNIS STAR Serena Williams has sparked a debate about the role of black women in society.

Williams, who appeared on the cover of Elle magazine in its Women of the Year, was speaking in the wake of the controversy that emerged following her heated clash with umpire Carlos Ramos during the US Open women's final earlier this year.

She told the magazine: "I've no research on how black women get from, in the workforce are — there are literally papers about it, how black women are named if they're angry, as opposed to white women, white men, black men," she said. "It is bottom of the totem pole."

Williams was vociferous after the Women an of the Year title after her triumphant return to the sport following the birth of her daughter last September.

By Vic Motune

A NATIONAL DAY of action is to be held next year to highlight the plight of families still struggling with the impact of the Windrush scandal.

BAME Lawyers 4 Justice, a coalition of leading black legal and community organisations, which is behind the event is also demanding a public inquiry into how members of the Windrush Generation have been treated.

RESULT

A spokesperson for one of the organisations told *The Voice*: "We have seen families suffer as a result of the Windrush scandal. People have not been able to work legally for years.

"Families have been torn apart after a relative has been deported and others have been made homeless as a result of not being able to prove their British citizenship.

"The National Day of Action is crucial because many Windrush Generation members are still frightened to come forward and we must support them so we can get their citizenship status sorted.

The spokesperson added: "Our organisations are uniting for this event to make our voice on this issue stronger and more powerful."

Story continued on page two

THE VOICE BLACK BUSINESS FAIR
WE INVITE YOU TO COME AND SUPPORT BLACK BUSINESSES

SATURDAY, 8th DECEMBER
10am - 6pm
Lambeth Town Hall,
Brixton, London, SW2 1RW
SEE INSIDE FOR DETAILS

Black lawyers organised a Windrush Day of Action and demanded an inquiry into the treatment of the Windrush Generation

happened. I am writing to apologise, explain how this happened and set out what we are doing to put it right.'

She said the Home Office measures were 'never intended to affect members of the Windrush Generation – all of whom are here legally. But, very regrettably, they have affected those who – through no fault of their own – never acquired any documentation.' May went on to explain that the Home Office had set up a taskforce with a dedicated helpline staffed by experienced case workers. She said: 'Anyone who wants to obtain documentation can meet with these case workers in person and be issued with that paperwork free of charge through an accelerated process.'

Shortly after May's letter was published, *The Voice* launched a campaign urging readers affected by the Windrush Scandal to help shape a proposed compensation scheme. The front-page headline of the September 6 2018 edition said simply: 'Please Come Forward.' The inside story quoted Arthur Torrington, Director and founder of the London-based charity The Windrush Foundation, who said: 'I urge everyone of Caribbean heritage to participate and add your own voice to the consultation. It's important that the Home Office hears from you. This will reflect the community's interest and our determination to assist those who need our support.'

Hundreds of readers did come forward as a result of *The Voice*'s campaign to give their views on how such a scheme might work. The Windrush Compensation Scheme was established in April 2019 and an estimated 15,000 people were thought to be eligible. However, there is still a significant backlog of cases still to be processed. And critics have claimed the compensation scheme has only added to the trauma experienced by those affected by the scandal. It is complex to navigate, there is a lack of free legal advice, claims take months to process and compensation and offers have been described as 'insultingly small'.

The Home Affairs Committee – a cross-party body of MPs that examines immigration and security – said that by the end of September 2021 only a fifth of the 15,000 people eligible had come forward and only a quarter of those had received any money. Among those who were caught up in the Windrush Scandal and felt cheated by promises of justice or compensation was Gladstone Wilson. The Wolverhampton resident moved to the UK from Jamaica in 1968 as a 12-year-old to join his parents. Like many children and young people who arrived as part of the Windrush Generation, he came on his parents' passports. After they returned to Jamaica Wilson settled in Wolverhampton, working for several years at a scrap yard before becoming a security guard at the city's New Cross Hospital.

However, his settled life came to a crashing halt when he received a letter from the Home Office in 2011 which said he had 'no basis' to stay in the country and that the Home Office had no records of him.

'The letter had a large photo of me on it and said that if I didn't report to the immigration centre in Solihull, I was either liable to be fined £5,000 or put in jail for six months, or both,' Wilson, 62, told *The Voice* in February 2020.

'It came as quite a shock. Every time I look at that letter with the photograph, I hang my head in shame – and I haven't done anything wrong.' He had no choice but to comply. Sadly, Wilson's mother died in December 2014. Not being able to fly out to Jamaica to attend the funeral because of the conditions imposed on him by the Home Office was a huge blow.

'I was unable to go because I wouldn't have been able to come back because of the situation concerning my British status in the UK,' he said.

'I was angry, annoyed and devastated. Not being able to go to your mum's funeral . . . you can't put a price on that. My sisters in America had to go over to Jamaica to make the arrangements. I explained everything to them and they did understand. But it was very hard.'

Just a few weeks later there was further tragedy for Wilson when his younger brother died. Both bereavements, coupled with the fact that he could not work or travel, began to have an impact on his mental health. Wilson's story was the front-page lead of *The Voice's* February 2020 edition. The dramatic headline 'I've been to hell and back' captured the pain Wilson felt at not being able to bury his late mother. The inside story told how Wilson received help from a local semi-retired solicitor who specialised in immigration issues, The lawyer was finally able to resolve his status marking the end of a seven-year battle. But an equally tough battle for compensation had only just begun.

Wilson applied for compensation under the Windrush Compensation Scheme. But the former security guard told the newspaper he found the process far from easy.

'I would not have known what to do if I hadn't had support from the Refugee and Migrant Centre in Wolverhampton. It's not that easy trying to understand it all' he said:

Without that support I couldn't imagine what would happen, I probably wouldn't be here today. It's a disgrace what the Home Office have done to me, they've ruined my life. I feel as though I've been treated like a criminal. It's racism, straightforward racism. They may deny it and say it's not but they could have easily checked to find out my status and the fact that I had a right to be here. They didn't bother to do that; they just made their minds up that I had no right to be here.'

The 'Windrush Lessons Learned Review,' an independent report released in March 2020, made it clear that the Windrush Scandal was the unavoidable outcome of policies intended to make life difficult for people without the proper documents. To prevent a repeat of the scandal, its author Wendy Williams, a solicitor who had spent two decades with the Crown Prosecution Service, recommended that the Home Office abolish its hostile environment policies, the root cause of the problem. Writing in *The Voice* about the Williams review, veteran equalities campaigner and author Patrick Vernon highlighted the challenges the government faced if it was to successfully implement the review's recommendations.

'There are many thousands of people that have still not come forward to resolve their status as there is still a lack of trust of the Home Office and the public bodies who implement the hostile environment policy and procedures' he said. 'The Home Office has not in the last two years developed a community engagement strategy, or funded grassroots and faith groups who are supporting victims' access to justice.'

Concerns about the lack of tangible progress in compensating Windrush Scandal victims were echoed in a March 2022 *Voice Online* report headlined 'Home Office on tipping point of another scandal, Windrush Review finds.'

Williams expressed her disappointment at the pace of change.

'In some areas, the [Home Office] has shown ambition and a commitment to taking forward my recommendations,' she said.

'But in others, I have been disappointed by the lack of tangible progress or drive to achieve the cultural changes required within a reasonable period to make them sustainable. Much more progress is required in policymaking and casework, which will be seen as the major indicators of improvement.'

'The department is at a tipping point and the next stage will be crucial in determining whether it has the capacity and capability to make good on its ambitions "to build a Home Office fit for the future, one that serves every corner of society".'

But amidst controversy there was also celebration. The scandal brought a renewed focus on the huge cultural and social impact on life in Britain that the Windrush Generation made. The seventieth anniversary of the arrival of *SS Empire Windrush* into Tilbury Docks, Essex, was marked in 2018. The government announced that an annual Windrush Day would be celebrated on June 22, to recognise and honour the contribution of the Windrush Generation and keep its legacy alive for future generations. To mark the seventieth anniversary *The Voice* produced a special 70-page anniversary edition that highlighted the cultural impact this group of pioneers had in areas such as politics, entertainment, sport, religion and the NHS. The edition featured interviews with men and women who arrived in Britain in the 1940s and 1950s such as Peter Braham, who built a successful TV repair business after arriving here as a 12-year-old from Jamaica in 1959, and Roy Walters, also from Jamaica, who went on to become Lord Mayor of Manchester.

There were also special messages from Prime Minster Theresa May and Lord Tariq Ahmad, Minister of State for the Commonwealth and the UN who wrote:

I doubt that there is a corner of Britain that has not been inspired and enriched by the Windrush Generation and their descendants. 'The fortitude shown as they overcame daunting challenges and built successful lives and businesses for themselves and their families has come to represent a strength in spirit that we continue to see today.'

It was a point reiterated the following year at a special House of Commons reception hosted by *The Voice* and Jamaica National to mark the first annual Windrush Day.

'Windrush Generation must not be characterised by scandal' was the headline of *The Voice* story that covered the June 2019 event. A number of high-profile individuals spoke at the event including Baroness Floella Benjamin, former Labour leader Jeremy Corbyn and the Bishop of Dover, Reverend Rose Hudson-Wilkin. Baroness Benjamin said the Windrush Generation had 'changed the face of Britain' and that the country was 'on the brink of something quite wonderful' because the whole nation was beginning to understand why Windrush was important.

Mental health is an issue that often leads many in the Black community struggling for long periods of time, as well as being misdiagnosed due to lack of culturally informed approaches to treatment. It has also often been at the heart of tragic deaths in custody cases. Figures released by mental health charity Mind illustrate several long-held concerns. Its research points to the fact Black people are 40 per cent more likely to access treatment for mental health issues through a police or criminal justice route, while also finding that Black people were 'less likely to receive psychological therapies, more likely to be compulsorily admitted for treatment and more likely to be on a medium-or

ON TOP OF THE WORLD: Hamilton is F1 king once more

THE VOICE

www.voice-online.co.uk   £1.00

CELEBRATING
35 YEARS
OF CHAMPIONING
A DIVERSE BRITAIN

Visit the Voice Exhibition at City Hall

'TOO MANY PEOPLE ARE SUFFERING'

A passion for fashion
British duo make their mark

The black maths pioneers
Innovators who thrived despite adversity

By Vic Motune

BOXING HERO Frank Bruno has criticised the way that people with mental health issues are treated in the UK and is urging reform of the system.

In an interview with *The Voice*, the former world champion said that too many people who are treated by NHS mental health services are needlessly suffering after being given powerful drugs that they don't want and which make their health worse.

Bruno himself has been sectioned three times and recalls how his experience of being given large doses of medication left him "feeling like a cabbage".

Now he wants to help change the system for others.

Former boxing world champion Frank Bruno spoke to The Voice *about the way people with mental health issues were being treated in the UK system*

high-secure ward? It also found that Black people were more likely to be 'subject to seclusion or restraint', with the figure standing at 56.2 per 100,000 people for Black Caribbean people, compared to 16.2 per 100,000 people for white people.

These were some of the issues on the mind of former world heavyweight boxing champion Frank Bruno when he sat down for an exclusive interview with *The Voice* in 2017. A picture of a solemn-looking Bruno next to the headline 'Too many people are suffering' dominated the front page of the November 2 edition. The popular fighter said he had been motivated to speak about mental health after his own experiences. He said the UK mental health system caused too many patients to suffer by forcing them to take drugs they often didn't want.

'I've been sectioned three times', he revealed:

The first time it happened, yes I had problems, yes I was going through whatever I was going through, but when I came out [of the mental health hospital], the dosage of medication they gave me numbed me out. They often give Black people a higher dosage than other people. When you go into the system they don't want to listen to you at all, they treat you as if you're nothing. They make out they care for you, but all they're not really getting to the root of the problem – why you're feeling down, what you're feeling from the medication. After taking it, you can be left staring at a wall like a crazy person.

Bruno continued:

Sometimes it would be about 60 different tablets, with doctors saying – 'take this one, that one, and take that one to counteract the side effects' or whatever. I told them 'this messes up my head; you don't know how I feel; I can't sleep at night; I'm having dreams. What you give me is very highly dangerous and it's hurting me and I can't focus. I asked them, 'Have you ever taken these medications? Do you know how it feels? You've got to know what you're giving somebody. If all you're worried about is getting paid, then all you're all doing is just making out that you really care for me.

The former boxing champ stressed that he wasn't telling people with mental health issues to stop taking medication entirely:

I'm not saying that everybody don't need some form of medication and what may be good for me may not be good for you. But it's the higher doses that mong you out and leave you with side effects. I don't know how people stick up for themselves. 'The government is looking at numbers and making the ching ching with pharmaceutical companies. I don't think they are too worried about what's happening.

Mental health issues faced by Black women has also been a campaigning issue for *The Voice*. Often the struggles and challenges of men are given more attention, while women's mental health issues are not given the visibility or resources they deserve. Campaigners have pointed to the cultural stereotype of the strong Black woman, the person who holds the family together, as a significant barrier to women being able to have open and honest debates about mental health. A story published in *The Voice* in January 2015 kicked off a long-running awareness campaign to

NEWS @thevoicenews voicenews www.voice-online.co.uk

THERAPISTS OF COLOUR: Main, therapists from the The Black, African and Asian Therapy Network (BAATN) with Eugene Ellis, centre, meet below, in discussion during a recent event

'WE CAN BEAT DEPRESSION'

Black organisations pave the way on mental health care tailored to women in the community

By Alannah Francis

BLACK WOMEN in the UK face an increased risk of self-harm and depression, according to research published in the British Journal of Psychiatry and NHS data.

When it comes to addressing the mental health problems of black women and the inadequate treatment they often face, the answers are coming from within the community.

Journalist Marverine Cole is one of the women driving the conversation around black women's mental health struggles and, importantly, the solutions into the mainstream.

Having recently opened up about her own experience with depression, and giving other black women a platform to

talk about their mental health in her documentary Black Girls Don't Cry, which aired last Friday on BBC Radio 4, Cole is proving black girls do indeed cry.

Like many, she the struggle of acknowledging what she was experiencing and concerns over how she would be perceived by others initially prevented Cole from speaking out.

DETRIMENTAL

But when she eventually told her friends, she discovered a number of them were taking antidepressants.

It took her longer to tell family members, however.

Mental health wasn't something that they discussed and she only told her mum of her diagnosis the day the documentary aired.

Cole is now urging other black women to speak out about their mental health issues and distance themselves from detrimental stereotypes.

"If we feel we're not handling things emotionally, we've got to speak up. We can't just keep saying 'I'm

fine, I'm fine, I'm fine' because that's when, sometimes, crises happen," said Cole.

One of the factors behind this reluctance to express concerns is the 'strong black woman' trope.

"The stereotypes are strong, they're perpetuated in the media – this whole strong black woman thing – we've just got to step out of that," said Cole.

Mainstream mental health services often lack the resources required to provide adequate care to black women. Instead of waiting for the services to wake up to their needs, black healthcare professionals and local groups are setting up their own services - and black women are finding them essential.

Cole, who saw a black fe-

> **"The stereotypes in the media show strong black women – and we have to step out of that"**

male counsellor, said: "People don't seem to understand us well enough to treat us properly."

Dr Isha McKenzie-Mavinga, a writer, poet and integrative transcultural psychotherapist and author of Black Issues in the Therapeutic Process, echoed Cole's feelings on the benefits of meeting with a black therapist.

It is important for black women to have "safe places where we can share our experiences and not feel mad and isolated".

Her work is an example of just that. She adopts what she terms a "black empathic approach" when a black woman is expressing issues affecting her mental health, creating an environment where her experiences are not denied.

"I believe her for a start and I assist her to assess, specifically, concerns about her identity and how that impacts her coping skills."

Dr McKenzie-Mavinga said institutional racism was behind the neglect of black

women's mental health, and cited what she called "ancestral baggage" as a cause for of their mental health conditions. "The first thing I would point to is racism, institutional racism and lack of attention to the mental health of black people," she said.

While black professionals and people with lived experience of mental health issues agree the NHS needs to do more to acknowledge smaller services that are helping black women, thriving initiatives from black psychologists are leading the way.

Calls from within the community were behind the creation of The Black, African and Asian Therapy Network (BAATN).

It is the UK's largest independent organisation specialising in working psychologically with people from black, African, Caribbean and Asian backgrounds.

It helps connect BAME people with counsellors who share similar ethnic backgrounds and an understanding of the cultural factors which can exacerbate mental health issues.

Eugene Ellis, the founder of BAATN, said: "The figures for BAME people accessing mental health services were pretty poor. The main motivation for me was people asking for therapists of colour."

Ellis works with those in the psychotherapy and counselling profession to meet the needs

of black people. His work involves encouraging people to face racial biases, something he describes as a difficult task. Funding is also a challenge.

"Trying to create the services ourselves, that's a big issue due to funding... we're trying to create safe spaces which do inspire other organisations," Ellis said.

EMOTIONAL

Nigel Stewart, the founder and director of The Centre for Pan African Thought, hosted the emotional emancipation circles explored by Cole in the documentary.

The initiative, in partnership with The Association of Black Therapists and the Community Healing Network, is another example of how black organisations are leading the way when it comes to improving access to tailored tools that tackle mental health issues.

Emotional emancipation circles give black people a space to share their stories and learn strategies to effectively respond to issues that aggravate mental health issues. A programme of the sessions will run for two years at the centre.

Stewart said: "It's our commitment to the community.

"The overwhelming response we get just across the board is people are very grateful for having a safe space to express some of the trauma and situations and discrimination they face on a daily basis."

The Voice also highlighted how the Black community were focusing on improving mental health care for women

encourage the sharing of stories and help break down some of the stigmas associated with mental health in the Black community.

Necola Hall joined the army in 2003, shortly after arriving in the UK from Jamaica. As a member of the 1 Black Watch Scottish Regiment in Warminster, Wiltshire, Hall's army career included a tour of Iraq during the Second Gulf War in 2004. But her dream career was soon to run into difficulty. When she got back home from Iraq, the unrelenting challenges of military life took their toll.

Hall struggled with her work in the army and found the experience of taking the exams required as part of her training difficult, something that led her to feel depressed. What she didn't know at the time was that her problems were due to her being severely dyslexic, a fact that only came to light after an army medical exam.

A year after returning from Iraq, Hall found out she was pregnant. Sadly, she experienced a miscarriage at 20 weeks. To add to her problems, she was also diagnosed with postnatal depression. Army doctors prescribed a course of anti depressants, but Hall refused. She feared that taking medication would force her to admit that her mental health had been affected which, in turn, would sink her army career, especially as one of a handful of Black and minority ethnic soldiers.

'I was afraid of the stigma in the Black community from my family and friends, if I admitted that I had mental health problems so I refused to take them,' Hall told *The Voice*. 'Also, as a Christian, I felt that if I was depressed, I was spiritually weak so my way of dealing with it was just to pray.' Over the following years, her depression worsened, leading to her emotional withdrawal from her family and her husband expressing concern at her erratic behaviour. Finally, in 2012 she was assigned a mental health nurse and Hall says that move turned her life around.

'It was the first time that I could really just talk to someone without the fear of being judged or stereotyped. She just believed me. She gave me a number of coping strategies and made interventions on my behalf which meant that I wasn't put back into stressful working situations.' One of those coping strategies was to write a daily journal in which Hall was encouraged to get the feelings she was experiencing down on paper. That daily practice turned into a book, *I Was A Soldier: Survival Against the Odds*, in which she detailed her struggles with depression and some of the factors that prevented her from talking about it. Hall welcomed the opportunity to share her story with readers of *The Voice* and during the interview she highlighted some of the projects she was working on to raise awareness, urging other Black women to speak up if they were facing difficulties with their mental health.

She said:

I know many Black women in the same situation. They may not have been in the army but they are struggling with issues such as stress and anxiety every day and it could be to do with looking after the children, money worries, holding down a job and very few of them have the courage to come out and talk about it for fear of what the church might say or looking like women who can't hold things together. I'm saying that is wrong and that it has to change. As Black women we may feel we always have to be strong in the face of emotional difficulties, but that's not the case.

Britain's top black weekly

ISSUE NO. 1836 | JUNE 14-20, 2018

**THE VOICE
CELEBRATING
35 YEARS
OF CHAMPIONING
A DIVERSE BRITAIN**

www.voice-online.co.uk £1.00

Civil rights leader Rev Al Sharpton addresses MPs

Grenfell a year on:

STILL RESILIENT, STILL UNITED

Community comes together to remember victims of the fire disaster

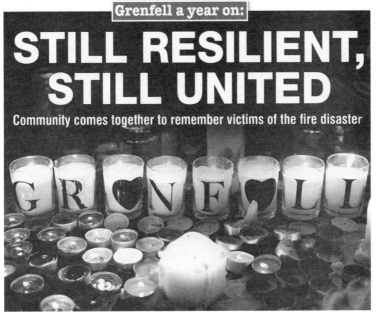

The Voice's

Windrush 70 Souvenir Edition
Out June 21 Interviews, personal stories, profiles and photos

A Windrush keepsake not to be missed!

Pick up a copy in your local supermarket / newsagent or email: subscriptions@thevoicemediagroup.co.uk

A year after the Grenfell fire, The Voice *commemorated the anniversary with a message of solidarity*

On June 14 2017, a shocking event brought home some hard truths about the nature of housing inequality in Britain. That day millions of people across the country saw the distressing scenes of Grenfell Tower, a 24-storey residential tower block in North Kensington, London on fire. There were many residents still trapped inside when the fire broke out. When the cladding caught fire, flames immersed the building and reduced people's homes to ash. In total, 72 people lost their lives in the tragedy.

It sent shockwaves through the construction industry and prompted an outpouring of grief and outrage as to how such a catastrophe could happen in the capital of one of the world's richest countries. What's more, Grenfell Tower is located in Kensington and Chelsea, a borough in which the rich live close to people struggling to make ends meet.

It's estimated that at least 34 of the Grenfell victims were from African, Middle Eastern or Asian backgrounds. Yet, during the inquiries, the issue of how housing inequalities impacted on people from minority communities was largely ignored.

On the first-year anniversary of the fire, *The Voice* reported on how people in the local community surrounding Grenfell Tower were providing each other with mutual support.

'Still resilient, still united' said the front-page headline of the 14 June 2018 edition.

In difficult times, people often look to local and national elected officials' leaders to provide stability and hope.

Instead survivors, bereaved relatives and justice campaigners were active in keeping up the pressure to get justice for the victims as the public inquiry into the causes of the fire opened. They organised a petition demanding a representative panel be added to the inquiry.

Among those who led the community response was Sierra Leone-born Kensington resident Tarek Gotti. The father of three self-funded 26 events for Grenfell Tower survivors, their families and local residents. To extend his philanthropic work he also set up a charity, Little Angels 4 Grenfell. Gotti said he decided to set up the charity after he witnessed his young children grieving following the loss of their school friends who died in the fire. On the night of the disaster Gotti and a group of friends were among the first individuals to enter the tower block, helping residents to escape during the initial stages of the fire at 1.05am on June 14.

But as the fire engulfed the tower block from two o'clock in the morning onwards the role of Gotti and the other first responders, as he described them, changed. Describing the night's events, Gotti told *The Voice*: 'As people evacuated the building I realised they would need water and chocolate to recover. That's when I told the guys from the local community who wanted to break through the police cordon to calm down and I helped to mobilise the community to ferry water, hot food and dates to the site.'

Speaking on the first-year anniversary, he wept as he repeated his children's reaction to their bereavement: 'I have to listen to my kids all the time saying, "I have lost my friends because of you. You're an army hero, why couldn't you save them?" I have been crying non-stop for the last year. I'm heartbroken. All I can do now is provide the love and affection for the local people and have an open house where I can feed them.'

Yvette Williams, campaign coordinator for Justice4 Grenfell, applauded the way in which the local community came together.

She told *The Voice*:

I don't believe many communities would have responded as positively to a similar disaster. Our resilience is a legacy of the Windrush Generation's achievements, which has helped release a unique community spirit. At times when I have felt weak there has always been local personalities available at marches or various events to add strength and provide encouragement for the cause.

2016 saw widespread Black Lives Matter protests in the US and UK following the deaths of two African American men, Alton Sterling and Philando Castile.

In the wake of those protests *The Voice* took a lead role in reporting on the rebirth of economic protest as a way of achieving racial equality. Equality campaigners who have been featured on the pages of the newspaper have long pointed out that the seemingly ever-widening differences in income and wealth between Black people and other communities invariably translate into similar disparities in political power and influence.

'Black Wealth Matters' was the headline on the front page of the 28 July 2016 edition. The story on the inside pages documented an emerging trend – thousands of Black Americans were moving their money into Black-owned banks in a powerful display of economic solidarity and boycotting big-name corporations as part of a pledge to support Black-owned businesses.

The report, headlined 'No respect without economic power', highlighted the efforts of organisations such as the Birmingham Black Pound Society who were trying to encourage a similar economic awareness in the UK.

At the time of the protests Black-owned banks could be found in several states across the US. There were none in this country.

However, this changed in October 2020 with the historic announcement that JN Bank had become the first 100 per cent Caribbean-owned retail bank in the UK. The news was splashed on the front page of the November 2020 edition under the headline 'New Digital UK Bank Launched'. The front page story told readers that the bank, launched by the JN Group, had opened its first branch in Brixton, South London, and was offering customers savings accounts and personal loans through the branch and its digital operation.

The headline on the inside story, 'At last – we've finally got a bank of our own in Britain', captured the feelings of *The Voice* readers and supporters of the bank.

'A moment of celebration for all and a decisive moment for the Black pound' the article said. 'For far too long, Black Britons have been poorly served by high street banks. For whatever reason, British banks have not treated their Black savers and borrowers equitably.' Advocates for a financial institution like JN Bank have long argued that it can play a critical role in community economic empowerment through providing loans for Black homeownership, capital for minority-led businesses or reinvesting in our communities. Now that dreamed-of bank had arrived, reader excitement about the news was clear. The article quoted Dean Fensome, CEO of JN Bank UK. He told *The Voice*: 'We intend to give back to the community primarily through the provision of scholarships/bursaries for tertiary education and the branch will be made available for community activities, workshops and seminars. We are excited to bring these values and behaviours to the UK and recognise the different financial needs of the population.'

The debate about how Black communities build economic muscle that followed the death of George Floyd in May 2020 occupied the mind of rapper Swiss at the height of the Black Lives Matter protests that year.

Swiss is well known to music fans as a member of the ground breaking South London garage collective So Solid Crew who bagged two MOBO Awards and a BRIT Award following the success of the chart-topping single '21 Seconds'. The protests that followed Floyd's death sparked memories of a conversation with friends that he'd had several years before.

'About 12 years ago, I had a passing thought about us galvanising ourselves and pouring back into our community economically' he told *The Voice* in May 2020:

> It was a strong inspirational thought I shared with my friend's older brother and that's where it stayed. It had always been lingering and I'm still surprised that no one actually came up with the idea of having a day where we're all thinking about going to support our own businesses and using that as a way to galvanise our community in thought and action. So, when George Floyd's murder happened it struck every corner of the world and people in many countries were protesting. But when I saw these protests and how the world reacted, I thought 'this is the same thing that happens every time'. There's an outpouring of emotion but I don't see any solution based practical actions that come out of that. I could see that this was a very strong, emotive signal that was coming from various communities, especially the Black community and I thought this was really a good time to redirect that energy. I wanted to do my part to create something positive out of this.

Britain's top black weekly

ISSUE NO. 1605 DECEMBER 5-11, 2013

FAMILY MATTERS: DO YOU KNOW WHO YOU ARE? p19-30»

THE VOICE

www.voice-online.co.uk £1.00

Bobby V Back with a vengeance

YV p23»

NEXT WEEK: A conversation with Rev Jessie Jackson

Angelic Angela

Bassett on her festive film role

p31»

Rallying Around

Bring back our Choice FM say listeners

p7»

WE WANT OUR CHOICE

MUM TOLD 'GO HOME'

Devastated Beverley Boothe ordered to return to Jamaica after 34 years in Britain

EXCLUSIVE p8»

Home Office

HEARTBROKEN: The woman fighting for her family

THE VOICE

www.voice-online.co.uk   £1.00

OUR
MADIBA

1918 - 2013

INSIDE: A special tribute p19 »

THE VOICE

www.voice-online.co.uk   £1.00

HAIR RAISING

Is natural hair a sign of cultural pride? p22 »

Fibroids nearly killed me p9
Emergency surgery recovered tumour the size of a six-month old foetus

INSIDE
Family Matters p27

FAMILY MATTERS

EXCLUSIVE INTERVIEW INSIDE

'I WANT TO TURN BLACK BRITAIN BLUE'

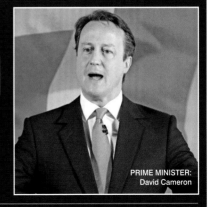

PRIME MINISTER:
David Cameron

Tory leader lays out plan to woo African and Caribbean voters

INSIDE: THE BET AWARDS IN PICTURES p26

THE VOICE

www.voice-online.co.uk £1.00

LIVING LEGEND
Beres Hammond on a 40-year career
.... p19 »

Lee 'Scratch' Perry
Reggae rebel
p23 ....

LS LIFE & STYLE

BERES HAMMOND
Real reggae royalty

Jamaican innovation
Legendary producer Lee Scratch
Perry on hitting the big screen

Rocking the runway
All the action from
Caribbean Fashion Week

Food for thought
Levi Roots becomes Life
& Style's new columnist

Kidnapped, beaten and tortured
Why this man was forced to leave Nigeria .... p6&7

HISTORY MAKER

How Baroness Valerie Amos, the young girl from Guyana, changed the face of higher education after being named the first black woman to lead a UK university

SEE INSIDE »

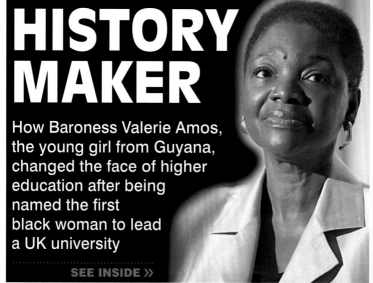

Britain's top black weekly

ISSUE NO. 1740 | JULY 28 - AUGUST 3, 2016

THE VOICE

www.voice-online.co.uk £1.00

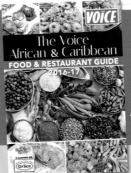

The Voice
African & Caribbean
FOOD & RESTAURANT GUIDE
2016-17

Food 4 thought...

Explore delicious African & Caribbean cuisine

To request your **FREE GUIDE** see inside

HIGHER LEARNING
Ten tips to get your child into a top school

UNIVERSITY FEATURE INSIDE: Your guide to Freshers' Week

BLACK WEALTH MATTERS

Community flexes financial muscle to gain equality

SEE INSIDE ›

PLUS

MANDELA TRILOGY
The major South African production is set to hit the UK stage

HIGH FLIER
Johnson-Thompson ready for Rio

THE VOICE

NEWSPAPER

OCTOBER 2019
ISSUE NO. 1901

YOUR FIRST 72-PAGE MONTHLY

WWW.VOICE-ONLINE.CO.UK

£2.50

Made by History essay competition returns

Free inside: UK Black Business Guide

Rudolph Walker: Celebrating an icon of stage and screen on his 80th birthday

'I'M STANDING FIRM'

EXCLUSIVE: Gina Miller speaks to The Voice about motherhood, courage, racism, campaigning and her fear over what will happen if we don't stand up for what is right **Page 6-7**

THE VOICE

JULY 2020 • ISSUE NO. 1908

BLACK LIVES MATTER

SEE INSIDE

NEWSPAPER

WWW.VOICE-ONLINE.CO.UK

£2.50

BEING BLACK IS NOT A CRIME

THE VOICE SAYS:

THE POLICE CONTINUE TO FAIL US

Met chief says things are improving but where is the evidence?

MILLIONS HAVE marched in the wake of George Floyd's death.

But systemic racism in policing is not just an American problem.

We are still five times more likely to be stopped by police than white Britons, more likely to be Tasered and a disproportionate number of black people die after use of force or restraint by officers.

In an exclusive interview Met Police Commissioner Cressida Dick told *The Voice* that the police have changed.

Our community's view has not – two decades after the Macpherson report was published there is still very little progress.

See full story inside

■ **THANK YOU TO OUR NHS HEROES AND KEY WORKERS**

SIMPLY THE BEST

Record breaker Lewis Hamilton – eight-page tribute edition

• Focus on the
Next Racing
Generation
• Hamilton
Commission:
Driving for
change
• Sporting Equals
pays homage to
the greatest of
all time
• fourth bullet
here

NOVEMBER 2020 • ISSUE NO. 1912

NEWSPAPER

WWW.VOICE-ONLINE.CO.UK

£2.50

SPECIAL FOCUS

Racism in Britain today
See pages 14, 18, 23, 41, 46

LEWIS HAMILTON
Greatest of all time
Tribute inside

NEW DIGITAL UK
BANK LAUNCHED

The first 100% Caribbean owned UK retail bank – JN Bank, was launched in Black History Month by JN Group. In keeping with its value to support communities, a flagship branch was opened in Brixton, South London. JN Bank has started by offering savings accounts and personal loans.

See pages 3 - 6 and 16

In 2020 the paper reported on the launch of the first Caribbean-owned UK retail bank

Swiss went on to create the first Black Pound Day, an event aimed at celebrating Black-owned businesses and giving the Black community a financial and emotional boost, after the anger at racial inequality in the UK evident by the protests that followed Floyd's death.

Falling on the first Saturday of each month, Black Pound Day encourages people to spend locally or online with Black-owned businesses and invest in communities that have been historically economically disadvantaged. The inaugural Black Pound Day attracted support from high-profile celebrities and quickly became the top-trending topic on Twitter in the UK. Now a regular event, it encourages Britons from all backgrounds to buy products or services from Black-owned businesses.

He said:

> I followed the inspiration I was given and here we are, many people getting behind this movement. I'm just so happy that people have been open to it. Black Pound Day does what it says on the tin, it's a very simple concept to understand.
>
> It's a day where we unify all cultures, not just Black, we utilise the emotional energy of recent months and turn that into an economic power as opposed to allowing those emotions to come and go as we know emotions do and nothing comes of it.

Following its June 2020 launch, several businesses shared on social media how they had experienced their biggest growth in sales after the event. Black Pound Day not only highlighted issues of systemic inequality in the UK, it held up a mirror to a major shift in how Black Britons supported Black-owned businesses. Among those who spoke about its impact was London-based company The Jerk Kitchen. Run by Natalie Dinning, the company was started by her father Neil in 2006. The Jerk Kitchen won hundreds of dedicated repeat customers before moving into other areas of business including producing a range of sauces called Lesley's, named after her mother. 'When I first heard about it, I was intrigued' Dinning told *The Voice*:

> I did a little bit of research, read what Swiss was saying and I was really excited about. But we didn't really know what was going to happen as a result of the day. The night before I didn't go to bed because I was creating some adverts to post on the actual day. But I also took the time to research other Black businesses and I was amazed at about how many there are out there. Then, at quarter to five in the morning on Black Pound Day, we got our first order. I was amazed and, to be honest, that day was a whirlwind for me. I was either answering a message on social media or replying to someone reposting us which was amazing. That day we sold our biggest ever number of sauces. Even though we have a lot of dedicated customers it's been hard to turn that into traffic to our website. Black Pound Day did that for us which was incredible.

However, Dinning told *The Voice* the impact must not stop there: 'I encourage people to not just stick to one day, we need to make sure that this message gets across because it's needed. One day is great but we need to make sure we are supporting each other 365 days of the year.'

For Swiss, this economic empowerment is a key part of what he wants Black Pound Day to achieve in the future:

> The day can help our community shape an economic agenda. When we have control of our economic agenda we can move from a position of power, we can make decisions from a position of power and achieve effective outcomes. Economic unity means we can effect change politically. This is really important. If we're a community that's not in a position of power we can't effect change in a way that can have a positive outcome for us.

Swiss's message seemed to have struck a chord. Research from the Black Pound Report 2022, produced by culture change consultancy Backlight, found that Black and minority ethnic consumers have become an increasingly important economic force. They have an annual disposable income of £4.5 billion – the figure for African Caribbean consumers alone is £1.1 billion. Importantly, they are increasingly vocal in using that sizeable buying power to challenge UK companies on the issue of race inequality. The report, which surveyed 3,500 people and is believed to be the most comprehensive study of its kind, found that 93 per cent of Black and minority ethnic consumers think brands have a responsibility to embrace diversity and inclusion compared to 74 per cent of those from a white background. And, the research found, multi ethnic consumers are around twice as likely as white consumers to favour and trust brands that are representative of different communities, have considered ethnic diversity in the creation of their products and services.

Business owners such as Georgina Fihosy, owner of Afro-touch Design, which produces African-inspired greeting cards, believes that the economic activism that Swiss set in motion with Black Pound Day will be around for a long time to come. 'Black consumers what to spend their money where they know they are being catered for' she told *The Voice*. 'I feel that this has led to some Black consumers spending more with Black-owned businesses and the Black Pound Day initiative has really helped to promote this. In my opinion, Black consumers will be loyal to and spend money on brands when that brand is seen as being culturally relevant, socially responsible and conscious as well as authentic.'

The Black community's desire for economic empowerment was a trend that *The Voice* had already identified leading to the launch of one of its most successful campaigns aimed at supporting Black-owned businesses. December 2018 saw the publication of the newspaper's first ever 'Black Business Guide' and the inaugural *The Voice* Black Business Fair, held at Brixton Town Hall. 'Community backs Black businesses' was the headline of the December 13 front-page news story about the event. Over 1,000 people gathered at the venue to buy from a diverse range of over 60 businesses and entrepreneurs. Attendees found there was everything from Black dolls and books for children, natural haircare and skincare products to authentic African-inspired clothing and Caribbean food and drink to choose from.

Among those who hailed the event was Joshua King, a business coach and speaker from London. He said:

Events like *The Voice* Black Business Fair are really important. They help consumers discover new Black-owned businesses, products and services. At the moment this happens predominantly online. While this is good it can be sporadic and decentralised. But having an event like this – with low barriers to entry, people not having to pay to attend and a good mix of businesses in the room – those that want to support Black-owned businesses will attend events like this. It's extremely needed and about time.

The growth in support of Black-owned businesses in the 2010s coincided with the emergence of another trend – the desire to celebrate Black achievement.

One of the most important manifestations of this is the *Powerlist* magazine and the annual *Powerlist* Black Excellence Awards. The *Powerlist* was established in 2007 when Michael Eboda, a former Editorial Director of Ethnic Media Group, left to start his own company, Powerful Media. Initially billed as a role model guide for young people, The *Powerlist* published a list of the UK's 100 most influential men and women of African, African Caribbean and African American heritage. Using his contacts in government Eboda managed to secure then-Prime Minister Gordon Brown for the inaugural launch, a feat that was to set the bar for the publication going forward. The following year, the *Powerlist* was launched at 10 Downing Street. At that time, Black people outside the realms of sport and entertainment were rarely given any recognition. Men and women such as Damon Buffini, Tom Ilube, Ric Lewis, Karen Blackett, Ken Olisa and Jacky Wright, all of whom have been hugely successful and influential in their respective sectors, were barely known until the *Powerlist* spotlighted them as number one on the list. The headline from *The Voice's* report on the 2020 Powerlist – 'We have the power' – in its November 2019 edition illustrated why so many in the community point to the *Powerlist* Black Excellence Awards as an inspirational event.

THE VOICE

www.voice-online.co.uk | £1.00

Dalton applies to stay in UK

X Factor champ to renew visa

New face in the sun

TV host Jean Johansson

TOP OF THE CLASS

the University of the West Indies hailed as one of the best in the world

See special 70th anniversary supplement inside

COMMUNITY BACKS BLACK BUSINESSES

SUPPORTING EACH OTHER: Some of the hundreds of people that attended The Voice Black Business Fair last weekend (photo: Thierry Lagrin)

The inaugural *Voice Black Business Fair* proves a success

By Vic Motune and Alannah Francis

THE AFRICAN Caribbean community came out in force at Lambeth Town Hall in Brixton last Saturday (December 8) to support black owned businesses.

Around 1,000 people vis-

ited the town hall between 10am and 6pm to buy from a diverse range of businesses and entrepreneurs who were present at the fair.

Eager shoppers came from across the UK to buy high quality unique products that ranged from black dolls and books for children, natural hair care and skin-

care products to authentic African-inspired clothing, Caribbean food and drink and professional services.

IMPORTANT

Charlotte Francis, who set up black doll and animation company Bizukho and Friends, told *The Voice*: "It's so important to have

events like this because funding black-owned businesses can sometimes be quite difficult. Having them all in the same room at one time means you can come out and support your community more easily."

Sonia Winnifred, Cabinet Member for Equalities and Culture, Lambeth Council,

also showed her support for the event.

She said: I really what to thank *The Voice* for putting on this event because it's important to show the community that we are good at business.

"We are entrepreneurs. you may not see us on the high street but we are there."

ONGOING ABUSE: Raheem Sterling

'National media too slow to react to racism'

THE MAINSTREAM media has been accused of being too slow to react to criticisms that its portrayal black footballers encourages racism in the game.

Earlier this week Manchester City forward Raheem Sterling prompted a major debate on the issue after he took to social media to address what he saw as the root cause of vitriol spouted from the terraces following his team's match with Chelsea.

In an Instagram post he said that th present helping to "fuel racism" by the ways in which they portray young black footballers.

In a statement the Black Collective of Media in Sport (BCOMS) said it hoped Sterling's comments would serve as a "wake up" call not just for newspapers but "all the media."

In his post, England international Sterling cited the markedly different ways his teammates Phil Foden and Tosin Adarabioyo were written about, with the latter portrayed in a markedly more negative light.

Sterling's comments come after he was abused by Chelsea fans at Stamford Bridge on Saturday (December 8). *See page 40*

In 2018 The Voice *organised its first Black Business fair in Brixton*

WE HAVE THE POWER

As the Powerlist 2020 is revealed, we take a look at those named in each category

A POSITIVE EFFECT ON PEOPLE'S LIVES: Clockwise from main, Ismail Ahmed's firm has changed how money is transferred; Cambridge has seen an increase in the number of black students enrolling since Stormzy announced his scholarship last year; Pat McGrath has been hailed as the world's most influential make-up artist

ISMAIL AHMED, founder and chairman of pioneering digital money transfer company WorldRemit, was named the most influential black person in Britain on the Powerlist 2020, the annual list of the 100 most powerful people of African, African Caribbean and African American heritage in the country.

Ahmed was born and raised in Somaliland during the country's civil war. He left for the UK in 1988, a journey that took over a month before he arrived in London.

One of his first jobs in this country was picking strawberries.

He also held down several jobs in order to send money to his family back in East Africa.

The challenges that came with sending international payments sowed the seeds of an idea that became WorldRemit.

Today the company employs 700 people across six continents and serves a diverse customer base that spans more than 30 nations from its London headquarters.

Ahmed said: "It is a real privilege and honour to win this award. When I was growing up in Somaliland, I saw how money sent back home by migrants could transform the lives of individuals and entire communities.

"When I came to London to study and started to send money back home, I was frustrated by the inconvenience and cost of transferring money through traditional agents. I was determined to find a better way and I set up WorldRemit in 2010 with the mission of making it easier and faster for migrants to send money home."

> **The Powerlist is delighted to celebrate these 100 amazing people – Ismail's story is incredibly powerful**

He added: "Today World Remit is one of the most global fintech firms and has attracted diverse and talented teams in London and around the world. This honour is testament to their hard work and passion for the company's mission."

Michael Eboda, Powerlist 2020 publisher said: "The Powerlist is delighted to celebrate these 100 amazing people.

Ismail is a true pioneer whose company is shaking up the remittance industry and positively impacting the lives of people around the world. His story is incredibly powerful and an inspiration to us all."

He is joined on the list by world renowned make-up artist Pat McGrath, founder of eponymous billion-pound cosmetics line Pat McGrath Labs.

McGrath has been hailed by American *Vogue* as the most influential make-up artist in the world.

This year she was among *Time* magazine's 100 most influential people alongside Michelle Obama and Facebook founder Mark Zuckerberg.

Beverley Johnson, hailed as the world's first black supermodel, described McGrath as a 'legend' and 'creative genius'.

She told *Time*: "When I started modelling there were no black makeup artists. It was a challenge to look our best. Pat McGrath allows us to be seen. Her make-up is not just nice make-up – her bold, beautiful colours make a statement. You usually don't get that with world-renowned make-up artists."

Also on the list is acclaimed grime artist Stormzy.

Described as the 'voice of the people' Stormzy, real name Michael Omari, began rapping at the age of 11. He turned to music full-time after working in quality assurance at an oil refinery in Southampton.

After gaining plaudits on the grime scene he later won Best Grime Act at the MOBO Awards.

He followed this feat by becoming the first unsigned rapper to appear on *Later with Jools Holland*.

Last year Stormzy announced that he would be funding scholarships for two students a year to attend Cambridge University.

It will fund tuition fees and maintenance grants for up to four years.

Another notable name on the list is the Duchess of Sussex, Meghan Markle.

New entrants on the Powerlist 2020 include model and activist Adwoa Aboah, *pictured left,* Michael Sherman, Chief

● Continued on page 59

The Voice also celebrated the Powerlist, *which names the most influential Black people in Britain*

The article featured an interview with Ismail Ahmed, founder and chairman of pioneering digital money transfer company WorldRemit, who was named the most influential Black person in Britain in that year's *Powerlist*. Also interviewed was world-renowned make-up artist Pat McGrath, founder of eponymous billion-pound cosmetics line Pat McGrath Labs. McGrath, who like Ahmed, was in the *Powerlist* 2020 top ten has been hailed by *American Vogue* as the most 'influential make-up artist in the world'. She was also among *Time* magazine's 100 most influential people alongside Michelle Obama and Mark Zuckerberg. As it has grown in recognition over the years, *Powerlist* has become the go-to publication for corporate organisations looking to diversify their board rooms. The *Powerlist* Black Excellence Awards, a very high-end Black-tie dinner, at which the *Powerlist*'s top ten is now launched every year, is widely recognised as the most important event in the Black professional calendar annually.

Two men that have been key to sports coverage in *The Voice* throughout the 2010s are Jofra Archer and Raheem Sterling.

Raheem Sterling is one of the nation's most precocious footballers, achieving renown while still a teenager, and has been instrumental in the turning around of England's football fortunes. Sterling, born in Jamaica in December 1994, travelled to Britain at the age of five, joining Queen's Park Rangers' academy aged ten. In 2010 he joined Liverpool for a fee of £450,000 and, two years later, would become the club's third youngest player. He came close to winning the Premier League title at Anfield and later began to accrue silverware following his £44-million transfer to Manchester City in 2015. When Pep Guardiola took the City reins in 2016, Sterling began to add further tactical flexibility to his game. He has won almost everything at the Etihad apart from the coveted Champions League.

Yet his success has come against a backdrop of racist abuse. An angry supporter got in Sterling's face at Stamford Bridge in 2018. After the incident, Sterling spoke eloquently and found support from most who listened. Here was another young, Black man forced to discuss his skin colour because of the intolerance of others. It was an issue that was forced on him and one he has handled with dignity throughout, including when the England team were booed by elements of their own support for taking the knee in support of Black Lives Matter. More often the abuse against Sterling was more insidious, such as when he was targeted by the British press for his supposed largesse, as well as his tattoos. Gareth Southgate's side represent a promising picture of multicultural society but this has done little to insulate Sterling from the worst elements of society.

By the same token, Archer's progress came at a time when English cricket's problems with institutional racism came to light in harrowing detail. Born in Barbados, he came to England as a 19-year-old with a view to representing the country of his father. In 2019, Archer stood atop the podium with England at the Cricket World Cup at Lord's and inspired a generation of young, aspiring cricketers in the process. He made his name first at Sussex, then in the Indian Premier League, where he was awarded MVP in 2020 despite his Rajasthan Royals' side finishing bottom that year.

Less than a year later, Archer reported hearing racist remarks at the Test match between New Zealand and England at Mount Maunganui. In 2022 former fast bowler Chris Lewis, another of England's contingent with roots in the Caribbean, smiled all too knowingly when discussing the notion that Archer, whose temperament was questioned following a breach of COVID-19 protocols, did not have the 'stomach' for Test cricket.

His 90mph pace at the crease and middle order menace are ready-made for limited overs but a continuation of his Test career beckons as soon as he returns from his long-term elbow injury. There was a buzz when recent images appeared of Archer bowling in nets with strapping around the offending elbow. He appears close to his long-awaited comeback.

Still, the issue of racism is never far away and Archer's defence of the England cricket team's decision to stop taking the knee, which was criticised by Michael Holding, has not stopped him calling for reform. For its part, the England and Wales Cricket Board continues to come to terms with what its CEO Tom Harrison called a 'very difficult set of truths' within the English game. The enduring problems with racism across sport and wider society remain, yet we can take a moment to celebrate the exploits of two sons of the Caribbean representing England.

As social media matured over the course of the 2010s, sporting stars increasingly became targeted by racist trolls. During the delayed Euro 2020 finals, Bukayo Saka, Marcus Rashford and Jadon Sancho all found themselves victims of trolls after England were defeated by Italy at Wembley Stadium.

Despite this, 19-year-old Saka said he was looking forward and not back. Some of the abuse came from disappointed England fans and harked back to when Chelsea's first Black player, Paul Canoville, was a target of the very fans he was representing. Saka, who has Nigerian heritage, has said that negativity won't break him and love always wins after torrid social media abuse followed his penalty miss during the final against Italy.

A man sadly used to social media abuse is Lewis Hamilton. His is a story of genuine triumph and inspiration. Since his arrival on the scene not a month has gone by when *The Voice* has not been contacted by a family friend or associate about a young, aspiring driver that wants to follow in Hamilton's tyre treads.

The 2010s has also seen an increase in the number of sporting clubs set up for the Black community. Organisations such as the British Black Golfers and the Black Swimming Association, who achieve so much with no profile or resources, have always had a place in our sports coverage. Their passion is every bit as great as those that are on our radar seemingly every day.

Football's Goals 4 Girls, founded by Francesca Brown; the sterling work of Bobby Kasanga at Hackney Wick FC; cricket's ACE Programme, the brainchild of the first Black woman to play for the England senior team, Ebony Rainford-Brent; and the S-Factor Athletics Academy, founded by Lisa Miller, are all honing the skills of sports' future.

There was a time when women's football was disregarded in favour of the men's game. But thanks to the achievements of the Lionesses, female footballers are finally receiving the acclaim they deserve.

Former international Hope Powell was dubbed the 'First Woman of English football' by *The Voice*. Now the Brighton Women's coach, Powell was the coach for the England women's team between 1998–2013 and played a key part in progressing the women's game. The Women's Super League has given genuine hope that, in time, it will attract the riches and profile of the Premier League.

The Voice also championed the career of Leicester City Women's player Holly Morgan. Over her 17 years at the club she was a defender, captain and then coach, while her brother Jonathan was team manager, her sister Jade was general manager and their father Rohan was chairman. The Morgan family were instrumental in Leicester City's rise to the Women's Super League – these are the stories that *The Voice* was born to tell.

As Black Lives Matter protests swept through the United Kingdom in the 2010s, they also raised questions about the country's education system. Calls grew for schools and universities to develop curriculums that better reflect a multicultural society, rather than, as many campaigners feel, stick with a curriculum that omits Black history. Indeed, there has been a long tradition of Black community activism in the education sector. Saturday schools, which trace their origins back to the 1960s, were founded by Black parents as a reaction to the racism and low expectations from teachers that saw their children experience racism in class. The parents, teachers and campaigners who were behind these volunteer schools say the activism they represent is needed now more than ever.

According to official figures Black Caribbean pupils are being excluded from schools in England six times more often than their white peers in some areas of England, analysis found. Schools have a statutory duty not to discriminate against pupils on the grounds of race. The pages of *The Voice* have featured several stories over the years of Black pupils unfairly targeted for things such as their hairstyles, kissing teeth and fist-bumping. Among them is Chikayzea Flanders, a 12-year-old who was forced to leave Fulham boys school in London on his first day in September 2017. He was told that his dreadlocked hair, which he wore tied-up, did not comply with the school's uniform and appearance policy and had to be cut off or he would face suspension. His mother, Tuesday Flanders, said his dreadlocks were a fundamental tenet of his Rastafarian beliefs and therefore should be exempt from the policy. Her son was taught in isolation and subsequently chose to leave the school to attend a nearby academy instead.

THE VOICE

SEPTEMBER 2020 • ISSUE NO. 1910

WINDRUSH HELPLINE campaign launched

Arrivals Waterloo Station 1948

SEE PAGE 4 – 5

NEWSPAPER

WWW.VOICE-ONLINE.CO.UK

£2.50

TRIBUTE TO
LORD MORRIS OF HANDSWORTH OJ
From shop steward to the people's hero

SEE PAGE 23–27

OUR CHILDREN'S EDUCATION
IS IN OUR HANDS

Following lockdown black parents are discovering that homeschooling is a way to challenge the low expectations and racial disparities of mainstream schools

SEE FULL STORY INSIDE

In 2020 The Voice *was inundated with messages from concerned parents who did not want their children to go back to school after lockdown*

However, in its September 2020 edition *The Voice's* front-page story told readers about an emerging trend it had investigated. 'Our children's education is in our hands' was the headline as it reported that while many families across the UK struggled with having to home school their children at the same time as coping with the demands of working from home, for Black families, lockdown had provided new opportunities. Quoted in the inside story was Cheryl Phoenix of the education campaign group Black Child Agenda. She said that a growing number of Black parents were more likely to continue with home-schooling after the end of lockdown.

She told *The Voice* that parents were increasingly taking their children's education into their own hands in a bid to protect them from institutional racism, stereotyping and a culture of low expectations of Black pupils from teachers.

'It's a massive trend. My inbox is filled with messages from parents asking, "How do I take my child out school? What do I do?" Every day I average about five to six messages from parents trying to find out what they have to do to ensure that their child doesn't go back to school in September.'

This trend of parents taking their children out of mainstream schools is an ongoing one as *Voice Online* reported in November 2021. The story, headlined 'Black Supplementary Schools are back and here to stay' said that there had been a dramatic increase in parents sending their children to Black supplementary schools following recent Black Lives Matter protests.

Among the campaigners that the newspaper interviewed was Nia Imara, who founded the National Association of Black Supplementary Schools (NABSS) website in 2007, which publishes a directory of Black supplementary schools across the UK.

Speaking to *The Voice*, he said: 'Since the rise of Black Lives Matter, there are more parents choosing to send their children to a supplementary school and I am seeing more schools opening to keep up with the demand.'

Davis Williams, founder of the Manhood Academy Global (MAG) – a registered charity committed to providing Black children with life-changing transformation opportunities said he also noticed soaring numbers of Black families reaching out to him for help. He told *The Voice*:

> We can't cope with how many parents are coming through our doors. We love what we do, but the amount of families we are seeing is showing us there is a bigger problem. A lot of parents have lost their patience and tolerance with the mainstream education system and are now home educating and are coming to us for support teaching their children about self-esteem, confidence and other key cultural elements.

The case of Child Q, the name given to the 15-year-old Black schoolgirl who was strip-searched by the police and wrongly accused of having drugs with her, reignited the concerns of parents about the way schools discriminate against their children. *The Voice* spoke to several education campaigners and teachers as part of its coverage of the story. Among them was Zahra Bei, a teacher with 20 years' experience and a member of the group No More Exclusions. She told the newspaper that the education system was inflicting 'state violence' on Black children. 'I see teachers acting more like prison guards and cops than educators' she said. 'I don't want to de-centre the story of Child Q, but also we know there are many Child Q's that have been treated like this.'

Black Lives Matter protests also prompted calls for greater race equality in higher education.

The decade saw some high-profile appointments – Baroness Valerie Amos made history as the first Black female head of a UK university when she was appointed Director of SOAS in 2015. *The Voice* also published exclusive interviews with former media executive Sonita Alleyne, who in 2019 became the first ever Black master of an Oxbridge college when she was appointed master of Jesus College, Cambridge University, and Lord Simon Woolley who became the first Black man to be elected head of an Oxbridge College. In March 2021 he was appointed principal of Cambridge University's Homerton College.

But despite these ground breaking appointments, figures from the Higher Education Statistics Agency (HESA) show that while the presence of Black students on campuses has improved, the number of Black professors has consistently remained below 1 per cent for several years. Speaking to *The Voice* about the lack of diversity in higher education, Baroness Valerie Amos said: 'Most universities will have action plans and strategies to tackle racial inequality, however this has not gone far enough. We should not be rewarding intent – we need to reward action and change.'

If the Windrush Scandal and racial profiling by police officers were key issues for equality campaigners in the 2010s, COVID-19 would reveal how these stark racial inequalities increased the risk of serious illness and death for people from Black and minority ethnic communities. After the World Health Organization (WHO) declared that the world was facing a pandemic in early 2020, Andrew Cuomo, Governor of New York talked about COVID-19 being the 'great equalizer'. He was referring to the notion that COVID was no respecter of demographics such as race, gender or age. But the tragic stories of Black healthcare professionals dying in what seemed like greater numbers than their white counterparts quickly proved this notion a fallacy. As news began to emerge about the impact of the pandemic in Britain and across the world, a 23 April *Voice Online* news report discussed what was quickly becoming a growing concern – why were people from Black, Asian and minority ethnic backgrounds at seemingly higher risk of suffering complications and death from the disease than white people?

Research from the Intensive Care National Audit and Research Centre examined patients critically ill with COVID-19 in UK hospitals. It found 35 per cent of almost 2,000 patients with COVID-19 were from a Black, Asian or minority ethnic background, despite forming only 13 per cent of the UK population. The article quoted Kamlesh Khunti, a professor in primary care diabetes and vascular medicine at the University of Leicester. He said: 'This is a signal and it needs to be looked at more carefully. We need to ensure that every individual, including the BAME population, are following social distancing instructions. We have anecdotal information that it might not be happening in certain BAME groups.' The following month a study of early COVID-19 deaths by the Health Service Journal found that 63 per cent of the first 106 deaths of NHS staff were from BAME backgrounds.

At the same time *The Voice*'s coverage highlighted the tragic impact of the pandemic on Black health professionals. Among them was Dr Alfa Sa'adu, who was described by his son Dani as a 'passionate man, who cared about saving people.' After working for nearly 40 years in different London hospitals before retiring in 2017, the well-liked and respected medic had returned to help the NHS in the battle against COVID-19. In March 2020 Dr Sa'adu started to show symptoms and immediately self-isolated. He sadly died a short time later. Tributes came from across the world, praising the Nigeria-born doctor's medical skill, warmth and dedication to helping others. Yvonne Coghill, director of the Workforce Race Equality Standard Implementation Team, NHS England, had worked with Dr Sa'adu and wanted readers of *The Voice* to know about the impact that her former colleague had on people from all walks of life: 'The presence that that man had when he was his authentic self, was phenomenal, I cannot even tell you. Alfa was a wonderful man, a wonderful human being.'

Among other stories of Black health professionals who died after contracting COVID-19 were Onyenachi Obasi, a nurse and health visitor from Barking and Dagenham, described by her family as an 'example of unconditional love' and Lewisham hospital nurse and mum-of-two Grace Kungwengwe. *The Voice* story included tributes from people who had known her and donated to her Go Fund Me page to raise funds for Grace's funeral. One of those donating, Teresa Borg said: 'This lady risked her live to help others, she's a hero.' As the UK went into lockdown, countless more heart-breaking stories of other Black key workers who died after contracting COVID-19 were emerging. The death of railway worker Belly Mujinga sparked an outpouring of anger. The mother of one, who had underlying respiratory problems, died on 5 April, 14 days after she was spat at by a man at Victoria Station.

In a column published that month in *The Voice*, headlined 'Belly Mujinga deserved more than being merely disposable,' Mayowa Ayodele wrote: 'That Belly Mujinga lost her life in the midst of the pandemic is a source of extreme sadness. That she leaves behind a husband is cause for even greater grief. It will lead to questions as to why, despite apparent knowledge of her respiratory issues, she was sent back out onto the concourse to complete her shift.' When UK grandmother Margaret Keenan became the first person in the world to be given the BioNTech-Pfizer vaccine in December 2020 it marked the start of the biggest mass vaccination programme in NHS history.

Health campaigners were also hopeful that this would halt the high numbers of people from Black and minority ethnic communities who were dying from the virus. These communities were high on the list of those leading NHS campaigns to encourage people to get vaccinated. However, after only a few months into the start of the vaccination roll-out it was clear that this was proving a challenge. Despite several studies highlighting COVID-19's dramatic impact on Black Britons they were among the hesitant groups to get a vaccine.

A YouGov poll published in March 2021 found that one in ten Black and minority ethnic Britons said they would not get vaccinated, a figure which rose to 19 per cent among people of African Caribbean origin. In contrast, another survey found that only 6 per cent of white Britons would refuse the vaccine.

Personal experiences of insensitive treatment by the NHS and a deep-rooted mistrust of authorities played a role in making many sceptical about the benefits of a vaccination.

On *The Voice*'s social media platforms and online forums, questions and fears circulated about the vaccine's safety. Dr Omon Imohi, a general practitioner in Newton-le-Willows, Merseyside, is among those who are passionate about challenging this mistrust. Dr Imohi is the co-founder of Black Women in Health, a non-profit partnership network for Black female healthcare professionals.

In the early months of 2021 her frustration at the relatively low numbers of Black people coming forward to get vaccinated led to her to innovate some new ways of connecting with an

Opinion

'Racism isn't getting worse – it's just getting caught on film'

Injustice and discrimination is nothing new to us – but the use of technology and social media means that people can be held to account more easily, says **Samuel Brooksworth**

IF ANDREW hit me, I had to hit him back. Growing up as a twin, like most siblings, we both had a simple rule. If he hit me, I had to hit him back and of course vice versa.

Until either one of us got our hit, there would be no resolution.

White people are hitting black people, but black people are not able to hit back. Ever.

Not in most court rooms, not in most places of work, and not almost anywhere. Being hit time and time again, but being told to stay calm, and not to react.

When you do react, you're the problem.

This is a vicious cycle of no resolution.

DIFFERENT

George Floyd's death feels different. Not because it has differed to any other unjustified murder that has been carried out by law enforcement on an unarmed black man, but it feels different due to the string of senseless racial discrimination that has occurred in this very same month.

Two names – Ahmaud Arbery and Amy Cooper.

Let's start off by saying racism isn't getting worse, it's simply getting captured.

The Ahmaud Arbery murder shows the pivotal role that footage plays in bringing justice after what is basically murder in broad daylight.

THREATENING

Additionally, incidents like that involving Amy Cooper; the white woman who was caught on camera telling Christian Cooper, a black birdwatcher, she was going to tell the police an African American man was "threatening my life" after he

> " The world can tune in front seat and view what many of us have to deal with on a day-to-day basis "

asked her to leash her dog in New York's Central Park.

Incidents like this, which most black people can relate to, are finally also being filmed.

No longer are these injustices simply things happening 'in our heads'.

PRIVILEGE

Instead the world can tune in front seat and view what many of us have to deal with on a day-to-day basis.

A white person using their privilege to make a black person feel lesser.

This particular incident angered many who saw it as Amy Cooper was an educated woman in a senior position within a top corporate organisation.

One can only imagine how many white people like Amy are in organisations blocking black people from progressing or getting promotions through their mindsets towards black people, only to hide behind the façade of 'work place equality'.

George Floyd's murder and the Amy Cooper incident go hand-in-hand. Floyd was killed

at the hands of racist law enforcement officers.

Black people's hopes and dreams are also being killed on a day-to-day basis by women like Amy Cooper in the corporate world and our culture is being stolen by organisations that want to profit from us but are then not willing to defend us.

We are being killed on the street, in the workplace and in courts rooms.

These two incidents highlight why frustration reached boiling point in the Western world due to the injustices we face every day.

UNJUST

Covid-19 has further highlighted this racism due to the unjust disproportionate rate of fatalities of black people compared to white people.

Is coronavirus racist? No.

Are black people more susceptible to contracting the virus? No.

What has been highlighted by this disproportionate rate of fatalities is the lack of care and attention given to those who have complained or have suffered.

Added to this, black, Asian and minority ethnic (BAME) people in England are 54 per cent more likely to be fined under coronavirus rules than white people are, again showing the disparity between how black people and white people are treated. Why is this?

Like everyone else, black people are at home in isolation, hopelessly watching these incidents take place around the world and seeing nothing being actioned.

With Ahmaud Arbery's death and Amy Cooper's incident bitterly stacking weight, George Floyd's murder is the straw that finally broke the camel's back.

ENOUGH IS ENOUGH: Top, the death of George Floyd 'feels different', says Samuel Brooksworth; left, video footage of Amy Cooper's encounter with black bird enthusiast Christian Cooper went viral

As Black Lives Matter protests swept the UK in 2020, The Voice *noted how social media had changed the nature of activism*

audience she was desperate to reach with clear, accurate information about the vaccine.

'In January 2021 we started creating short one or two-minute entertaining TikTok videos about the vaccine, what it contains, the benefits and the possible side effects,' she told *The Voice* in January 2022.

> She explained further: We also organised several Zoom webinars, and Facebook Live and Instagram Live events with other Black doctors, nurses and pharmacists and people who were involved in the clinical trials when the vaccine was being developed. Through social media and platforms such as WhatsApp we've been able to reach a wide audience, answer questions and help people understand why they need the vaccine. Addressing some of the key doubts and conflicting advice found in several online platforms has been a key part of this strategy. We know that normally vaccines take about five years to create. Now we have a vaccine that was created in less than a year, so of course, people will be sceptical Every webinar we conducted had a panel of people from different medical specialities and non-medics such as faith and community leaders. What we did was to take the questions and myths we were hearing such as the belief that the vaccine contains microchips and create slides to use in the webinar. Then someone on the panel with a medical background would explain why the vaccine doesn't contain microchips.

The collaborative efforts of medical professionals like Imohi, local health authorities and community organisations to create a culturally sensitive approach to the vaccine rollout appeared to have had a positive effect.

According to NHS data, the number of non-white people vaccinated in the UK rose from 2.4 million to 7.6 million between February and April 2021.

Nottingham became home to the first Black Lives Matter branch in Europe in 2015 after it was founded on Twitter in 2013 by three Black women, Patrisse Cullors, Alicia Garza and Opal Tometi. In the early years of Black Lives Matter UK, *The Voice* was an important outlet at a time when much of the mainstream media was largely unsympathetic to its cause. The prevailing view was that there was little need for such a movement in this country because race relations were better here than they were in the US. In July 2016, a crowd of about 300 people gathered in Windrush Square, Brixton, bringing traffic to a standstill as they marched to the police station and through neighbouring streets, chanting 'Black lives matter' and 'hands up, don't shoot'. This march followed widespread anger at the deaths of two Black men, Philando Castile in Minnesota and Alton Sterling in Louisiana, in the United States following police contact. Speaking exclusively to *The Voice*, Marayam Ali, the founder of the Black Lives Matter movement in London, echoed the views of those who felt that racism and police brutality is as prevalent here as it is the US.

The 18-year-old said: 'By these people coming here to stand and unite, they are showing that they are against police brutality and that's the most important thing. I think people forget that racism is a worldwide thing. It's still very prevalent. This is ultimately a cry for help.'

Unlike the Black Lives Matter demonstrations of 2016, the death of George Floyd in May 2020 sparked an unprecedented

Opinion

'ALL I EVER DID WAS BE BLACK'

We might be 'safer' in Britain than our US counterparts, but we're still under attack, says **Abigail Ogunjobi**

DISCRIMINATION: For Abigail Ogunjobi, racism manifests itself in everyday interactions

THE BRIT in me is whispering, "Be quiet Abbie, be PC", whilst the black in me retorts, "Speak up! If not now, then when?"

I wrote this piece and held on to it for weeks because honestly, I've been protective of it.

I've been guarded against those who are 'bored' of the topic, those who in their hearts and homes have the luxury of undermining struggles that they will never be subject to.

Just under three months ago, the world witnessed the cold-blooded murder of yet another black man, victim to an archaic yet ever-present regime of skin politics. For many

> **If an individual like Derek Chauvin doesn't suffocate you, oppression will**

black people in America, the heart-breaking reality is, if an individual like Derek Chauvin doesn't suffocate you, the weight of a four-pronged (institutional, structural, interpersonal and internalised) system of oppression will. Quick

history lesson: upon the abolition of slavery, black Americans found themselves at a severe economic disadvantage.

Housing authorities and banks would not grant them the loans that they required to thrive and maintain a quality standard of living.

DISPARITY

This led to an increase of run-down neighbourhoods and a stark disparity between black and white communities as well as limited resources to build and sustain their businesses.

Redlining meant that government agencies defined cities that they deemed to be attractive for

investment, usually categorising black neighbourhoods as undesirable.

Low property values and low tax contributions from black neighbourhoods meant that less money could be allocated to local black schools resulting in the recruitment of underqualified teachers, inadequate educational material and large student/teacher ratios – the perfect set

up for failure. Larger classes become harder to control, students disengage and become disruptive. The consequence? Suspension and expulsion.

OBLIGATION

With extra time on their hands and no obligation to be in school, is it any wonder that some of their kids get caught up in bad company? Is it sur-

prising that they end up in juvenile detention centres, gradually inducting themselves further into the criminal justice system, which we already know (as guided by negative media propagation) has its biases against black people?

Upon release, many of these offenders struggle to find jobs.

Continued on page 45

In the aftermath of the death of George Floyd, The Voice *provided a platform for Black journalists to speak honestly about their personal experiences*

discourse about the nature of systemic racism in the UK. Commentators not only highlighted grim statistics illustrating the extent of racial inequality in this country but also the more subtle ways that racism had an impact on the lives of Black people.

Among them was *The Voice* writer Abigail Ogunjobi.

'The Brit in me is whispering, "Be quiet Abbie, be PC", while the Black in me retorts, "Speak up! If not now, then when?"' she wrote in an August 2020 column headlined 'All I ever did was be Black':

> Living Black in Britain is having my petrol pump switched off at the petrol station and being asked to pay first when the other customers didn't have to. It's having myself and my siblings accosted on our way out of a restaurant by the manager wanting to 'double check' if we had covered the bill. It's me holding my groceries at almost arm's length, so the security guard who is 'keeping an eye on me' can see that I'm not stealing.

Back in 1982, founder of *The Voice* Val McCalla had a goal from the very beginning that Britain's rapidly growing Black community should have a platform to campaign against the discriminatory policing and champion its rights amidst the racial tension that marked life in Britain in the early 1980s. In the second decade of the twenty-first century, that radical campaigning platform that McCalla envisioned back in 1982 adapted to the digital communication age.

Following the Black Lives Matter protests that swept the UK in 2020 after the death of George Floyd at the hands of police officers, that platform became even more important in providing Black people with a voice to challenge racism in policing. Thousands defied the government-imposed lockdown to join the largest anti-racism rallies ever seen in this country, easily exceeding the 80,000 who attended the Rock Against Racism concert in East London in April 1978. Protests took place in towns and places where there were very few Black people.

In the days immediately after Floyd's death, *The Voice*'s Twitter, Instagram and Facebook pages quickly signposted readers to information about planned demonstrations across the UK campaign while also posting news stories, comment pieces and video footage on *Voice Online*. For thousands of activists social media, unlike any tool available in the 1980s and 1990s, has given the younger generation faster access to people and information than their predecessors could have imagined. If you want to share a video of a protest or a violent police arrest, you might post it on TikTok or Instagram, for example. If you want to let people know about an upcoming march, you may use WhatsApp, Twitter or Facebook.

For people like *The Voice* reporter Leah Mahon, social media is a key part of activism. She said:

There was lots of information being shared and conversation on Instagram, and that's where I was often direct messaging my friends and finding out about where a lot of the protests were taking place. I'd say 'I'll be going to this Black Lives Matter protest here in Manchester, that one in Birmingham, who else is going? And then we'd all agree. It was personal as well. At the time I was dealing with a lot of racism in my previous workplace, getting called the N word and other microaggressions and I just thought, 'I'm tired of this and I want to do something quickly.'

Column

WHY WE MUST EMBRACE OPTIMISM AMID TURMOIL

2020 has been one of the most difficult years we have ever had to endure. But, says **David Olusoga**, despite this, the anger and frustration we feel can only benefit us in the long term – and we've already started to see that

A S WE enter the final months of 2020 – the year of Black Lives Matter, toppled statues and an unprecedented national conversation about race and racism – how should we feel about it all?

Should we be generally optimistic or pessimistic about the future?

Should we conclude that what happened this summer - here in Britain and across the world – was an historic moment of change, loaded with potential for yet greater transformation?

Or should we draw the opposite conclusion and assume that what we have just witnessed was merely a passing moment, an event rather than the beginning of a process?

INGRAINED

As so often the case for pessimism is the easier of the two to make. Pessimism is justified because of what it is we are up against - the idea of race.

Centuries-old and deeply ingrained within our society race casts a heavy shadow over the modern world.

Like many of the most powerful and most toxic ideas it has become so normalised that many of those who are advantaged by it are unaware of their privilege.

To make the case for optimism is to ask that millions of people who live their lives under the shadow of race to believe that

> " Companies big and small now acknowledge the structural nature of racism "

in the near future they might escape into the light. That is quite an ask.

Optimism is often dismissed as wishful thinking but this year the case for optimism has to be made because in 2020 events have taken place that no one would have predicted back in January.

If, for example, someone had told me nine months ago that by Black History Month 2020 the statue of the slave trader Edward Colston, that had stood for 125 years in the centre of Bristol, would be lying on its back in a council lock up covered in graffiti and scratches, having been

down by protestors, I would have dismiss them as a fantasist.

Yet in June we all witnessed Colston's bronze effigy, all eight foot three inches of it, dragged to the pavement and thrown into the harbour from which over 2,000 slave trading expeditions set sail.

From that moment onwards 2020 has been a year of impossibilities made possible.

Another unimaginable event took place in September when the Colston Society, which for 275 years had celebrated and memorialised the reputation of Colston voted for its own dissolution.

WORSHIP

After the events of the summer the excuses and self-rationalisation that for so many years had been successfully deployed to justify the worship of a man who traded in human flesh were simply no longer viable. The game was up. The cause was lost.

But perhaps the most significant changes of 2020 have been those focused on changing the future rather than reassessing the past.

At the beginning of 2020 thousands of British companies, corporations and institutions talked-the-talk about diversity and inclusion but could not find the institutional will to change their internal cultures and recruitment practices.

Now, in the final months of 2020, companies big and small and whole sectors of the economy now acknowledge the structural nature of racism and have committed themselves to new courses of action on diversity and inclusion that in some cases are radical and potentially transformative.

Some did much more than

PANDEMIC PROTEST: Bristol's statue of slave trader Edward Colston was torn down in June

> " In 2020, a year unlike any other, the arrival of Black History Month should inspire us to seize the possibilities Davis speaks of and demand change "

issuing statements in support of Black Lives Matter and launched internal audits of their processes in order to better understand how their cultures

condemned the dance troupe Diversity for performing a routine inspired by Black Lives Matter on *Britain's Got Talent*. ITV not only offered their

backing to Ashley Banjo, *pictured far left*, and his dancers, the broadcaster took out full-page advertisements in national newspapers affirming their determination to and defend the rights of this group of young black people to use dance to express their feelings about the historic events we are all living through.

More is needed but the commitments made in 2020 exceed what anyone realistically expected might be achieved at the beginning of this year.

In my own industry TV a host of new initiatives have been launched and just this month ITV stood up to the critics who

year something like that might have been the outcome. But not in 2020.

In an interview in June the legendary American activist Angela Davis described 2020 as the year in which "we are finally witnessing the consequences of decades and centuries of attempting to expel racism from our societies".

MOMENT

The rise of Black Lives Matter, she argued, has created "a moment of possibility".

"What we are offered," Davis counselled, "is the possibility of reimagining and recreating" the future.

In 2020, a year unlike any other, the arrival of Black History Month should inspire us to seize the possibilities Davis speaks of, and demands, change that up to now we have dared to even imagine.

If ever there was a year to put pessimism aside and embrace optimism this is it.

On Black History Month 2020, historian David Olusoga wrote in The Voice *about how the year's events should inspire optimism for change*

As Mahon's experience highlights – Floyd's death resonated deeply with Black Britons. Long-standing concerns about the deaths of Black people in police custody and discriminatory use of stop and searches meant that many marchers wanted to challenge the view held by much of the mainstream media, that the UK is more progressive on race than America. A *Voice Online* story about one of the first big demonstrations in the week following Floyd's tragic death reflected the anger of protestors who defied strict lockdown regulations. The report was accompanied by a dramatic photo of a young man crouching, his head in his hands in seeming despair, being comforted by a fellow protestor. A week later, protestors began targeting monuments of historic figures long associated with racism. A bronze memorial statue of one of Bristol's most famous slave traders, Edward Colston was torn down and thrown into the harbour.

The newspaper went on to report that they knelt on the neck of the statue, re-enacting the way that police officers had knelt on the neck of George Floyd before throwing it into the harbour.

'It says 'Erected by the citizens of Bristol, as a memorial to one of the most virtuous and wise sons of this city''local protestor John McAllister told *The Voice*. 'The man was a slave trader. He was generous to Bristol but it was off the back of slavery and it's absolutely despicable. It's an insult to the people of Bristol.'

After initially being silent on the Black Lives Matter, and with demonstrations quickly spreading across the country, Prime Minister Boris Johnson responded to the news with an article written exclusively for *The Voice*. He acknowledged the 'incontrovertible, undeniable feeling of injustice' motivating the rallies, while condemning those who have flouted social distancing to attend them during a 'time of national trial'. Johnson's article was widely quoted in the national media. But his efforts to build a dialogue with the Black community also brought an angry response from equality campaigners who pointed to previous articles he'd written in which he described African people as having 'watermelon smiles' and women in burqas looking like 'bank robbers'.

'He should begin any speech he gives on this subject with an apology for his past mistakes and a personal vow to do better,' said playwright and campaigner Bonnie Greer.

If social media was key to helping campaigners quickly organise mass protests it also shaped debates about the relationship between the police and the Black community. Throughout its 40-year-history, *The Voice* has documented the anger that Black people feel about racial disparities in policing, and especially about police use of stop and search. The 2010s saw the newspaper highlight an emerging trend – people using mobile devices to document racial disparities in policing in real time and post the resulting videos to social media platforms.

In some instances, this has led to officers being suspended or sacked.

The Voice columnist Samuel Brooksworth drew attention to this trend. 'Let's start off by saying racism isn't getting worse, it's simply getting captured,' he wrote. 'The Ahmaud Arbery murder (a 25-year-old Black man killed while jogging in Satilla Shores, Georgia) shows the pivotal role that footage plays in bringing justice after what is basically murder in broad daylight. Incidents like this, which most Black people can relate to, are finally also being filmed. No longer are these injustices simply things happening 'in our heads'.

In 2020, several stories featured in the pages of *The Voice* and *Voice Online* about stop and searches captured on mobile phone. One involved charity founder Sayce Holmes-Lewis. One morning in early May, during lockdown, he was driving through South London on his way to deliver food to a friend who had recently lost a loved one to COVID-19 when he was pulled over by police officers. They suspected he was carrying drugs.

'After the officers pulled up alongside me, they asked me to get out of the car,' he told *The Voice* in an interview for its You Tube YouTube channel. 'When I asked them what was the reason one of the officers told me they were stopping me under the Section 23 Misuse of Drugs Act. I told them they had got the wrong person. At that point one of the officers became very aggressive telling me they needed to see what was in my car.' Holmes-Lewis refused. Like many young Black men in London, he had good reason to mistrust the police.

When he was 14, he was assaulted by a Metropolitan Police officer on the way home from school. Despite having CCTV footage and witnesses to the assault, the case was thrown out by the Crown Prosecution Service due to lack of evidence.

The injustice he felt remained with him and in the years since, he has been stopped and searched over 30 times. This time however, he was decided to do something differently. After getting out of his car and agreeing to be searched, he walked back to his car, got his phone and began filming the encounter with the officers.

'I just thought "enough is enough"' he said in the interview. 'I just wanted to document it. But I also want to showcase what they were doing to me as an upstanding Black man in the community.'

The resulting video went viral after Holmes-Lewis uploaded it online. He later received an apology from the Metropolitan

News

Met police chief: 'I recognise that there is further to go'

Commissioner Cressida Dick recognises anger with the force – but is working on change

**EXCLUSIVE
by Vic Motune**

MET POLICE Commissioner Cressida Dick has acknowledged some of the criticisms of the force by the black community which has accused it of discriminatory policing.

In a wide ranging interview with The Voice, Commissioner Dick answered questions from community organisations such as StopWatch and Access UK and collated by the newspaper's news editor Vic Motune.

The questions covered areas such as police community relations, ethnic diversity in the force and racial disparity in the use of stop and search.

ANALYSIS

A recent analysis by Dr Krisztian Posch, a lecturer in crime science at University College London for The Guardian found that officers enforcing the coronavirus lockdown were more than twice as likely to issue fines to black people as to white people.

The common sentiment shared by the organisations The Voice spoke before interviewing the Met Police chief was that no progress had been made since the publication of the Macpherson Report in 1999 to end the kind of discriminatory policing that has traditionally been such a point of contention between the police and the black community.

The Macpherson Report famously described the Met Police as "institutionally racist".

When asked if the force was still institutionally racist she said: "I fully recognise that there is further to go, and that some people will see us as a service which hasn't changed as much as they would like. And we are, of course, working in a society that is going through an awful lot of questioning itself right now.

"One of which we recognise,

> **We've done a huge amount against hate crime, and I'm proud of that**

that racism has existed and does exist.

"We've done a huge amount against hate crime, and I'm proud of that. I have a long history, personally, of being antiracist.

"I'm passionate about this. And I've been working very hard on it personally in the last two or three years as Commissioner. But we've got further to go. And it's for others to judge where they see we now are."

PROUD

She added: "I'm very proud of so many of the changes that we've made in terms of the way we police our communities. We've always been a service which has tried to involve the public, but we've been doing that more and more over the last few years.

"We have been trying to make sure that we are sensitive in the way that we police, that we listen to the public, and that

we recognise where people may feel that they want a different police service than what they're receiving right now."

Asked about ethnic disparity in stop and search, Commissioner Dick again acknowledged community concerns.

She said: "I do understand that if you're living in a high violent crime area and you might be from African or Caribbean heritage, you're feeling that your son is more likely to get stabbed, hugely more likely to get stabbed than, you know, white people a mile up the road, because that's the shocking disproportionality.

CONFIDENCE

"If you're seeing that and you're seeing lots of officers, and on occasion you're seeing lots of stop and search being done, that may be a really uncomfortable feeling. And I want people to feel more confidence in their policemen, to see us as there to protect them, and not there in any way other than as a friend and a protector. And that's the bit I know we've got further to go."

She added: "In areas of high violent crime, you will have police officers.

"It would be a racist thing to withdraw police officers from an area which has both high violence and minority communities. We wouldn't ever do that.

"We are there. And we are trying to protect people. And we're trying to target individuals who we know are violent drug dealers who are carrying knives, who are carrying firearms and so forth. And one of the ways we do that is through Stop and Search."

HELD TO ACCOUNT: Met Commissioner Cressida Dick says that while figures have improved in the UK, there is still a long way to go in ridding the force of racism – and that the people must be the judge of improvement

However, she highlighted the fact that there was greater transparency on the issue.

"One of the changes that I've

> **We use minimum force. We only use force which is necessary**

seen so strongly in the last 10 years is that we are now more transparent. We're now more accountable. We are now more heavily scrutinised than we ever have been, and probably than any other public service in this country. And certainly

the UK police services are more so than any others in the world. And I'm proud of that.

"Also we look at our figures all the time, including through the lens of race and disproportionality. So you have readily available to you our figures on stop and search, on use of force, on the usage of Taser and use of firearms.

CONTRAST

"And let me just contrast that with, for example, the United States. It's extraordinarily hard to get figures on any of those subjects there. Secondly, many of the tactics that they use routinely there we don't. Because we use minimum force. We only use force which is necessary. Some people have talked about choke holds. We don't

use those. We don't use gas in crowds. We don't use baton rounds. We use our firearms incredibly sparingly."

Dick continued: "If you come to Stop and Search, you have to remember that we are policing in an environment which sadly is unequal, and in an environment in which violent crime affects some places and some people hugely more than others. And it breaks my heart that some places which were subject to high violent crime when I started as a police officer, still are. I was an Inspector in Peckham for five years. And Peckham has changed a lot, but there are parts of the Borough of Southwark, which is subject to really high violent crime on occasion. And that was true nearly 30 years ago."

You can help us bring an end to systemic racism in Britain

Over the past two months, hundreds of thousands of people all over the world have marched in mostly peaceful protests led by the Black Lives Matter movement.

While the protests have been sparked by the death of George Floyd in the US, campaigning organisations

in the UK, including this newspaper, have been clear to say that systemic racism is not just an American problem.

Over two decades after the publication of the Macpherson Report, there are many who believe that the force remains institutionally racist.

Although improvements have been made post-Macpherson, such as hate crimes now being identified, black officers are disproportionately subjected to discipline compared to their white counterparts. We still have disproportionality in stop and search, with a black person five times more

likely to be stopped by police than their white counterparts. A black person is 20 times more likely to be stopped under section 60 roadblocks and more likely to be Tasered.

These figures may be down to unconscious bias. But even if so, the fact that police officers know these

figures but decide not to question why they are happening is institutionally racist.

We're urging you, our readers, to contact police watchdog, the Independent Office for Police Conduct (IOPC) and let them know of your concerns.

In an interview with The Voice, *Met Police Commissioner Cressida Dick admitted more needed to be done to tackle racism in the police force*

Police. Following the incident, the charity founder was invited to work with the Met on a ground breaking training programme that taught new officers how to better interact with young Black people during stop and search.

Another *Voice Online* headline from May 2020 read: 'Child screams for help as dad is Tasered by Manchester police officers.' The story was accompanied by a still image captured from a mobile phone video showing a Black man who appears to have nothing in his hands in heated discussion with two Greater Manchester police officers while a small boy looks on. The video, which was shared on *The Voice*'s Twitter page, shows the man being tasered by one of the officers while the child screams 'daddy.' The person who took the video is heard responding in shock while the police officer shouts 'get your hands behind your back now,' all the while continuing to send pulses through the device.

With the number of these reports growing through the summer, MPs asked the Met ropolitan Police Commissioner Cressida Dick if her force was still institutionally racist. She replied that institutional racism was not a 'massive systemic issue.' But a quick look at some of *The Voice's* recent archives highlights the fact that many in the Black community feel strongly that systemic racism is still at the heart of long-standing tensions between the police and the community. For a start, there is the issue of poor recruitment. Or, in other words, a police force that doesn't look much like the city it claims to be serving.

'It is unacceptable that in the twenty-first century less than 5 per cent of police officers in England and Wales are from Black and ethnic minority backgrounds,' former president of the National Black Police Association Charles Critchlow told

The Voice in April 2013: 'British policing must adopt radical approaches across the service, if issues of race and diversity are to be successfully addressed.'

As the 2010s progressed, serious concerns about the deaths of Black people in police custody continued to grow. Leon Briggs, Shekou Bayoh, Rashan Charles and Dalian Atkinson were among just some of the tragic cases that featured in the pages of *The Voice* since 2013. And for family members and protestors quoted in the newspaper's stories, these tragic deaths were another reminder that discrimination was still prevalent within the police service despite the findings of the Macpherson report in 1999. Faced with increasingly strident criticisms of its policing of diverse communities in the wake of George Floyd's death, Dick reached out to *The Voice* in July 2020 for an exclusive interview, the same month she had told MPs that she didn't think institutional racism in the police force was a significant systemic issue.

The interview was part of her efforts to build dialogue with the Black community and reassure people that fair policing was at the top of her agenda. In a wide-ranging interview with *The Voice*, Dick answered questions from community organisations such as StopWatch and Access UK, which had been collated by the newspaper's editorial team. Asked if the force was institutionally racist, she began by saying: 'I fully recognise that there is further to go, and that some people will see us as a service which hasn't changed as much as they would like. And we are, of course, working in a society that is going through an awful lot of questioning itself right now.'

Dick went on to say that she recognised that 'racism has existed and does exist,' but stopped short of admitting the force was institutionally racist.

'We've done a huge amount against hate crime, and I'm proud of that. I have a long history, personally, of being anti-racist. I'm passionate about this. And I've been working very hard on it personally in the last two or three years as Commissioner. But we've got further to go. And it's for others to judge where they see we now are.' Asked about ethnic disparity in stop and search, Commissioner Dick again acknowledged the Black community's concerns.

But she added: 'It would be a racist thing to withdraw police officers from an area which has both high violence and minority communities. We wouldn't ever do that. We are trying to protect people. And we're trying to target individuals who we know are violent drug dealers who are carrying knives, who are carrying firearms and so forth. And one of the ways we do that is through stop and search.'

Following the interview, *The Voice* put the Commissioner's responses to the community groups whose concerns it had shared with her. A consensus quickly emerged, one that was reflected in the uncompromising headline that dominated the front page of the July 2020 edition. 'The police continue to fail us,' it said. 'Met chief says things are improving but where's the evidence?'

The editorial said: 'Systemic racism in policing is not just an American problem. We are still five times more likely to be stopped by police than white Britons, more likely to be tasered and a disproportionate number of Black people die after use of force or restraint by officers.'

Following *The Voice*'s interview with Cressida Dick, calls for policing reform continued. In December 2020, reporter Izin Akhabau included eye-popping statistics from UCL research for a *Voice Online* story about continuing racial disparities in stop and search. The research found that Black men aged between 18 and 24 were almost 20 times more likely to be stopped and searched between July and September of that year. Dick's resignation as Met Police Commissioner in February 2022 following a series of racism and sexism scandals came as a relief for many who had been calling for a reform of policing.

London Mayor Sadiq Khan, who made it clear he had no confidence in her leadership in the wake of growing dissatisfaction with the Met, saw her departure as an opportunity for a fresh approach that would win the confidence of Londoners and minority communities. 'It's clear that the only way to start to deliver the scale of the change required is to have new leadership right at the top of the Metropolitan Police' he told *The Voice*.

But as a March 2022 investigation into policing by *The Voice* found, the need for that fresh approach didn't stop with Met officers.

Greater Manchester Police were also facing demands from Black police officers, equality campaigners and the public, to get to grips with a canteen culture of racism in the ranks.

Former Home Office criminologist and Manchester resident David Dalgleish told the newspaper:

The most recent data in Manchester shows that despite white British people representing over 80 per cent of the city-region's population, they make up less than half of those stopped and searched by police. Greater Manchester's latest stop and search figures will do little to assure people that much has changed since recording was introduced as a result of the Stephen Lawrence Inquiry.

Paul Obinna, a teacher and educational consultant who taught in Manchester's Moss Side during the late 1980s and early 1990s told *The Voice*: 'Police are only as good as the communities from which they are drawn. Police from towns and areas with low non-white populations carry negative stereotypical beliefs and ideas which affect their expectations and policing delivery.'

In the January 2022 edition of *The Voice*, Lord Simon Woolley, reflecting on the legacy of the newspaper, said: 'The whole story of modern Black British history, in particular the struggle for justice and equality can be told in the pages of *The Voice* newspaper.' As we look to the future, what are those pages likely to reveal as the twenty-first century progresses? Already, there are prominent voices who are somewhat pessimistic that race equality will be given prominence by those in authority. Certainly, one reason for the pessimism stems from the events surrounding the March 2021 report from the Commission on Race and Ethnic Disparities.

Launched by Boris Johnson at the height of the Black Lives Matter protests in the summer of 2020, Commission members were recruited by political adviser Munira Mirza who had previously denied the existence of structural and institutional racism. Among those appointed were education consultant and former *The Voice* columnist Tony Sewell, space scientist Maggie Aderin-Pocock and Keith Fraser, chair of the Youth Justice Board. Its findings controversially concluded that the claim the country is still institutionally racist is not borne out by evidence. It argued that family structure and social class had a bigger impact than race on people's life chances and that racial discrimination has often been misapplied to 'account for every observed disparity' between ethnic groups.

Critics of the report said it deliberately tried to minimise the prevalence of racism in British society and institutions.

'The report reminds me of the ones done in the 1960s and 1970s. Those reports suggested that immigrant children could survive the colour bar of their parents if they worked hard and were grateful to be British' wrote Patrick Vernon in a column for *The Voice* a few days after the report's publication. 'Instead of being forward-thinking and adding a new debate on race, the report is almost stuck in a time warp or even 'lost in space'. It does not face the true realities of 2021.'

Lord Woolley was far more direct in his assessment: 'That report marked the worst time of my political career. I've campaigned for Black and brown people to be in power. And it was Black and brown people that were throwing other Black and brown people under the bus, desperately cozying up to Boris Johnson for political favour. It was about as heart breaking as Black politics could be.'

So, was the hope for progress that marked the widespread Black Lives Matter protests of 2020 misplaced? Or are those who claimed that we witnessed a genuine landmark moment in the battle for equality right? Popular historian and broadcaster David Olusoga was keen to address both sides of the debate in a *Voice* column from the October 2020:

> Should we conclude that what happened this summer - here in Britain and across the world – was an historic moment of change, loaded with potential for yet greater transformation? Or should we draw the opposite conclusion and assume that what we have just witnessed was merely a passing moment, an event rather than the beginning of a process? As so often the case for pessimism is the easier of the two to make. Pessimism is justified because of what it is we are up against - the idea of

race. To make the case for optimism is to ask that millions of people who live their lives under the shadow of race to believe that in the near future they might escape into the light. That is quite an ask.

Olusoga quoted legendary American activist Angela Davis who described 2020 as the year in which 'we are finally witnessing the consequences of decades and centuries of attempting to expel racism from our societies'. Olusoga concluded by telling readers that we should be inspired 'to seize the possibilities Davis speaks of, and demand change that up to now we have dared to even imagine'.

Notes

Foreword

xi   Henry, Lenny and Ryder, Marcus, *Black British Lives Matter: A Clarion Call for Equality* (Faber & Faber, 2021)
New Faces [tv show] ITV (1973–1978)

xii   Walker, Tim, *BAFTAs were a disgrace for not celebrating Black talent, says Lenny Henry* [article] *Daily Telegraph* (13 May 2013) https://www.telegraph.co.uk/culture/tvandradio/10057059/Baftas-were-a-disgrace-for-not-celebrating-black-talent-says-Lenny-Henry.html

Anisiobi, J J, *'What were the judges doing?' Lenny Henry blasts BAFTA for not recognising Black talent at this year's television awards* [article] *Daily Mail* (15 May 2013) https://www.dailymail.co.uk/tvshowbiz/article-2324994/Lenny-Henry-blasts-Bafta-recognising-black-talent-years-television-awards.html

Introduction

3   'I shall leave it to history, but remember that I shall be one of the historians', Churchill, Winston, quoted in Reynolds, David, *In Command of History: Churchill Fighting and Writing the Second World War* (Allen Lane, 2004) p.xix

[**journalism is the**] 'first rough draft of history' Graham, Philip, speech to the overseas correspondents of Newsweek in London (April 1963)

4 'For the longest time the central distraction for Black Britons...' Younge, Gary, writing in Fryer, Peter, *Staying Power* (Pluto Press, 2010)

1982-1992: A Defiant Voice in the Wilderness

11 'Injustice anywhere is a threat to justice everywhere' Luther King Jr, Martin, *Letter from a Birmingham Jail* (1963)

12 'It was springtime in London...' McCalla, Val, quoted in Burnett, Derek, *Millennium People: The Soul of Success* (Hibiscus Books, 2003)

51 Baxter, Carol, *The Black Nurse: An Endangered Species* (National Extension College Trust Ltd, 1988)

72 Bowie, David, 'Ashes to Ashes' [music video] (RCA, 1980) directed by Bowie, David and Mallet, David
Gilroy, Beryl, *Black Teacher* (Faber & Faber, 2022)

78 Bob Marley and the Wailers, *Concrete Jungle*, (Island, 1973), music and lyrics by Marley, Bob
Musical Youth, 'Pass the Dutchie', (MCA Records, 1982) music and lyrics by Mittoo, Jackie, Simpson, Fitzroy, Ferguson, Lloyd
Bob & Marcia, 'Young Gifted and Black', (Trojan Records, 1970) music and lyrics by Simone, Nina, and Irvine, Weldon

80 Thompson, Carroll, 'Simply in Love', (Santic Records, 1981), music and lyrics by Thompson, Carroll and Chin, Leonard

Thompson, Carroll, *Hopelessly in Love* (Carib Gems, 1981) produced by C&B Productions

Kay, Janet, 'Lovin' You', (Pye Records, 1978) music and lyrics by Riperton, Minnie and Rudolph, Dick

Kay, Janet, *Silly Games* (Scope, 1979) music and lyrics by Bovell, Diana

Mama Dragon, [musical] (1981), music and lyrics by Dhondy, Farrukh, Kay, Janet and the Government

81 *No Problem!* [TV show] Channel 4 (1983–1985) created by Black Theatre Co-operative

82 Paris, Mica, 'My One Temptation', (4th & Broadway/Island Records, 1988) written by Leeson, Mick, Waters, Miles, and Vale, Peter

84 *The Real McCoy* [TV show] BBC (1991–1996) produced by Charlie Hanson

1993-2002: The Black British Middle Class in 100 Letters

91 *ITV News At Ten* [TV show] ITV (1967-present) founded by Cox, Geoffrey

100 Headley, Victor, *Yardie*, (Pan Books, 1993)

105 Macka B, 'Buppie Culture' (Ariwa, 1983) music and lyrics by McFarlane, Christopher

111 *Dance Energy* [TV show] BBC (1990–1993)

Desmond's [TV show] Channel 4 (1989–1994) created by Worrell, Trix

123 *The Crying Game* [film] Palace Pictures (1992) directed by Jordan, Neil

Mama I Want To Sing! [musical] (1983) music and lyrics by Naylor, Wesley, Higginsen, Vy, and Wydro, Ken

Troy, Doris, 'Just One Look' [song] (Atlantic, 1963) music and lyrics by Troy, Doris and Carroll, Gregory

150 Duncanson, Neil, *The Fastest Men on Earth: The Inside Stories the Olympic Men's 100m Champions* (Welbeck Publishing Group, 2021)

151 Bruno, Frank, *Let Me Be Frank* (Mirror Books, 2017)

2003–2012: Has Anything Changed?

204 Zephaniah, Benjamin, *Too Black Too Strong*, (Bloodaxe Books, 2001)

206 *The X Factor*, [TV show] ITV (2004–2018) created by Cowell, Simon

Fame Academy [TV show] BBC (2002–2003) based on *Operación Triunfo*, created by Cruz, Toni, Mainat, Josep Maria, Mainat, Joan Ramon

208 *EastEnders* [TV show] BBC (1985-present) created by Smith, Julia, and Holland, Tony

210 *Skins* [TV show] Channel 4 (2007–2013) created by Elsley, Bryan, and Brittain, Jamie

Get Out [film] Universal Pictures (2017) directed by Peele, Jordan

Black Panther [film] Marvel Studios (2018) directed by Coogler, Ryan

2013–2022: The Voice in the Social Media Age

253 Hall, Necola, *I was a Soldier: Survival Against the Odds* (Hansib Publications, 2014)

259 So Solid Crew, '21 Seconds' [song] (Relentless, 2011) music and lyrics by Maffia, Lisa, Megaman, Skat D, Kaish, Synth, Mac, Face, Asher D, G-Man, Romeo, Harvey

About the Authors

Richard Adeshiyan

Richard Adeshiyan started his journalism career at *The Voice* in 1983, where he worked for a decade. He was the founding Editor of *New Nation* newspaper in 1996 and has also worked in television, including the BBC's *Black Britain* and *Windrush*.

Dotun Adebayo

Dotun Adebayo arrived in the UK from Lagos aged six in 1965. After studying at the universities of Stockholm, London and Essex, he worked at *The Voice* for six years before launching The X Press, the most successful Black-interest book publisher in Britain. Today, he presents on BBC Radio 5Live.

Winsome Cornish MBE

Winsome Cornish is a former editor of *The Voice* and worked at the paper for 12 years. She managed Spectrum Radio for five years and worked with Operation Black Vote for a decade. In 2011 she was awarded an MBE for services to Black and ethnic minority communities.

Vic Motune

Vic Motune is a former news editor of *The Voice* and still writes for the paper on trends in Black tech entrepreneurship. He was previously a producer with BBC Radio 5Live and appeared as a newspaper reviewer for BBC News. He has won a MIND award for his reporting on mental health.

Rodney Hinds

Rodney Hinds has been sports editor of *The Voice* for more than 20 years. He has written three books and presented his own show on Colourful Radio and ABN Radio. In 2019 he won the Lifetime Achievement Award at the National Diversity Awards.

Index

Note: page numbers in **bold** refer to *The Voice* covers.